The City of Today Is a Dying Thing

Des Fitzgerald is Professor of Medical Humanities and Social Sciences at University College Cork. He was awarded the Philip Leverhulme Prize for sociology in 2017, and named a 'New Generation Thinker' by the BBC and the Arts and Humanities Research Council. He lives in Cork with his wife and two children.

Further praise for *The City of Today Is a Dying Thing*:

'A social scientist offers a witty and sceptical view of our obsession with greenery in urban spaces . . . Counterintuitive, funny and provocative . . . We could all use a little more of Fitzgerald's scepticism.' Edwin Heathcote, *Financial Times*

'An amusing, sceptical and refreshing journey through the past and future of urban life. Fitzgerald has an eye for the incongruous, and a talent for teasing out grander themes from unlikely or lacklustre settings . . . [his] engagements with his surroundings are compelling . . . [and] he has an entertaining cattiness throughout . . . A compassionate and lively venture, a robust defence of the messiness of cities, and a noble corrective against those who insist on a managerial view of nature, urban spaces and human beings.' *Daily Telegraph*

'Fitzgerald's style is spirited and outspoken, poking fun at the absurdity of received opinion, mad initiatives and confused policies with energy and charm. He writes in the style of pro-urbanists such as John Grindrod and Barnabas Calder, both of whom have drawn general readers into debates about architecture and cities which many would prefer to be left to insiders . . . an entertaining book.' *Spectator*

'Satisfyingly compelling . . . funny, well-researched, personable, and unlike city planning elites both past and present – dare I say it – accessible.' *Irish Times*

'Urban planning might not spark joy in every reader's heart, but it's a topic Des Fitzgerald explores with gusto in *The City of Today Is a Dying Thing* . . . Fitzgerald surveys a rich array of ideas about nature and analyses the power dynamics at play in urban planning . . . A gifted wordsmith, [he] trips nimbly across history and architecture, moving from figures such as Le Corbusier (from whose writings comes the book's title) and Frank Lloyd Wright to Jonas Salk, the discoverer of a polio vaccine . . . [a] learned and entertaining book.' *Irish Sunday Independent*

'An examination of the past, present, and future of urban life . . . an insightful read.' *Irish Independent*

'Fitzgerald keeps us engaged through his off-beat, irreverent style . . . Throughout this eclectic book, Fitzgerald's contrarian outlook is a touchstone.' *Irish Examiner*

'A curious but alluring publication . . . filled with anecdotes and familial musings, while also a thorough historical analysis of the green city ideals. I will never look at the poor old urban tree in the same way again.' *London Society*

'It reads like Jon Ronson let loose on city planners: endlessly funny, outrageously caustic and seriously smart.' John Grindrod, author of *Concretopia* and *Iconicon*

'In this lively, irreverent and insightful study, Fitzgerald helps us see that concepts like "nature" and the "green future city" stand in for anxieties about urbanisation, the psyche, and the threat of the Other – and asks what kinds of cities we want to build and inhabit.' Lauren Elkin, author of *Flaneuse*

'Incendiary . . . a sharp critic and a stone cold realist. His stimulating book is a reminder that there are no simple solutions to global climate change.' Eric Klinenberg, author of *Palaces for the People*

# THE CITY OF TODAY IS A DYING THING

## IN SEARCH OF THE CITIES OF TOMORROW

# DES FITZGERALD

faber

First published in 2024
by Faber & Faber Limited
The Bindery, 51 Hatton Garden
London EC1N 8HN

This paperback edition first published in 2025

Typeset by Faber & Faber Limited
Printed and bound by CPI Group (UK) Ltd, Croydon, CRO 4YY

A CIP record for this book
is available from the British Library

ISBN 978–0–571–36222–6

Our authorised representative in the EU for product safety is
Easy Access System Europe, Mustamae tee 50, 10621 Tallinn, Estonia
gpsr.requests@easproject.com

2 4 6 8 10 9 7 5 3

For Neasa!

# Contents

# Introduction

In September 1868, forty-six-year-old Frederick Law Olmsted, already the most prominent landscape designer and conservationist of his day, sat down at his desk in New York City to compose a report on a new suburb proposed for the banks of the Des Plaines River, about nine miles from Chicago – a site to which the developer, E. E. Child, had given the deceptively bland name Riverside.[1] To understand the possibilities for this site, in Olmsted's account, you had to understand not so much the environmental but rather the social conditions that would encourage people to live there. You had to understand, he wrote, that the middle of the nineteenth century was a period of what today we would call urbanisation. People were coming together in booming towns and cities. They had developed a taste for the luxuries and refinements that you only get from city life. And yet, from the vantage point of his desk in New York, Olmsted could sense something in the air. 'There are symptoms of a change,' he wrote to Riverside's financial backers, who had contracted his and his partner's firm, Olmsted, Vaux & Co., to design the site from scratch – 'a counter-tide of migration' away from the city and back towards a different kind of life. You see this phenomenon, he said, in the common desire to live near parks. You see it in the desperation to plant rows of trees, 'little enclosures of turf and foliage' in every newly laid street. It has been established,

Olmsted went on, by a Dr Rumney of the British Association for the Advancement of Social Science, that simply living near other people can make a person ill, even manifesting in a kind of 'nervous feebleness'.

It was the *suburb*, according to Olmsted, that was truly the city of the future. And not just any suburb, but rather a suburb that could successfully recreate that very particular feeling of being not in the city at all – that could recreate the feeling of being in the countryside, with its pure air, its shade, its open spaces, its 'distance from the jar, noise, confusion and bustle of commercial thoroughfares'.[2] A realisation was dawning: there was something just a bit off about city life. The city was not, in fact, a very good place to live in at all. Some new way of living, not quite the city, not quite the country, now loomed on the horizon. As Olmsted put it the following year, in a letter to the author and journalist Edward Everett Hale, the key thing now was to create a space for living that was some mixture of the two. '[I] urge principles, plans and measures,' Olmsted wrote effusively, 'tending to the ruralizing of *all* our urban population and the urbanizing of our rustic population.'[3]

Olmsted was neither the first nor the only person to have such thoughts. The fantasy of the city that was not really a city at all, of the landscaped park that still maintained the rugged virtues of the open frontier – this was already a guiding theme of American public life in the nineteenth century. It was a fantasy, indeed, the historian Dorceta Taylor reminds us, that was held on to with special fervour by urban elites, like Olmsted, anxious about what city life was doing to their own waning sense of racial superiority.[4] Through different, often overlapping waves of urbanisation across the globe, this idea has never fully gone away. My interest in this book is in following its contours into the present day, as a new kind of anxiety about the city, and a new kind of desire for the countryside, begins to rise again. This desire is, of course, in many ways very different from the racialised anxieties of Olmsted's day. And yet also maybe not so different.

Things ultimately went south for Olmsted and Vaux at Riverside: their plans were not followed exactly, the developer went bust, and Olmsted had to take payment in lots, which quickly collapsed in value. And yet somehow Riverside, a surprisingly sturdy green village on the banks of an unloved river, began to take shape. Olmsted was by then out of the picture. But there was another figure, then living in obscurity in Chicago, who may well have seen Riverside under construction, and who would carry this urge articulated by Olmsted much further in the decades that followed.[5] This was Ebenezer Howard, the unlikely founder of the Garden City movement, who would go on to establish two new urban centres on his return to his birthplace in England: first there was Letchworth Garden City, founded in 1904; and then the new town of Welwyn Garden City, which followed in 1920.

On an unseasonably warm day in mid-September 2021, I caught a train at King's Cross in London, admired the station's spectacular new glass and steel dome – now arced over the frantic concourse like an upturned glass on an ant colony – and travelled twenty miles north, to the sleepy commuter county of Hertfordshire, and into a different world entirely. My destination was Welwyn Garden City – England's second and last true 'garden city', once part of a great international movement to shift urban planning in the twentieth century towards new, medium-sized satellite towns, surrounded by green space. Just as Frederick Law Olmsted had dreamed, these towns were to be new places for living that were not quite urban and not quite rural, with decent housing and work for all, and underpinned by an economic system (this was not part of Olmsted's dream) that would reinvest the proceeds of increasing land values for everyone's benefit. Though it never really worked out like that, and the broader movement has long since faded away, the busy and prosperous town of Welwyn was nonetheless happily celebrating its hundredth anniversary, as well as its small but critical role in the history of urban planning. And so I went along, curious to see what the one-time city of the future looked like, now that that future had, unambiguously, if rather unceremoniously, arrived.

Having founded Welwyn with his collaborators and backers in 1920, Ebenezer Howard quickly appointed a Montreal-born architect, Louis de Soissons, to create the town's master plan. De Soissons, who had just graduated from university, would end up spending his life as the chief architect of Welwyn Garden City, dying there in 1962. In his original plan, de Soissons laid out the green heart of the town a bit like a sideways 'T', where the horizontal bar, Parkway, is longer than the vertical bar, Howardsgate. At the north end of Parkway, de Soissons added a small, bulbous park, rather pompously known as The Campus. Seen from above, the whole thing looks a bit like a gun or an erect penis.

The idea behind Welwyn, and behind garden cities more generally, was not simply to remake urban spaces on the basis of green and healthy country life. It was an attempt to reform how land was owned and who made money from it – to stop increases in land value from benefiting solely private owners, and instead to use that rise for the collective good of the residents. But the movement was also about creating a new kind of person. Or at least it was a serious attempt to return the benighted inhabitants of industrial cities to some more natural state. 'Men', Howard wrote, quoting the eugenicist philosopher Herbert Spencer, 'are equally entitled to the use of the earth.' What they want is the 'practical life', the fruits of their toil, an equal share, a short commute, a patch of grass to call their own, neither rural simplicity nor urban drudgery, but something somehow in between. If planners would just use 'the resources of modern science', Howard wrote, 'Art may supplement Nature, and life may become an abiding joy and delight'.[6]

Today, though, I realised as I exited the ugly 1990s shopping mall that somehow contains the train station, if central Howardsgate is still a lush, green, formally landscaped city-centre park, it's also more or less a taxi rank. A line of cars crept around the edges, like flies on a cake, collecting passengers from the station and the nearby chain shops. Mutual ownership, meanwhile, disappeared in the 1980s. Today, houses are available on the open market – many of them, I saw in estate agents' windows as I walked around, going for well over a million pounds. Welwyn Garden City might still represent a kind of utopia, I reflected as I tried not to get run over by the speeding commuters in their SUVs, but *whose* utopia, exactly, was not quite so clear.

I had come to Welwyn because I'd been thinking about urban planning and the future of the city for some time. I

wanted to know why so many people in that field were convinced there was something about our cities that was simply
bad for us, and especially that there was something about
them that was psychologically or even morally bad for us. I
was trying to imagine what this future would look like, and
how it might be different from previous attempts to fix these
problems. I was also trying to figure out why it was that so
many planners, architects and policy-makers were so fixated
on *nature* as the solution to all of the city's problems – why
they seemed to think that treating the city as if it was a kind
of organism, a living thing, would finally bring planning and
architecture into the twenty-first century. As I traipsed around
international events on future cities, healthy cities, green cities
and so on, it began to feel as if there were no issue in city life,
from air quality to mental health, that couldn't be fixed by a
line of trees, a green roof, a biomimetic office block, a forlorn
plant growing through the cracks in some derelict wall.

And yet by the time I arrived in Welwyn, I was starting
to find the whole 'green city' rhetoric extremely unconvin-
cing. Too often, it seemed to me, an urban park was just a
nice-looking taxi-rank-in-waiting. Carefully tended green
space was just another way of pushing up house prices and
creating exclusive communities, where the lush trees act as
pretty effective symbolic gates. Maybe the reality is that, however the rest of us feel about it, lots of people find their joy
not so much in digging vegetables or caressing the bushes,
but rather in driving ugly cars at great speed through exclusive commuter towns.

And it seemed to me, too, that what a place like Welwyn
symbolised was perhaps not really an attempt to transform

urban space. Rather, it was an attempt to do away with the lively, messy, unpredictable city altogether. 'The city of today is a dying thing,' wrote the architect and planner Le Corbusier, as the first streets in Welwyn were taking shape. We must learn, he insisted, to build garden cities 'in the open', guided by a spirit of uniformity, regularity, and discipline.[7] Across the Atlantic, the American architect Frank Lloyd Wright was similarly starting to sketch out his 'broadacre city'. This, too, was a new kind of urban space, one that was, in fact, no kind of urban space at all. Instead, it was an endlessly rolling open suburb without a centre, dotted throughout with little prairie homesteads, each standing proudly alone, connected only by a hot, strangling mesh of twentieth-century freeway. 'To look at the cross-section of any plan of a big city', Wright wrote feverishly in *The Living City* some years later, 'is to look at something like the section of a fibrous tumor.' A city like New York is really a kind of 'vampire' – a monster that 'must renew itself from our farms and villages'.[8] In other words, what had looked like a simple desire for green suburbia was at its heart a decidedly *anti*-urban philosophy. It's true that this school of thought, a strange mixture of eugenic pastoralism, frontier 'individualism', and the desire for order and rationality, was largely held at bay by the unpredictable boom in urban living that swept through many countries in the mid-twentieth century. But it was now returning, with more and more force, in the queasy opening decades of the twenty-first.

Here's an example: one very boring afternoon, just a couple of weeks before I went to Welwyn, I saw a tweet from the hugely successful Danish architecture firm BIG, announcing its participation in a major new project.[9] A US billionaire called Marc Lore, who had made a good part of his fortune through his co-ownership of the baby accessories website diapers.com, announced that he was going to finance the building of a new city called Telosa, somewhere deep in the Arizona desert. Telosa, I found out from a link in the tweet, was an attempt to reform capitalism around a philosophy that Lore termed 'equitism'.[10] The core of this notion comes from the Victorian economist and reformer Henry George, who, in a much earlier period of rapid urbanisation, argued for using the increasing value of residential land for community benefit rather than private gain (it was George's ideas that had also inspired Ebenezer Howard).[11] To design his own utopia around these principles, Lore had hired the celebrity Danish architect Bjarke Ingels, BIG's founder. Ingels had made his name in the early 2000s by building a housing block in Copenhagen, VM, modelled on Le Corbusier's *Unité d'habitation*. The idea behind VM was that the twisting angles of two buildings (one in the shape of a 'V'; the other more like an 'M'), added to skilfully cantilevered balconies, meant that instead of simply gazing into each other's windows, residents could look out onto green fields. In a book setting out his design philosophy, Ingels spoke of work like this in grand, Darwinian terms. 'Human life evolved through adaptation to changes in the natural environment,' he wrote. 'With the invention of architecture and technology we have seized the power to adapt our surroundings to the way we want to live . . . as life evolves, our cities and our architecture need to evolve with it.'[12]

When I googled 'Telosa', I saw, okay, many of the urban futurist clichés that you might expect from a man who'd made a fortune from small children shitting themselves, but I saw something else too. In the promotional materials, people were shown hanging out in parks, surrounded by trees, lazily dipping their feet into pools. In busy street scenes, the artists had been careful to show that the pavements were lined with local Arizonan plants (or at least my possibly problematic idea of Arizonan plants; anyway, they looked like really big cactuses), making clear that there would always be views into the distant mountain range. The website assured would-be residents that they would 'always be connected to nature' and that abundant 'city parks' will 'host carefully managed reservoirs which store water for the city and provide all residents with open space within minutes of where they live'.[13]

Things began to escalate. In July 2022, a video popped up in my social media feed, showing an artist's rendering of *another* new city, to be built this time in the desert north-west of Saudi Arabia. It was called The Line, though in the video it just looked like a giant nightclub corridor: two enormous mirrored walls, each 500 metres high and 170 kilometres long, were apparently going to be erected 200 metres from one another. In the gap in between, the designers imagined a hyper-futuristic urban space, filled with trees and flowers, with – here and there – a few modern-looking buildings peeking out. In the publicity material, The Line was described as 'the future of urban living . . . a civilizational revolution that puts humans first, providing an unprecedented urban living experience while preserving the surrounding nature'.[14] This place will eventually be home, say the Saudi government, to nine million people. There will be no roads or cars; no emissions of any kind; the city will operate wholly on renewable energy; and nature will be fully integrated throughout. In one sense, this all seems like pie in the sky, something that can be easily dismissed. But also it isn't. Because The Line is just one part of a new urban mega-project under way in Saudi Arabia called NEOM: a giant new smart city to be built from scratch, including not only The Line, but also a floating octagonal port city, an airport and a ski resort.[15] There may also be, according to the *Guardian*, 'a huge artificial moon, glow-in-the-dark beaches, flying drone-powered taxis, robotic butlers to clean the homes of residents and' – this final flourish seeming to tempt fate somewhat – 'a *Jurassic Park*-style attraction featuring animatronic lizards'.[16] Despite the claim that it is being built on empty land, Indigenous people have claimed they have been violently evicted from the area since the project began. In October 2022, it was reported that three members of a tribe who refused to leave their land had been sentenced to death.[17]

If Telosa and NEOM are visions of the future, they are nonetheless both oddly familiar. From the parks to the tree-lined streets, from the references to Henry George to the weird concern with civilisation, from the interest in Darwin to a violent relationship with Indigenous people, these two places offer a vision of the future city, of the future *green* city, wholly rooted in the ideologies and anxieties of the nineteenth century. What if this connection between the past and the present, I wondered, between techno-science fantasy and pre-modern dreamland held up for green urbanism more generally? And also thinking about powerful billionaires, and celebrity architects, and the autocratic leaders of petrostates, what if we weren't importing just the urban and environmental aesthetics of the nineteenth century, but also the social and political structures that those aesthetics were very explicitly designed to convey? Were we, in fact, returning to the pre-modern city in more ways than one?

This book, I should say at the outset, is *against* green cities. It's also more or less against the idea of the urban future – not least because, as is becoming clear in Saudi Arabia, visions of the future city are always violent for someone.[18] I'm writing against these things not because I'm sceptical about the positive effects of green space, or the need for some kind of environmental transformation as climate change starts to really bite, but because I think the science and politics of green urbanism is a great deal more complex than we want to admit. With this in mind, I'm going to talk to scientists and architects in what follows; I'm going to meet people doing meditation work in forests, activists trying to protect city trees, and individuals carrying out serious policy work on cities and happiness. These are all *good* people. And yet there's something else going on too – something more unsettling in terms of the grand, overarching visions of the urban future with which we are ceaselessly bombarded. Because despite the science-fiction visual rhetoric that green urban futures so often trade in, despite the critical work that lots of activists and planners are doing in cities today, I'm worried that what is really at stake, ideologically as well as aesthetically, is a decidedly nineteenth-century vision – a vision in which the primal urge of grasping city dwellers needs to be tamed by the stern hand of nature; in which social elites, anxious once again about the lively, convivial mass of urban humans that surround them, have suddenly become really interested in covering streets with forests, in turning bustling neigh-bourhoods into sterile parks. What I realised, in the course of researching and writing this book, is that the future of the city looks very weirdly like its past. And I began to wonder if there wasn't something worth valuing and protecting about the city as it is now. Cities are messy, unequal, often violent for sure. But in terms of our capacity to think and build and plot collectively, to improve our situation materially, to impose ourselves, and our ideas, and our homes on the world around us, the city *as a city*, it seemed to me, was a space where the political and moral goods of late modernity, at least for some people, for some of the time, could feel powerfully close to hand.

I emailed Bjarke Ingels's office to see if someone might talk to me about all of this. They sent back a polite response thank-ing me for reaching out, but regretting to inform me that they weren't doing interviews right now. Maybe I could circle back in six months? Maybe. In the meantime, I decided to start with an architect who had inspired Bjarke Ingels, surely the most interesting, most influential, most problematic and simply the *strangest* person to take the problem of nature and the city seriously in the century just gone. I decided to start with Le Corbusier.

# 1: Living in the City

Corbusierhaus, Berlin.

In the late summer of 1933, a group of architects and planners boarded a steamship, the SS *Patris II*, in the port of Marseilles. The passengers were all members of CIAM, the Congrès internationaux d'architecture moderne, a movement founded in 1928 to create a new architecture, one better attuned to the forms and rhythms of the machine age.[1] The 1933 Congress – CIAM's fourth – had been planned for Moscow, where the Communist Party had once shared the group's revolutionary approach to remaking the built environment. By the early 1930s, however, Stalin had his own ideas about the monumental architecture of the new century. Spurned, CIAM decided to make for Greece by boat – for what would become one of the most influential urban planning meetings of the century.[2]

On board was the great modernist architect and planner Le Corbusier, who was then becoming CIAM's most visible figure.[3] Le Corbusier was at a creative high point: having made his name – and a great public scandal – with his *Plan Voisin* to more or less level the centre of Paris in 1925, he had then proposed a similar plan for the rebuilding of Algiers. This would have meant, among other things, surrounding the city's world-famous Kasbah with a forest of skyscrapers and a highway suspended above the ground at a height of about fourteen storeys (alas, the mayor of Algiers went in another direction).[4] Also on board was the Finnish designer and architect Alvar Aalto, who had just completed his Paimio Sanatorium in south-west Finland, a hugely influential modernist intervention in hospital design, where the building itself was designed to be part of the healing process.

These were serious times for modern design. Two weeks before the ship left Marseilles, the Bauhaus school in Berlin, then the world's most famous design institute, had voted to dissolve itself following raids by the Gestapo and increasing pressure from the Nazi government. László Moholy-Nagy, the Hungarian-born photographer, film-maker and designer who had taught at the Bauhaus in the 1920s, was also travelling on the *Patris II*. Moholy-Nagy had even brought a 16mm camera, shooting footage that he later edited into a twenty-nine-minute silent film, *Architect's Congress*. The movie still floats around online today, a remarkably watchable and yet deeply melancholic document of the voyage. In wavering, silent images, earnest planners paste schemes for cities like Detroit and Zaandam to the ship's heaving bulkheads; serious young men crowd the sunny decks for talks by Le Corbusier and CIAM's chair, the Dutch planner Cornelis van Esteren; excitement overcomes the passengers as the ship approaches the Isthmus of Corinth; then we see Moholy-Nagy himself, smiling warmly as he greets the Greek delegation at the port; and, finally, there is the grand opening of the Congress, with 1,500 hopeful people in attendance. Looming overhead, we see the Acropolis of Athens, lit for the occasion and brightening the night sky – like a promise, from history, of great things to come. Within the decade, both the city that these architects set sail from and the one they had just arrived in would be under fascist occupation.

In 1933, the future of Europe and the future of the city seemed like two halves of the same equation. CIAM had been founded on the idea that in the age of the machine, architecture could no longer be neatly separated from political and economic realities. Now more than ever, thinking about what buildings should be like, how towns should work, meant confronting the starkest political, ethical and even biological questions of how humans were going to make their lives in the century to come.

This was, to say the least, a politically ambiguous and awkward project. In the years that followed, Le Corbusier – a long-time fascist affiliate and anti-Semite, despite being widely associated with the left – would move to Vichy, the capital of occupied France, and collaborate actively with its Nazi-backed puppet government.[5] In 1943, he anonymously published his *Athens Charter* in occupied Paris, formally recording the findings of the 1933 meeting in his inimitable style.[6] The cities that CIAM had examined, he argued, were pictures of total chaos, leading to nothing but misery for their poor citizens. Modern cities are failures; they 'do not fulfil their purpose, which is to satisfy the primordial biological and psychological needs of their populations'. The urban citizen is even 'molested' by the machine age: they are stifled, crushed, trodden underfoot; green space is devoured by the unplanned growth of the suburbs; the air is foul and the transport makes no sense.

The solution, Le Corbusier says, summarising the findings of the Congress, is to divide the functions of work, play, housing and movement. With high-speed motor cars you can keep factories and offices far away from houses, with green open space (and a multi-lane highway) in between. That also means building upwards, making the city vertical, but doing so, perhaps counter-intuitively, to preserve vast tracts of open land for rest and play, for making a pleasant vista, even for growing vegetables.

For the members of CIAM, the hyper-modern city is not – as it was so influentially caricatured in the film-maker Fritz Lang's 1923 masterpiece *Metropolis* – a place of endless speed, efficiency, production and toil. As the historian Peder Anker points out, avant-garde architecture in the 1930s was deeply concerned with biological science and humans' place in nature.[7] The delegates in 1933 were interested in leisure, good living and what we might today call 'wellbeing'. They were bothered about sunlight and green spaces and play areas, and what someone would do for entertainment when they got home from work. 'A town is a tool,' Le Corbusier had written in 1924. In the modern age, we are confronted with an 'immense step in evolution, so brutal and so overwhelming' that we will either grip that tool firmly and put it to use or we will perish. We have to 'burn our bridges', Le Corbusier declared. We must 'break with the past'.[8]

Exactly eighty-five years after the delegates of CIAM set sail from Marseilles, I travelled in less elegant fashion to Athens for another congress on the future of the city in troubled times. Amazingly, I had booked a late flight without it having occurred to me that Athens is quite far from London. I landed, deeply confused, in an empty terminal smelling of smoke at 4 a.m. and took a taxi that drove at great speed down the deserted motorway, before arriving in an alarmingly fancy hotel, where I briefly collapsed. I woke three hours later, bleary-eyed, and headed to an open-air breakfast deck filled with sun, yoghurt, cold meat, and Americans. The morning heat was up, the magpies had started to circle – and there, overlooking the city as if nothing at all had happened, was the same Acropolis that had been lit in hope for Le Corbusier, Moholy-Nagy and the architects of CIAM all those decades ago.

I was in Athens for the first-ever meeting of a new group that was also interested in urbanisation, wellbeing and the good life: the World Congress on Forests for Public Health. I had tagged along because I wanted to see, up close, a loosely organised 'movement' that I had been following for a while – a movement that, it seemed to me, was also rethinking the shape and fabric of modern life, albeit with more subtlety, and perhaps a little less bombast.

This was still a movement of architects and planners, but now psychologists, public health people and politicians were also involved. They, too, saw something potentially catastrophic in the modern city, but not so much because of bad planning, or because architects were too timid – which was Le Corbusier's diagnosis. I was following people who were instead convinced that living in cities was actually *in itself* fiercely bad for us: that the literal brick and stone and speed of urban life were making us stressed, lonely, depressed, *ill*. And their vision for remaking the city wasn't one of geometrically ordered skyscrapers, helipads, ten-lane highways and the latest synthetic materials. It was the opposite: a vision of the city remade as a *forest* – a pastoral space of parks, streams and hedgerows, of otters in the river and trees on the streets.

Le Corbusier once wrote that we should think of the city as 'the grip of man upon nature' – even as a 'human operation directed *against nature*' (my emphasis).[9] A century later, the ambitions of architects and planners seemed to be very different. Instead of exalting the city as a triumph over the natural landscape, here was a vision of urban space as a kind of anti-city, a place that hides its own basic *citiness*, embarrassed, beneath a canopy of trees.

In the weeks and months surrounding the congress, London formally declared itself a park. A week or so after that, there was a story in the news about wild boars taking over parts of Barcelona. Singapore announced that it was turning its airport into a botanic garden, complete with orang-utans. Indonesia said that it was going to rebuild its new capital as a forest city. What was happening here? What was this shrubby, green, urban future that seemed to be coming into global existence – and doing so almost without notice? How and why was the fabric of city life being transformed before our eyes?

Here's the thing that surprises you about Athens: it's very modern. Ancient ruination is everywhere, obviously. There's still the agora and the library; there's the Temple of Athena Nike and the Theatre of Dionysus; here and there you can even find a still-functioning Byzantine temple; and if you stand in the right place for long enough, you will hear the low, uncanny hum of Greek Orthodox chant, the distant sound of a pre-medieval world that can gently unhook your bones from your nerves. So the slightly rickety, jerry-built air of the twentieth-century city takes you by surprise, hastily bolted together over the decades, without much planning regulation, as people came in from the countryside seeking work and a better life.

More incongruous are the great monumental modernist constructions that dot the Athens skyline: the serene American embassy by the Bauhaus founder, Walter Gropius; the Hilton Hotel, with its reliefs by the Greek artist Yiannis Moralis; the great hulking passenger terminal at the ancient port of Piraeus, built in the early 1960s by Ioannis Lapsis and Elias Scroumbelos.[10] Athens is a city where the ancient and modern slide over one another in sometimes eerie ways. On a day off, I tried to take a photo of the ruined Temple of Olympian Zeus – a row of colossal, fifty-foot columns, standing in rigid formation against the sky – and my phone, mistaking the giant pillars for a close-up of a barcode, began frantically searching the internet to find me a better deal. It was a strange reminder that while our symbols may move around, the visual grammar they rely upon has surprisingly long roots.

The congress was meeting at one of the great symbols of modernist Athens, the Hellenic War Museum, a square-looking building topped by a thick, overhanging rectangle of concrete, like a giant stone mushroom. I had come early to see the keynote speaker and main attraction, a scientist and author whose name has become synonymous with the idea that getting out of the city to 'bathe' in the forest is vital for your psychological and emotional health: Dr Qing Li from the Nippon Medical School in Tokyo, the then president of the Japanese Society for Forest Medicine.

'People like forests,' Li told the assembly, as the room gradually filled with foresters, planners and public health people from all over the world. The air, he said – I am paraphrasing here from my notes – the atmosphere, the sense of calm, all of it produces a preventive effect against some of the most well-known illnesses associated with our modern lifestyle. The practice known in Japanese as *shinrin-yoku* – literally, forest-bathing – reduces the amount of adrenaline in the body, thus bringing down stress and ultimately making us less prone to depression, anxiety and anger. 'Forest medicine', Li told us, is a 'new science'.

As images of ancient Japanese forests flashed up behind him, he described the role of phytoncides, the organic compounds found in the natural oils that trees sometimes use as a defence against insects and fungi.[11] Releasing phytoncides into the air, he told us, is also how trees communicate with one another – and, in fact, this is often what you smell when walking through a forest. In his book extolling the virtues of *shinrin-yoku*, Li describes a study in which he took twelve volunteers and slipped phytoncide oil into a diffuser as they slept, but otherwise changed nothing else about their lives. All of them slept better and had fewer stress hormones, as well as higher levels of some immune-system cells.

Li has been interested in this topic since 1982, and has been collecting data in earnest since 2004. In his best-selling book *Into the Forest*, he talks about how we modern humans have become estranged from nature as we have moved towards life as an urban species. We live, he writes, in dense, overcrowded cities, packed onto subways, crammed on footpaths, corralled in our offices and air-conditioned houses. We've allowed ourselves to become overworked, stressed out, tied to screens in small rooms. The city might be an exciting place, he concedes – but it's a stressful one too, and that stress plays a role in heart attacks, strokes and cancer.[12]

Even more insidious is the effect of this urban mode of life on our mental health – on loneliness, isolation, depression. 'A two-hour forest bathe', writes Li, 'will help you to unplug from technology and slow down. It will bring you into the present moment and de-stress and relax you.' It will boost your energy, improve your mood, bring down your blood pressure and help your immune system. Simply being in the atmosphere of the forest – breathing in the organic compounds emitted by the trees – can have major effects on your health.

Shuffling in my beautifully designed but strikingly uncomfortable 1970s seat, it would be fair to say I was sceptical. What would the utopian skyscraper architects on the *Patris II* have made of it all? And yet speaker after speaker came

A beautiful but uncomfortable seat at the Hellenic War Museum, Athens.

to the podium and told a similar story. Groups of people with mental health problems had been led into the woods in Poland, Ireland, Serbia, South Korea; with the help of trained guides, they'd been taken on structured walks through the trees; they'd breathed in the phytoncides; they'd touched the trees. And over and over again their stress had gone down, their mood had gone up.

Several other speakers outlined plans for giving city dwellers more opportunities to experience nature in their daily lives. There were discussions of the mental health benefits of increasing tree cover in cities, of creating the conditions for more birdsong, of producing 'micro-forests' in otherwise forlorn pockets of urban space, of the psychological benefits of people simply tending their own gardens, and so on and on. Overwhelmed by it all, I skipped the conference dinner and went out for sausages and *bifteki* on my own, flicking through the scientific literature and brooding over what seemed to be an unavoidably green, leafy future for the modern city.

The thing is, none of this can be dismissed, even if, like me, you're inclined to dismiss it. It's true that the scientific literature is still quite new and hasn't really settled down yet, but generally it does seem to support these conclusions, showing fairly consistently the positive effects that being around green space has on health, and especially mental health. In one striking study a group of Danish researchers used historic satellite images to track the amount of green space around the childhood homes of Danish adults; they were able to show, remarkably, that the more green space you had around your house at the age of twelve, the less likely you were to be admitted to a psychiatric hospital as a grown-up.[13] Another study, reported in many newspapers, showed that taking just twenty minutes out of your day to be around nature – strolling through a park on your lunch break, say – is enough of a 'nature dose' to measurably reduce your stress levels. Scientists even suggest that doctors should write prescriptions for this, instructing their stressed-out, city-dwelling patients to take twenty-minute 'nature pills' and improve their mental health.[14]

There's something incredibly seductive about all this. When I got home, I moved into the back bedroom of our house and opened the big window wide before going to sleep. When I woke, I was no longer looking at the grey slate of my neighbour's roof but instead had a view onto the thick canopy of trees and bushes that our small row of terraced houses hides behind its back. And it's true: I slept better. I *felt* better.

*

It's that feeling that I want to try to understand – that sense of calm and stillness that comes from looking out of a bedroom window onto a slowly waving group of trees. For a lot of people, that feeling is hugely important, even vital for their physical and emotional wellbeing. Some scientists have shown that our bodies heal quicker when we can see trees. Others argue that being around nature is such a core part of our evolutionary inheritance that, in its absence, many of us will entirely lose our reason.[15]

Such claims have now found their way into the worlds of architecture and urban planning, and thereby into the political and financial institutions that ultimately decide how cities take shape. In London, leading architectural theorists are currently trying to design buildings that function like biological organisms, so that they are more in tune with our natural rhythms and preferences. In Shanghai, the city authorities have approved an enormous residential and retail complex in the centre of the city that will be literally built into an entirely new tree-covered hill. (The designer is Thomas Heatherwick, who once designed a grand new 'garden bridge' in London. That project, alas, controversially ran aground due to cost overruns and a growing realisation that what had been sold as a new 'floating paradise' for the city was in reality a privately owned, gated space, to be hired out for corporate events, among other activities.[16]) All of this seems to be very much at odds with what – until very recently – most of us assumed the future of the city would look like. From the most avant-garde science fiction to the most banal planning documents, a shared agenda has emerged: for the good of humanity, the city of the future must be woody and green.

It is no coincidence that we are living in one of the greatest periods of urbanisation in human history. The much-cited UN statistic is that nearly 70 per cent of the world's population will be urban dwellers by 2050.[17] Make of that what you want. It's certainly true that there are more cities in the world today than there have ever been, and that the sizes of some – the 24 million people of Shanghai, the 18 million of Karachi – have grown at scales that would have been unimaginable until quite recently. And part of me wonders if much of this desire to entirely reimagine the city as a green space doesn't also reflect a kind of cultural anxiety about that – a growing fear that we have perhaps pulled ourselves out of reach of our natural roots, that we have wandered too far from the garden.

This is perhaps a good moment to remember that this is not the first point in history when there has been, at the same time, a great movement of the population to the cities *and* a large, official anxiety about what that might mean for the minds and bodies of those who have moved – *and* a large cultural turn towards greenery, trees and wilderness. In fact, there is a striking historical correlation between, on the one hand, romantic ideas about nature, and on the other, periods of mass urbanisation.

In the early 1860s, during the violent displacement of Indigenous North American people from the central Sierra Nevada, travellers into the west of the still-expanding American empire were reportedly struck by the awe-inspiring beauty of the area we now call Yosemite. Reports filtered back to the cities of the east, and so the first white tourists started to come – and with them, the early stirrings of a tourist infrastructure, with large consequences for the ecology of the area.[18]

This was also a time when hundreds of thousands of people were arriving every year into the exploding cities of the north-eastern United States, cramming into the manky streets of New York, Boston and Philadelphia, making a new life as best they could in the unsanitary, overcrowded cities. The historian Dorceta Taylor argues that at the meeting point of these simultaneous developments – rapid urbanisation in the east, colonial conquest in the west – the *idea* of wilderness emerges in North America. So, too, does a new kind of person with a new kind of aim: a self-consciously robust man or woman given to wandering westwards, away from the dank metropolis, and into what they thought of as a pristine, natural landscape. This ideology of North American wilderness was, needless to say, reliant on erasing Indigenous people from both the territory and the history of the landscapes that were then being colonised.[19]

Yosemite was declared a national park by Abraham Lincoln in 1864. A commission was appointed to study the ecology of the new park and make plans for its effective management, with Frederick Law Olmsted as the commission's chair. Olmsted, as we noted in the Introduction, is known to many today as the 'father' of American landscape architecture. In 1864, he was already the co-designer of New York's Central Park, a prolific writer and anti-slavery campaigner, and a decorated former head of the sanitary commission during the Civil War.[20] But Olmsted was also a journalist (he co-founded the magazine *The Nation*) and a hugely influential writer about nature. He was someone who not only shaped natural spaces; he also shaped how we think about those spaces in the first place, and what we think they are for.[21]

Albert Bierstadt, *Valley of the Yosemite*, 1864.

Olmsted wrote his first report on Yosemite the following year. It was vitally important, he argued, for Congress to secure the area, before some rich individual acquired it for himself and, in pursuit of personal gain, spoiled this 'union of the deepest sublimity with the deepest beauty of nature'. Olmsted makes two arguments for governments acquiring spaces like Yosemite. One is purely financial: people were already coming from Europe to see the area, and it would be enormously advantageous to the finances of the new state of California, and to its enterprising citizens, to preserve the thing that these travellers were coming to see. But the other argument is more psychological in nature. 'It is a scientific fact,' he writes in the report,

> that the occasional contemplation of natural scenes of an
> impressive character, particularly if this contemplation
> occurs in connection with relief from ordinary cares, change

of air and change of habits, is favorable to the health and vigor of men and especially to the health and vigor of their intellect beyond any other conditions which can be offered them, that it not only gives pleasure for the time being but increases the subsequent capacity for happiness and the means of securing happiness.

In other words, without the opportunity to contemplate nature there could be no happiness – and this in a nation founded on precisely the notion that achieving happiness was the central object of human existence. But it gets worse: urban people do not have the opportunity for the contemplation of natural scenes, Olmsted writes, and the result is

a class of disorders, the characteristic quality of which is mental disability, sometimes taking the severe forms of softening of the brain, paralysis, palsey [*sic*], monomania, or insanity, but more frequently of mental and nervous excitability, moroseness, or irascibility, incapacitating the subject for the proper exercise of the intellectual and moral forces.

What we see here is a key moment in the cultural reimagining of the great outdoors as a psychological object – a moment in which influential figures are cementing a deep connection between the human psyche and the environment. This isn't any kind of deliberate plot; Olmsted, I am certain, is wholly sincere. But nonetheless there's something in the air, as he and his fellow commissioners tramp through the valleys and caverns of Yosemite. They are simply very ready to see a deep relation between mind, body and nature; they are eager to believe that being immersed in nature might have a profound effect on a person's nervous system.[22]

In Olmsted's writing, then, we can begin to grasp some of the deep roots of the cultural connection between nature, urbanisation and the psyche – to understand that what may look to us like a finding from recent science goes well back into the nineteenth century.[23] And it goes back not only into early versions of scientific research, but also into landscape design, architecture, conservation and government bureaucracy. It is a collective anxiety about the mental states of these new citizens – from Ireland, Italy and what were certainly seen as the less 'civilised' parts of Europe – that Olmsted is partly channelling when he writes about Yosemite and what it could do for Americans; a sense that deprivation of nature was bad for these weak urban dwellers' general character, that without what the feminist theorist Donna Haraway once called a 'prophylactic dose of nature', urban life would produce nervous disorder, anxiety and a general sense of degeneration; that the new nation had to act – and it had to act fast.[24]

On the other side of the Atlantic, at more or less the same time, an identical concern had already manifested itself – with a strikingly similar solution. In London in 1833 – a hundred years before the delegates of CIAM set sail from Marseilles – a parliamentary committee had been set up to investigate the lack of green space in the United Kingdom's rapidly expanding industrial cities.[25] We are 'convinced', the committee wrote in its first report, 'that some Open Places reserved for the amusement (under due regulations to preserve public order) of the humbler classes would assist to wean them from low and debasing pleasures . . . it must be evident that it is of the first importance to their health on their day of rest to enjoy the fresh air.'[26] In other words, parks should be provided for the benefit of the lower orders on Sundays. And the committee was very frank about what the purpose of such parks would be: the control of the burgeoning working classes. 'A man walking out with his family among his neighbours of different ranks, will naturally be desirous to be properly clothed, and that his Wife and Children should be so also . . . this desire duly directed and controlled, is found by experience to be of the most powerful effect in promoting Civilisation, and exciting Industry.'

Anxieties about urbanisation, green space and the proper conduct of man had been circulating in Britain even before the Indigenous people of Yosemite were being torn from their land. In fact, it was an 1850 visit to Britain's first urban park, at Birkenhead in Merseyside, that partly inspired Olmsted's later work: 'this magnificent pleasure ground is entirely, unreservedly, and forever the People's own', he marvelled in an article for *The Horticulturalist* the following year. 'The poorest British peasant is as free to enjoy it in all its parts as the British Queen.'[27]

Birkenhead Park had been designed by Joseph Paxton and opened to the public in 1847. An improvement initiative by the wealthy merchants of Liverpool, Birkenhead was a small-scale intervention in the grand scheme of things, and more aimed at the wealthy classes than the slothful day labourer. But it was also the tipping point of a movement that had begun to grow and swell as the century proceeded: a movement to get more green spaces into Britain's exploding cities, and to do so not for aesthetic reasons, nor particularly out of the munificence of the urban authorities, but rather as an intervention in the health – including, to use a term that didn't exist then, the mental health – of the urban poor.[28]

The city park, in this sense, should be understood as one thread within the thick weave of moralism, reform and improvement that characterised the great public institutions of the age.[29] The rapid expansion of green space in the city was partly born out of a genuine sense of patrician duty, it's true, partly out of a moral objection to the base pursuits of drinking and dog fighting (and thus the desire to provide a healthy alternative), and partly, in this era of revolutions, out of an attempt to channel any insurrectionary feeling into more tranquil and, indeed – where appropriate – more amorous, even reproductive, pursuits. It was also simply about getting people out walking and breathing in the fresh air, keeping them physically healthy and rejuvenated, all the better to be ready for the following week's work once their day of rest was over.

All of this is well and good. But the history of England's great nineteenth-century parks – Victoria Park in east London, Moor Park in Preston, Stanley and Sefton Parks in Liverpool, Philips Park in Manchester, Peel Park in Bradford – is also the history of an attempt to mould and create a new urban citizen; to intervene in and even to alter the 'character' of that citizen, to affect what we might today call their 'mental state'. We should think of the urban park in Victorian England not as a neutral space but as a technology for soothing people, for calming them, even for *civilising* them, in quite explicit terms.[30]

This attempt to use the city park to intervene in the body and the mind – to keep the humble urban citizen both physically fit and morally good – is perhaps best seen in the work of the National Health Society, a philanthropic and reformist health promotion society formed in London in 1871. The historian Clare Hickman, drawing on the society's archive, has shown how its members' wide-ranging interests in public health became embroiled in the growing 'open space' movement, which promoted the creation of urban parks, among other kinds of healthy spaces, even turning into a kind of early environmental activism.[31]

The urban park, Hickman says, was thus where two anxieties about the new class of urban worker came together. In one sense, the desire to get people out walking came from a *medical* concern to keep the urban worker fit and well (not least so they could keep working without the inconvenience of illness or death). But the same development can also be seen as a *moral* concern that the worker be a person of good character, that they not be brought low by nervous agitation, melancholy or insanity. And this was the case not only for the park, but also for the allotment, the vegetable patch, the domestic garden, the arboretum, and so on. This was an age marked by a generalised concern with the 'social question': how to keep booming industrial capitalism on the road, despite the enormous and highly visible violence and injustice it produced, and do so without creating the conditions for revolution. For many among the governing classes of the day, the urban park was a major part of the answer.

These developments had at least partly grown out of a connection between green space and the mind that had been established half a century earlier, in the then new practice of asylum architecture.[32] As asylums for the insane gradually stopped being spaces of confinement and punishment, they morphed into restorative, therapeutic retreats, generally in rural areas, where interaction with nature was at the heart of the new system of treatment. In Britain, this development was pioneered by the Quakers William Tuke, who established the York Retreat in 1796, and his grandson Samuel, who popularised the method with a book he published in 1813. Frederick Law Olmsted also worked on plans for mental institutions in Hartford, Buffalo and western Massachusetts. His plan for the last of these – the McLean asylum in Belmont, which is still functioning today – was thrown into poignant relief when he himself became a patient there at the end of his life.[33] Who knows how much of Olmsted's own agitated thinking was soothed by the woody calm of his new surroundings. By the time he died there, in 1903, the debate about nature, the city and the mind had barely started.

A few months after I left Athens, I was in Paris. I hate Paris. It's something about the mix of imperial pomp and saccharine cutesiness in the streetscape. It's also the terrible food, I think. And though quite a few European cities confuse rudeness with having a personality, in Paris there is just something about the sheer *frequency* of interpersonal unpleasantness that, over time, becomes wounding to the human spirit. Mostly, my hatred of Paris is a reaction to a very dull and conventional city's vastly inflated reputation. I'm broadly with Le Corbusier here: raze the centre, build a highway and some skyscrapers, then fill the space in between with gardens and vegetable patches. That at least would be interesting.

I was in Paris, nonetheless, for a gathering of global 'thought leaders' interested in the benefits of making the modern city more green. It was, in fact, an auspicious location. The mayor had just announced a plan to surround the city's major landmarks with trees, creating an 'urban forest' that would help meet the goal of Paris being 50 per cent covered by trees by 2030. This was no small endeavour: 'the city imagines turning the square in front of city hall into a pine grove', wrote the journalist Feargus O'Sullivan, 'while future springtimes will see the opera house's back elevation emerge from a sea of cherry blossom. The paved plaza at the side of the Gare de Lyon will become a woodland garden.'[34]

The conference I was attending – a self-described global 'movement', in fact – was a forum for scientists, planners, political leaders and others to come together around a shared green-city agenda. It was big: several hundred attendees from around the world were at the Sorbonne, including many of the major figures from the world of urban ecosystems, who were treated to an art programme, an accompanying book of 'flash fiction' and a 'farm to table' banquet. For an event happening on a university campus, it was slickly choreographed, with a rolling programme of public 'dialogues', 'microtalks' and 'seed sessions', ranging from how to finance green infrastructure to how to meditate with plants. There were speeches from various French political and business figures, a wordless performance about street trees that I didn't understand, and lots of talk about biodiversity and the psychological benefits of nature. I went to one session where you got to wear a VR headset to see what your green roof might look like, and another where you had to pretend to be a place and then be psychoanalysed as if you were that place. An artist gave a talk on how she likes to dance with nature in the city, and later I saw her weaving her body, with great deliberation, through the array of small potted plants that lined the meeting's entranceway.

There was something very charming but also oddly *evangelical* about all of this – like a weird mix of Silicon Valley and Christian revivalism. 'Your project is so sacred and so wonderful,' said one speaker to another. Someone else said to a panel of presenters, 'Your talks are so beautiful and poignant.' A planner told the crowd, with great seriousness, 'My job is to be a healer.' You get the idea. At the beginning of each day, everyone had to stand up, look around and introduce themselves to the people nearest to them – it was *that* kind of conference.

Amid the fervour and the enthusiasm and the – I wrestle with my own cynicism here – basically *good* desire to fill the city with trees and birds, to plan in a more ecologically sustainable way, and so on, I was struggling with a larger problem, one that tracks the work of the great park designers of the nineteenth century, the revolutionary modernists of the twentieth and, as we will see, a whole host of other major urban movements and philosophies. That problem has a lot to do with my own suspicions about this entire scene and is one of the major issues I want to help myself understand as I move around this world.

The problem is that everyone in Paris basically seemed to think more nature was good. But no one ever actually said what they meant by 'nature' in the first place. What they meant by this term was, I guess, what most people mean by it: green things, trees, parks, birds, open space, clean air. This was never actually said, though, and so I was left wondering. We're all convinced that there's something wrong with contemporary city life. Equally, we're all convinced – I think – that much of what's wrong has to do with an absence of nature somehow. And that absence seems to go in two directions. On the one hand, there's not enough natural *stuff* in cities – too few trees, not enough otters. On the other, a kind of unnatural *way of living* has taken hold among city people – too much sitting in air-conditioned buildings, too much concrete, too much stress and speed. All of this is, I believe, fairly uncontroversial.

But it was unclear to me then – it still isn't clear now – what it is, exactly, that makes the city so unnatural in the first place. Maybe this seems like hair-splitting, but truly, if put on the spot, I don't think I know what 'nature' actually is. And while we're at it, I'm not even sure I know what counts as 'the city' and what doesn't. Walk as far as you can in a city like London or Shanghai. Walk through Swansea even. Where does the city actually end? At what point – exactly – do you enter the great 'outside' of modern urban life?

In an influential 1938 essay, Lewis Mumford, maybe the greatest American critic of urban planning, defined a city as that place where 'the diffused rays of many beams of life fall into focus'.[35] Cities, says Mumford, are the culmination of humankind's domination of the earth; they're where the need for industry and co-operation have come together. Cities are the great sites of monumental and public life – they are living museums of themselves, cathedrals to their own glory and the forms of life they make possible; cities are where vastly different kinds of people can come together, with different functions and desires and needs, which somehow get orchestrated into the great four-dimensional fold of human social life.

This seems like a fine description of Rome in the fourth century, or London in the nineteenth. But it tells us more or less nothing about daily life in a mid-sized regional city in the early twenty-first century – which is to say, it tells us nothing about the mundane, unremarkable, badly planned and more or less ugly places where almost all urban life gets played out today. 'The future of the city' sounds like a fine topic for discussion, until you realise we are talking about a category that includes Beijing, Poughkeepsie, Byzantium, Atlantis and Limerick.

Airy talk tells us little about what actually counts as 'the city' and what doesn't – about what is urban space, and what is a natural environment, and what actually marks the break between these categories. This really matters. In Paris, lots of people were convinced that the future of the city inevitably meant bringing healthier, greener, more natural, non-city things into it, even reshaping and replanting the city itself around those things.

But take a concrete tower block – for many people, the epitome of unnatural urban living and the great icon of modern, nature-conquering architecture and planning. There's nothing obviously unnatural about concrete. Even the raw *béton brut*, the concrete that gives its name to the distinctive style we call 'brutalism': the chalk, clay and various chemical admixtures that make up cement; the sand, gravel and slag of aggregate;

the water that binds it all together . . . all of these things are unambiguously of this earth. All of them are found in, and harvested from, the wild outdoors. All of them have been bobbing around in the surface gloop that covers this planet at least as long as we have, and likely longer. To rub one's face against a concrete wall and to rub it against a leaf are, no doubt, different sensory experiences. But it is not a difference that is obviously marked by contact with 'nature'. Yes, some might say, but surely there is something in the processing of these raw materials that somehow shifts the end product into the category of the unnatural. This does not seem convincing: just as with moral panics around 'processed food', the act of mixing and processing and combining is complex, but it is not doing metaphysical work – there is no process that can make things unearthly, no churn that lifts them out of the same chalky, debased realm that humans, along with every other living creature on the planet, have always inhabited. 'The dams of beavers and the webs of spiders are presumably natural,' says the environmental philosopher Steven Vogel – so then 'why are the dams built by humans or the polyester fabrics they weave not so?'[36] If we feel things to *be* unnatural – if on principle we dislike a modern art gallery, say, or a cup-a-soup – well, we are entitled to our moralism, but no one is obliged to grant this feeling any philosophical or scientific status.

And anyway, as much as the urban things don't seem obviously unnatural, so the natural things are not necessarily un-urban. The languid mother fox who took over a tyre yard next to a flat I once lived in in south London, and who would raise her head, cautious but unafraid, whenever the outside light hit her rubbery throne – she was no less a creature of the city than I was myself. I once lived in Cardiff, which, like a lot of cities near the sea, is regularly terrorised by roaming packs of gulls. You'd see them strutting in groups around town, like a bunch of big Welsh lads, angrily guarding their ill-gotten chips and pizza. Or you'd go home to find them screaming angrily from behind your chimney pot. I truly hated those gulls. But still, I could recognise that not only were they city creatures, they had even adopted a specifically urban mode of life. They were urban*ists*, those gulls, as fiercely identified with that status as any bearded gentrifier. These kinds of awkward co-habitations are only going to become more common. A new wildlife ordnance in Los Angeles means you might just see a mountain lion hanging out at your country club – and this might be your problem, not the lion's.[37] In Asheville, North Carolina, the local black bear population know which day is bin day.[38]

When we think about how life has developed in the city – especially when we think about that development in relation to nature, or our own place in nature – we are often thinking about a set of material traces, traces that seem to lead us back to an artificial turn in the development of human society. At such moments, the city appears to us as a synthetic density of concrete, glass and medium-density fibreboard; of slate, chrome, and liquid crystal; of synthetic fabric, industrial carpet, air conditioning, high-pressure sodium, rubber, petrol, polyester – all the human things of the late modern world, all of which seem to have carried us very far from a more innocent age of trees, birds, otters, air, wood, water and soil. The problem is that the distinction between these sets of things is not obvious. MDF is held together by a wax that comes from palm trees. The town is already full of otters. 'Nature', it turns out, is not necessarily a natural category.

Go back about two hundred and fifty years, the environmental historian William Cronon once wrote, and there's no such thing as 'wilderness'.[39] No one's going off wandering around pristine lakes and canyons in 1700, and any traveller encountering Yosemite in this period would most likely have understood it as a deathly space of horror and fear. It was the Romantic poets and their contemporaries in the eighteenth century who came up with the idea that untouched nature was a way to encounter the 'sublime' – to have a sort of religious experience, even to attain full personhood, in an increasingly industrial and urban age. This Romantic ideal, as it flowed into what became the environmental movement, is at least partly embedded in a suspicion of – even a hostility to – the modern urban world as such. Nature is the central symbol of this hostility; it comes to signify the things and objects that are furthest away from human development. Nature, according to Cronon, is in this sense a fundamentally negative concept: it describes 'the places where humans are not'. We might say that nature, for many urban thinkers today, is only the place where the *city* is not.

And this is a big part of my problem: I'm worried that we're over-investing in nature as a panacea to what are actually fairly mundane urban problems; that we have mistaken what is really only a historically specific malaise – or a side show to the wider sense of melancholy that has often accompanied the modern world – for some kind of biological problem. And it's not that the biology is meaningless. It isn't. Nonetheless, as this book goes on, I'm going to think in a slightly different way about the relationship between humans, wellbeing and the urban environment. I'm going to suggest that whether and how we live well in some place might not have much to do with the relative artificiality or naturalness of that place; that in fact (and here we can learn something from the twentieth-century modernists) there are ways of thinking about planning and design in which natural, organic things and high-tech, industrial things do not move in different spheres.

I'm also worried that we have given too much weight to people who don't actually like cities very much and probably never did – people who maybe don't even like the modern world itself very much. But I *do* love that world. I love its unromantic insistence on always looking forward, always moving on, always going *somewhere*, even with all its jaggedness, its hardness and its capacity for awfulness. I love the cities that absolutely embody that sensibility. I spent the first seven years of my life living in remarkable proximity to an actual bog, and I have never had much time for pastoral scenes.

Before I left Paris, I walked down to the river, to the cathedral of Notre-Dame, which had been wrecked by fire only a few months earlier. The cathedral was cordoned off and closed to visitors, and yet still the ruined structure was a tourist landmark. People crowded round the temporary fence, trying to get a good angle for a photo of the gaping hole in the roof, snapping away at the empty space where the spire used to be. There the cathedral stands now, like the Acropolis of Athens, a melancholy tribute to the urban mode of life, a monument to the glorification of the city, but also to its ruination as time, hubris and – yes – nature take their inevitable toll.

Following a general invitation from President Emmanuel Macron for new ideas to repair the structure, a well-known French architect, Vincent Callebaut, proposed not simply rebuilding the cathedral's roof but transforming it into a garden, complete with a park, a contemplation space and an aquaponic farm, producing its own energy and twenty-one tons of fruit and veg every year. The cathedral, if it were to follow such a design, wrote Callebaut, 'would become an exemplary eco-engineering structure, and the church a true pioneer in environmental resiliency'.[40]

This is a purely speculative design that seems unlikely to be realised, in this space at least: the French Senate has since insisted that the cathedral be rebuilt exactly as it was, despite Macron's grandiose vision. And yet even just as an idea or a wish – to remake the cathedral as a park – this proposal makes clear just how much nature has become an object of both psychological and spiritual repair in the contemporary city. If we can recognise the cathedral as an iconic symbol of the city in previous centuries, with the spire its towering sign of authority and transcendence, then today we just might see the richly landscaped rooftop garden as playing a similar role. It's no longer towering Gothic stonework we look to. Today it's a little copse of waving trees, or a raised vegetable garden, looking onto the streets below, that offers the urban citizen a promise of moral purity, spiritual repair, even something like eternal life.

# 2: The Garden Bathed in Sunlight

Port Sunlight, the Wirral, Merseyside.

In May 1984, the Indian architect Charles Correa arrived in London to attend an event celebrating the 150th anniversary of the Royal Institute of British Architects. Correa was regarded as the most important architect of independent India. Which was not a minor accolade. Ever since Jawaharlal Nehru – India's first prime minister – had invited Le Corbusier to design a new capital for the Indian portion of the partitioned territory of Punjab, architecture had been central to the projection of twentieth-century Indian identity.[1] And the MIT-trained Correa, who had returned to practice in then-Bombay in 1958, was perfectly suited to it: his signature blend of contemporary and 'traditional' materials demonstrated, as one obituary put it, 'an authentic Indian modernity'.[2] In fact, so well recognised was Correa by this time that not only was he attending the RIBA gala as a guest, he was also to be awarded the institute's highest prize: its Royal Gold Medal. This is a big deal in the architecture world. The medal is, as RIBA puts it rather pompously on its website, 'approved personally by the Monarch', and can be given, once a year, to 'a person or group of people who have had a significant influence either directly or indirectly on the advancement of architecture'.[3]

The event was to be held at Hampton Court Palace, on the banks of the River Thames. Given its own various royal entanglements and desires, RIBA had invited the then Prince Charles to give the keynote address. What was required of Charles, we might imagine, was the issuance of some standard royal emollient – a general blessing of the occasion, its fine attendees, the noble profession of architecture, etc., etc. When the prince stood up, however, it was quickly apparent that he had other ideas. 'For far too long, it seems to me,' he began, 'some planners and architects have consistently ignored the feelings and wishes of the mass of ordinary people in this country.'[4] The delegates must have stirred in their seats. What? *What indeed*, Charles asked, had they done to the fine historical city of London, with their ugly modern buildings? He described the winning design to extend the National Gallery in Trafalgar Square as looking 'like a municipal fire station, complete with the sort of tower that contains the siren'. The building, he said, in a now-famous phrase, would end up looking 'like a carbuncle or a wart on the face of an old friend'. One can almost hear the vol-au-vents and thick slices of quiche Lorraine catching in people's throats. One writer later said that the RIBA president's face froze into 'a glazed mask'.[5] Warming to his theme, Charles described another proposal for a tower near the Mansion House in the City of London as 'a giant glass stump'. And anyway, he went on, why has everything these days got to be straight and vertical and functional? Why not use curves or those nice arches that you see on old buildings?

Consider London before the war, Charles continued (which is to say, before his audience had got their hands on it). Building to his speech's highest rhetorical moment, Charles asserted that it was at this time that 'the affinity between buildings and the earth, in spite of the City's immense size, was so close and organic that the houses looked almost as though they had grown out of the earth'. To ensure his audience would not misunderstand the insult, Charles closed by quoting Goethe, effectively saying that there was no point in having imagination without taste. He acknowledged that the association was probably regretting having asked him to speak. Still, he concluded, he hoped the next 150 years would see some improvement. And then he sat back down. As someone put it in RIBA's journal some years later, Charles 'might as well have dropped the mic as he walked off'.[6] That other Charles who had travelled from Mumbai – still somewhere in the room, we have to assume – was by now wholly and entirely forgotten.

From the moment of this speech and up to the present day, the now-King Charles has been one of the most influential and widely discussed figures in architecture and town planning in England. The guiding points of his vision have remained much the same: a kind of jocular but still biting hostility to twentieth-century building materials; a sly fetish for not only the physical but also the social order of the pre-modern city; and a loosely theological idea that anything not built in his own lifetime probably grew out of the soil. But this being England, and he being the longest-serving heir apparent, Charles has had many opportunities to air and expand upon these notions. In particular, as with many institutes and writers who have followed in his wake, Charles has been committed to the idea that this vision of the city as a sort of pre-modern, organic, human-scale construction is simply *better* for the people who live in it, including better for their health; that there is something in the built fabric of late modernity that has jolted people out of the social and biological groove that they had been squatting happily in for some centuries, and that we now need to put this right.

A few years after his speech, Charles expanded on his views in a paranoid and, for the son of a monarch, rather self-pitying volume, *A Vision of Britain*. 'For a long time,' Charles wrote, opposite a picture of a watercolour he had painted at his mother's Balmoral estate, 'I have felt strongly about the wanton destruction which has taken place in this country in the name of progress; about the sheer, unadulterated ugliness and mediocrity of public and commercial buildings, and of housing estates, not to mention the dreariness and heartlessness of so much urban planning.' Modern architecture is the obsession of a shadowy, powerful group of architects that had captured key institutions and produced 'deformed monsters which have come to haunt our towns and cities, our villages and our countryside'. He went on: 'we have ended up with Frankenstein monsters, devoid of character, alien and largely unloved, except by the professors who have been concocting these horrors in their laboratories'.[7]

King Charles is well known for his strong architectural views. He is understood by many in the profession to be simply a kind of idiot dilettante. For others, no doubt – perhaps for people with more conservative leanings – he represents a rare voice of reason and sanity on urban design. But there is something more interesting – more troubling – in the King's view that is less often noticed, which is his idea that the modern cityscape is not simply ugly or badly constructed, rather it is *unnatural*; that unlike the traditional buildings of previous centuries, the architecture of our age has somehow become confected and artificial. Charles looks at Georgian doorways and little stone cottages like a farmer might approvingly regard his soil or his vegetable patch – as the rich and loamy stuff of natural growth and replenishment.

There is a history here. In fact, Charles is reanimating some quite old and distinctive ideas about the relationship between humans and the urban environment, ideas found in the history of garden cities, hygienic cities and the weird utopian cities built by wealthy industrialists. In this view, it is as if cities are not simply the places we make to live in; they are, in fact, environments for making and growing humans. The town thus becomes a kind of ecology, the street a sort of petri dish. Once we start thinking like this, of course, the question of the city and its design becomes transformed: we are no longer faced with an aesthetic question of what kind of city

47

we do or don't like; we are confronted instead with a political and biological question of how cities can be best adapted to human life – of what *kinds* of humans, exactly, we want our cities to produce.

In the late 1980s, the town of Dorchester in south-west England wanted to expand to the west. The land that Dorchester wanted to expand *into*, however, was owned by the Duchy of Cornwall – a territory, and a set of accompanying rights and responsibilities, that had been inherited, as it happens, by the then Prince of Wales. Fresh from the popular success of his book and accompanying BBC programme, Charles took the opportunity to 'work with the council to create a model urban extension to this ancient market town', as the website of that new extension, now called Poundbury, delicately puts it.[8] He immediately appointed the Luxembourgish architect Léon Krier, a well-known opponent of modernist town planning and a noted expert on the work of Hitler's architect, Albert Speer.[9] Krier was the man for the job. Having once worked for the modernist architect James Stirling, Krier, says the writer Owen Hatherley, 'became fixated by the existentialist, rural-romantic philosophy of Martin Heidegger and increasingly disenchanted with the results of postwar reconstruction'.[10] As opposed to the clearly zoned modernist city – where there is one space for living, another for industry, a third for retail, and so on – in *traditional* urban planning, wrote Krier in 1987, one finds instead 'the totality of urban functions within a comfortable and pleasant walking distance'.[11] In his vision, the traditional city is 'a complete and finite urban community, a member of a larger family of independent urban quarters, of cities within the city, of cities within the country. The traditional city is economical in the use of TIME, ENERGY and LAND. It is by nature ECOLOGICAL.' Drawing on such principles, Krier delivered his master plan to Prince Charles the following year, and construction of the first phase of the new town began just four years later.

It's easy to make fun of all this, and easier still to read it as a very conservative, reactionary kind of vision, a squeak of aristocratic terror at the jostle and possibility promised – however ephemerally – by the twentieth-century city. But what does it actually look like? To find out, I went to Poundbury with my wife and son, as well as my father, who, unexpectedly, had decided to visit for the weekend. So we took his rented car on the scenic route towards Dorset, and somewhere in the Mendip Hills, my then one-year-old son vomited all over his child seat, himself and the back of the rental. We brushed him down at the side of the road, pulled half-digested porridge from his hair and made a collective decision to press on. It was Remembrance Sunday, a day when melancholy and nationalism get weirdly entangled in the English psyche, and I had been worried about taking my father – a socially awkward rural Irishman – out for lunch in what was then, after all, still very much the domain of the former Prince of Wales.

The day was grey, and Dorset greyer still. From Dorchester, where elderly men with Union flags were already heading for the pub and a Vera Lynn singalong, we drove up Bridport Road and into Poundbury itself. We carried on through the heart of the new town, towards the recently completed

Queen Mother Square, all four of us staring at the bleakly empty streets like teenagers in a zombie movie. Whatever you think about Poundbury, its aesthetics or its politics, it is an undeniably *weird* place. The main part of town is shaped a bit like a human kidney split into four quadrants; in each, there is a mix of housing, a few shops here and there, and even some small industry. The houses themselves are all 'traditional', meaning in most cases that they follow an aesthetic caught somewhere between the eighteenth and nineteenth centuries. But they're also all pretty new and well kept, so the effect is less like being in a well-worn Georgian street in, say, contemporary London and more like being transported to the historical moment when these styles were new. The effect is a bit uncanny.

That's not the architects' fault, in fairness. But it struck me, as we walked up and down the empty residential

A street in Poundbury, Dorset.

streets, that much of what people find so charming about old houses is that they're *old*. It's not so much the design of a Georgian house that people like specifically; it's just that we live in an age when Georgian houses happen to be old. Not in Poundbury, though. Here, old and new are sort of pressed awkwardly together, rather like a couple skipping the period of getting to know one another and getting straight down to some very public sex. There's a round, commercial-looking building in an area called the Butter Market that houses a coffee shop, as if some part of an old butter market had been repurposed for twenty-first-century tastes. I don't know if anyone ever actually sold butter in this area, but at least it feels like someone created a 'repurposed' building from scratch in the absence of the original purpose, and then named the area after the purpose that may or may not have existed. That's the Poundbury vibe.

Queen Mother Square, though, is where the town goes full Las Vegas. Elizabeth Bowes-Lyon herself is resplendent on an enormous plinth at its centre, a large protruding feather in her hat giving her, from a distance, the unexpected form of a defiant figure holding up a fist. The public and commercial buildings around the square, meanwhile, abandon the English vernacular of the surrounding streets and offer something more like imperial Russia in one of its less self-effacing moments. The square itself, Hatherley again notes, is now 'a free car park, to encourage visitors to the town so that they can inject some life into a rather eerie place, and maybe look at some real estate'.[12] There's a Waitrose and a pub and, nearby, a rather forlorn little playground. Above it all, the Queen Mother gazes benignly down on the Range Rovers

51

and other SUVs. 'It's what she would have wanted, really,' said my father.

It seems hard to deny that Charles's urban vision is, whether one admires these qualities or not, thoroughly Ruritanian, anti-modern, nostalgic and often strikingly vicious, for all the King's image of doddery amiability. At one point in *A Vision of Britain*, he shows an image of himself actually demolishing a block, with the caption: 'I am told that crushed tower block, mixed with soil, makes a very good basis for growing roses.' Later, he waxes lyrical about N. M. Lund's 1904 painting of the Bank of England, *Heart of Empire*, which, says Charles, 'says everything about the harmony and scale of a City of London where the Lord Mayor's Mansion House and the houses of God were given appropriate prominence – all finding their place comfortably in the landscape'. God, empire and capital, in other words, all nestled together, as unchanging – and unchangeable – as the very soil in which they are grounded. In his writing, Charles emphasises 'hierarchy' in design and describes how the scale of buildings should reflect the hierarchy of 'our social organisations'. He likes 'harmony' and 'enclosure', and emphasises 'our indigenous roots'. Some of the ideas in his book – and we might recognise, in Charles's defence, that the book is more than thirty years old – are almost comically reactionary. The things that he values – hierarchy, enclosure, order – are like a paean to feudal privilege, to the point where it seems hard to sustain the idea that we are only (or even mostly) talking about buildings here. All I'm saying is, if I was the undeserving heir to a rich and influential monarchical institution, I too would spend a lot of time talking about the virtues of hierarchy, and God's wishes, and the natural order of things.

This idea of soil, though, or of urban space as potentially *organic* – the idea that the modern city is a problem precisely because it is *not* organic, that the past is to be preferred not so much for aesthetic but rather for biological reasons – is what drew me to Poundbury in the first place. The week before I visited, I had attended an online conference on traditional architecture, and seen a talk by the well-known mathematician and architectural theorist Nikos Salingaros, who argued that humans' relationship to older-style buildings is neurological and subliminal. Beauty isn't about aesthetics, Salingaros had suggested; it's about healing. Old-fashioned buildings draw the eye and engage our attention; natural materials are encoded with fractal patterns that human beings are attracted to; evolution drives us to seek out the deep symmetries that classical architecture offers. More modern buildings, he went on, with their minimal look and their synthetic design, actually repel people at the neurological level (this is an argument that we will encounter in more detail in the next chapter).

What are we to make of all this? It's not an argument I find particularly compelling, but I do get why people might be convinced that the modern built environment is . . . at least at something of a remove from human beings' evolutionary origins or our general biological inclinations. Personally, I don't think it's interesting or useful to say that Trump Tower, for example, is objectionable because its sheer brute ugliness offends our instinctive desire for trees, water or open space, but okay – I get it. The extension of this argument into a claim that, on the other hand, there *are* some buildings that are somehow closer to nature, and better for *our* nature, is where I come unstuck.

'Buildings', says Charles at one point in *A Vision of Britain*, 'should look like they belong.' And then, later: 'There is no need for London to ape Manhattan. We already possessed a skyline. They had to create one.' What could this possibly mean? Does he imagine that St Paul's Cathedral or the Bank of England sprang from the earth? Does he think buildings from before the twentieth century have somehow always been there, without any intervention from humans – that the pre-modern skyline of London has some kind of affinity with the landscape, even that it *belongs* to that landscape? The classical column, Charles says later, began life as a tree trunk propping up a roof; in this sense, the column-as-trunk offers 'a mysterious sense of well-being and a kind of contentment'. In Charles's fantasia, in other words, classical design elements are not simply more biologically appealing to humans; they actually fade back into the earth itself, as if classical buildings are only minor elaborations on already-existing natural forms.

What's at stake here is an idea that the modern cityscape is not simply bad because it's ugly or because lots of people just don't like the look of modern buildings, but that it is *inherently* bad. The claim is that disliking the minimal steel and glass of modern construction is not only an aesthetic judgement; it is, in fact, a kind of biological repulsion, an aversion encoded in one's very genome, passed down from generation to generation as humans became more and more displaced from their natural habitats. In this logic, a person does not dislike downtown Manhattan in the same way they might dislike a book or a film, but rather as they would dislike a snake or a stinging plant.

'There are two principal things that appeal to me about classical architecture,' George Saumarez Smith said to me over lemon tea, in his office at the back of a beautifully restored sixteenth-century manor house in Winchester. I had come to see Saumarez Smith partly because he's one of the most lauded and well-known architects working in the classical tradition in Britain, and I thought he might help me understand its appeal. But I had also come to Winchester because Saumarez Smith, along with the designer Ben Pentreath, is the architect behind a good deal of what's been built in Poundbury over the last ten years or so. His work ranges from art galleries in London's swish Bond Street to rather grand villas in the country, as well as streets of more ordinary-looking homes. Much of his work centres on an appreciation of what classically minded architects call 'the five orders', derived from architectural treatises first published in Renaissance Italy that formalised the different 'orders' of classical architecture (Doric, Ionic, and so on). These were principally focused on the design of columns, but also on the precise relationships between the different elements: the correct ratio of width to capital height, and so on. This kind of architecture, Saumarez Smith told me, has 'essentially been made irrelevant in [today's] architectural education'. Classical architecture, he said, 'by which I mean something that has its roots in Greek and Roman antiquity, had its expression originally in temples, but was developed into other sorts of building types and is bound up in its architectural expression in the orders'.

I nodded as he rather beautifully sketched some column types on a napkin in front of me. 'But it also originates,' he went on, 'in the way that society is organised, and the way that cities are designed and built as well.'

We talked about architectural education and how, as a student in Edinburgh, he had tried hard to reconcile his interest in the city's more traditional buildings with the rather fixed twentieth-century training he was getting from his university tutors. 'The people that I was being taught by,' he said, 'I guess had probably been trained in the 1980s. And the people they were trained by would be, as it were, first-generation modernist. And so I think that they would have received an extremely dogmatic training, in which classical architecture would have been deliberately excluded.'

I asked him what made these older, more traditional styles still relevant today then. 'One thing is that it has its roots in the natural world,' he replied, sipping on his tea. 'And wherever you look, whether it's the shape of moulding on a glazing bar' – he tapped the very nice wooden sash windows next to where we were sitting – 'or the way that materials throw water off them or the way that shadows are cast on architectural forms . . . it's all to do with a symbiotic relationship to the natural world. Light and the effects of weather and the passing of seasons and all those sorts of things are programmed into the classical vocabulary.' Right, I said. Huh. 'And the second thing,' he continued, 'is that classical architecture is able to organise buildings and places in cities, in a way that has a civilising effect on society.

Ultimately, I just think that it's much more humane than the alternatives.'

We talked a lot about his work in Poundbury, and about Krier and the then-Prince Charles, who I was surprised to learn were still very much involved. 'Right from the outset,' Saumarez Smith said suddenly, 'Poundbury was an experiment. The Prince of Wales had written *A Vision of Britain* and had come under fire from the architecture profession. And he said, "Well, the best thing to do is to try and put these ideas into practice." The Duchy of Cornwall owns a huge amount of land in the south-west of England and other places as well. And they had been selling off land for development for years. And that parcel of land on the west side of Dorchester was going to be developed at some point. Had the Prince of Wales not intervened, the Duchy would probably have done a deal with one of the major house builders, and it would have been developed with very little design oversight. And it would be a completely bog-standard housing estate by now. It would have probably been built in half the time, and all the houses would be essentially the same. There would be no mixed use. No attempt at something out of the ordinary. And nobody would bat an eyelid at all. It would just be . . .'

'Unremarkable?' I said.

'Like any other modern suburb in any other market town anywhere else in the rest of Britain,' he replied. 'So I think one ought to approach Poundbury within that context: that it is an experiment in trying to do a whole lot of things which are out of the ordinary. And if that is the point by which one measures success, then I think it has been very successful. There are as many workplaces in Poundbury as there are houses. That is quite incredible. Find another development anywhere in the country in the last fifty years that you can say that about.'

He talked about how so much housing, and so many cul-de-sac estates, were essentially guided by housing regulations, and how Poundbury had worked around these to create a permeable, walkable space. 'There's no signage,' he said. 'There's no street parking regulation. And we put all of the services through the rear courtyards so the streets don't get dug up to get at the services. And the whole development benefits from an anaerobic digestion plant nearby in order to make it as off-grid as possible. And all of those are really extraordinary, pioneering things to have done. And amazingly difficult to achieve. A measure of how hard they are to achieve is you see that it hasn't been done elsewhere, despite the fact that many people have attempted it, you know? But Poundbury really goes to extremes.'

We were finishing up by now. Despite my misgivings about the place, I found myself oddly moved by Saumarez Smith's defence of what Poundbury was trying to do, and also sympathetic to his light sense of frustration that people wouldn't take it seriously, treating Poundbury as a kind of Georgian Disneyland, cut off from the world. 'I was in Poundbury last week,' he said, as I was leaving, 'just walking around. And somebody opened their front door and said, "Are you George? Did you design our house?" And I said, "Yes!" They said, "Oh, come in. We'd love you to see what we've done with the house." And then I got sort of attacked by the family dog in the kitchen, and they were telling me how much they love living there, and how everybody has great pride in their gardens, and how it's really nice on a Sunday morning. Everybody walks their dogs and has a chat to one another. And how there's a residents' association, and you walk past the school and the children are out in the playground, playing. And you kind of think, "Architects say that Poundbury is make-believe, but you know, *it's all real life*."'

Let's go back to a little over a century before the Prince of Wales got up to speak in Hampton Court Palace. It's October 1875, and a noted physician and writer, Benjamin Ward Richardson, has been asked to give an address on urban planning to the annual meeting of the Social Science Association in Brighton. Now more or less forgotten, at the time the association was one of the UK's largest and most influential civic organisations. It wasn't interested in 'social science' as we might understand it; the association was really a vehicle for social reformers, politicians, journalists and the civic-minded bourgeoisie more generally, to think publicly through the problems of the day, establish commissions and reports on them, and then try to influence the government. Who should be allowed to vote? What's an effective deterrent against petty crime? How can we clean up the cities? How can public health be improved? These were among the topics analysed by its five well-regulated 'departments'. The association's annual congress, meanwhile, went around the country like a travelling circus of liberal reform. People attended in their thousands, while what was actually said at the meetings was lavishly reported in the newspapers.[13]

Richardson's address to the 1875 meeting covered two topics close to the hearts of many Victorian reformers: the condition of the city and the problem of public health. By the middle decades of the nineteenth century, the sanitary situation in English cities had become so bad that in Liverpool, about 3.5 per cent of the city's population (roughly one person in every twenty-eight) died each year.[14] Most of this was a product of the sheer dirtiness of everyday life in the industrial Victorian city, and people's inability to access basic sanitary facilities. Families lived more or less on top of one another, with no ventilation or space, limited access to laundry equipment or hot water, sewage flowing in the streets, often no separation of living and working spaces, and the chemical by-products of heavy industry hanging in the air. All of this produced a public health disaster that was so bad that even the urban rich were no longer insulated from it. In 1875, Parliament finally passed the Public Health Act, which tried to alleviate the appalling urban mortality rate by at least mandating the use of sewers, creating new housing controls and regulations, and setting up a public health bureaucracy made up of medical officers and sanitary inspectors.

Such was the scene when Richardson got up to speak in Brighton. He didn't offer a proposal for new sanitary techniques or any medical theories for why urban living might be bad for people, or even a polemic against the complacent urban bourgeoisie. What Richardson offered, instead, was science fiction. With vivid, often hyper-real detail, he described a future city that he had invented called 'Hygeia'.[15] Hygeia, in Richardson's mind, is a city of 100,000 souls, built across 4,000 acres of land (roughly the size of the London Borough of Islington, current population about 240,000). No building in Hygeia is higher than sixty feet, which allows for the free movement of air. In fact, water and air are critical to Richardson's construction. He imagines his city on a slope, like a gently subsiding house, with an angled subway running the full length underneath, so that all water and waste flows down to a gravel layer at the south-eastern edge of town. At street level, the pavements are also tilted, with slits every few yards for dirt and water to fall through. 'Gutter children' are thus nowhere to be seen, Richardson points out, because – one can almost feel him beaming – there is no gutter. 'Instead of the gutter,' indeed, 'the poorest child has the garden; for the foul sight and smell of unwholesome garbage, he has flowers and green sward.'

Elsewhere, the gridded streets are built wide to maximise sunlight; shrubs and trees line each side, with gardens to the rear of every house; the city is mostly silent at street level because there's an underground railroad ferrying everything around; all sewage and power, all slaughterhouses and sanitary works, all refuse dumps and mortuaries, are built at a distance from the city; animals are kept away from places of human habitation and killed humanely; in the residential areas of town, houses are glazed in grey brick to keep the water out, prevent damp and rest the eyes; inside, chimneys go through a central furnace that removes the carbon before smoke is released; kitchens are always built on upper floors, which gives light so that you can quickly detect dirt and also allows cooking smells to disperse out of the house; rubbish goes through a hidden slot in the wall; every room has hot and cold water, while the roofs, which are flat, are covered in flower beds; clothes are washed and disinfected at large public laundries – nothing is dried indoors; there are pools, gymnasia, libraries and lecture halls, but no alcohol for sale, and no tobacco either.

Watching over all this with a kindly but unblinking eye is, Richardson imagines, a system of total medical supervision, under the command of a principal sanitary officer, who receives reports from the town's doctors, records all births and deaths, keeps an eye on animal disease, inspects samples of food and conducts chemical analyses. For those who, in spite of all these measures, still insist on dying, burial takes place outside the city. Corpses are placed in the earth with only a shroud. Vegetables are grown in the fertile soil left by the city's decomposing former residents.

This sounds mad – and, of course, it *is* mad. But Richardson is deadly serious. If you build Hygeia, he says, you remove the conditions for cholera, typhus, diarrhoea, croup, rheumatic fever and smallpox. There would be no deprivation, hunger or scurvy. Liver disease, kidney disorders and delirium tremens would be the stuff of fairy stories. Parasites would be eradicated and insanity virtually unknown. Tuberculosis would simply float away through open windows and down well-ventilated streets. Sure, it might not be a very *joyful* place – but at least death rates would plummet.

It maybe tells us something about the anxious climate at the time, and of the real deep fears around unhealthy urban environments, that Richardson's talk was an enormous public success. Newspapers at home and abroad reported on it, and the whole speech was published as a pamphlet, *Hygeia*, the following year. 'Rich old ladies', wrote the historian James Cassedy in 1962, 'began to build "Hygeian residences"; tradesmen advertised Hygeian goods.'[16] Early ideas for a national health service, meanwhile, began to draw on Richardson's arguments for a public medical infrastructure. The pamphlet was taken up particularly enthusiastically in the US, as cities like Chicago and San Francisco entered a wave of enormous growth. But then, Cassedy reports, just as *Hygeia* was reaching the height of its fame, it disappeared. In 1876, the same year as Richardson's pamphlet was published, the German physician and biologist Robert Koch discovered the bacteria that cause cholera and tuberculosis. With the growing acceptance of germ theories of disease, public health tilted on its axis. Who cared about huge, costly schemes of urban design, when laboratory scientists could simply eradicate these newly discovered microorganisms? There was no need for a contentious social reorganisation. People could still enjoy beer and tobacco, they didn't need to be ruled by medical superintendents, and, okay, landlords could continue to exploit people, but at least now with fewer fatalities. Richardson's triumph ended almost before it began.

The dream did not quite die, however. One person in Chicago who surely *did* read *Hygeia* was Ebenezer Howard, a British-born clerical worker and stenographer who had arrived in the city five years earlier. In the building boom that came in the wake of the Great Chicago Fire of 1871, Howard might well have seen something of Frederick Law Olmsted's planned suburb of Riverside. This was, as we saw in the Introduction, a landscaped suburban utopia of colonial houses, surrounded by parks and greenery.[17] When Howard returned to England later the same year, he began to formulate the plans that would not only bring Hygeia closer to reality than anything else, but would have a transformative effect on urban design and planning, and their relationship to health, for at least the next century.

Back in London, Ebenezer Howard found a job at Hansard – the organisation that makes the official record of the UK's parliamentary debates – and began to move in reformist and dissenting circles. He met figures as diverse as the playwright George Bernard Shaw, the anarchist Russian dissident Peter Kropotkin, and Beatrice and Sidney Webb, the founders of the Fabian Society; he read J. S. Mill on new cities, Henry George on urban economics, and Herbert Spencer on biology and eugenics. From this array of influences, Howard distilled an assortment of political and quasi-biological ideas, a melange of notions about good health and proper morals, and crystallised it into the new discipline of city planning – something he had neither experience nor expertise in.

In 1898, Howard published *To-Morrow: A Path to Peaceful Reform*. What he would propose as the 'garden city' in that now famous text is something strikingly close to Richardson's Hygeia. It is a mixture of town and country: a dream-city built in a garden, surrounded by green space, well governed, with light industry and reasonable rents, a kind of city without the city, brought together within a similarly weird spatial fantasy.

It is *land*, says Howard, a renewed relation of people *to* the land, that will solve 'the problems of intemperance, of excessive toil, of restless anxiety, of grinding poverty' that characterise modern urban life.[18] Think of the city as a kind of magnet, he says, and human beings as so many tiny needles drawn towards it. The force of the magnet, or what attracts people to the city, is made up of high wages, a good social life, better living conditions compared to the countryside. At the same time, that force is weakened by the downsides of city life – long hours, bad air, noise, and so on. The countryside has its own attractive powers – low rent, decent air, sunshine. But here, too, the force is weakened, and perhaps fatally so, by isolation, lack of work, and social stagnation. It is through the balance of these forces of attraction and repulsion that people end up in one place rather than another. But what if, says Howard, there was a *third* magnet – one that would hold together all the advantages of the city (stuff! friends! a job!), but do so while also keeping the attractions of the countryside (fields! cheap things! air!). This third magnet is what Howard calls the 'garden city'. 'Human society and the beauty of nature are meant to be enjoyed together,' he says. 'The two magnets must be made one. As man and woman by their varied gifts and faculties supplement each other, so should town and country.' This weirdly heteronormative sex imagery is a constant in Howard's writing, and it is no mere metaphor. The capacity of the town and country to come together and reproduce, and in the process make healthy new people, is central to his vision and, indeed, to the generally eugenic urges that guide it. 'Town and country *must be married*,' he says elsewhere, with the emphasis included, 'and out of this joyous union will spring a new hope, a new life, a new civilisation.' One can almost see him standing approvingly over the conjugal couple, encouraging them here and there in their movements.

What Howard is trying to create is a new kind of environment, something completely different from the 'crowded,

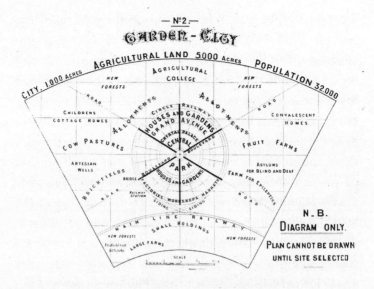

A diagram of the garden city, from Ebenezer Howard,
*Garden Cities of To-Morrow*.

ill-ventilated, unplanned, unwieldy, unhealthy cities' that
were like 'ulcers on the very face of our beautiful island'.
What would it mean to make a city that had all the 'natural healthfulness of the country'? For Howard, remember,
health is not only physical, it is *moral*, and it is *beautiful*.
A man of his time, he is in conversation not only with
eugenicists and agriculturalists, but also with vegetarians
and biologists and racists. He wants the city to be a petri
dish for physically fit people and also good people and also
beautiful people, and he equates physical fitness *with* beauty
and *with* goodness. Immersion in natural surroundings, in
Howard's view, is unique in its capacity to produce all three.
You might see the garden city as a sort of fusty aesthetic

object, a boring, very White suburb, with some extra trees and a kind of inchoate hostility to whatever its inhabitants imagine urban life to be. In all fairness, this is often what places that call themselves 'garden' cities, suburbs, villages and so on actually *are*. But this is not how Ebenezer Howard imagined them. His was a much stranger, much more radical, and much more troubling vision.

In 1902, the Garden City Association held a meeting in the planned community of Bourneville, near Birmingham, sponsored by the Quaker chocolate magnate (and Bourneville founder) George Cadbury. As well as Cadbury, the delegates included George Bernard Shaw, Earl Grey (the grandson of the prime minister Charles, the second Earl Grey, later the governor general of Canada, for whom the bergamot-scented Chinese tea blend is named) and, of course, Howard himself. From this meeting, the Garden City Pioneer Company and then the First Garden City Ltd emerged, with £300,000 in authorised share capital. A site at Letchworth in Hertfordshire, England, was selected and ultimately purchased by First Garden City Ltd. In 1904, Raymond Unwin and Barry Parker, devotees of William Morris, were appointed as architects and master planners of the new city. By 1905, two thousand people had moved to Letchworth, and the population grew slowly but steadily thereafter.

The movement, too, continued to grow, if in similarly unspectacular fashion. In 1919, with World War I ended and the scent of Bolshevism in the air, there was a widespread political interest in providing better living conditions for returning soldiers. Howard, who by this time was at the margin of events in Letchworth, raised the money to buy 1,500 acres near Lord Salisbury's estate in Hertfordshire. Salisbury sold the newly formed Second Garden City Company another 700 acres, and in 1920, Welwyn Garden City was born.

A few years ago (I mentioned this in the introduction) I attended an event to mark the town's centenary, but after a dispiriting morning tramping around cod-pastoral laneways with some of the well-heeled residents, I abandoned the second half of the tour and instead went around taking photos of the town's weirdly eroticised statuary, which gives the place a kind of harvest bacchanalia, *Wicker Man* vibe. Suffice to say that if I'd stayed the night – I did not – I'd have made sure the door of my room was well locked.

Later, though, as I was reading through the history of the movement's early days, one of the names at the 1902 meeting in Bourneville leaped out at me. It wasn't Earl Grey or George Bernard Shaw; it was William Lever, later Lord Leverhulme, who in addition to being a director of the First Garden City Company Ltd was a co-founder of the Lever Brothers soap operation. This highly successful company would eventually join with a Dutch margarine conglomerate to form Unilever, the global corporation that today produces a truly wild array of toothpastes, breakfast cereals, toilet cleaners, ice creams and laundry detergents. It's also still the world's number one manufacturer of soap.

Having been born into a successful grocery family in Bolton, Lancashire, Lever became a partner in his father's firm, which he significantly expanded, before leaving to set up his own soap-manufacturing concern.[19] Though the soap had some genuine advantages – his chemist used vegetable rather than animal fats – Lever's real gift was for branding. His soap was the first to be sold in standardised tablets, wrapped in the company's distinctive insignia and bearing the brand name Sunlight. When he eventually left Bolton, Lever established his new soap works on the banks of the River Mersey, a few miles downstream from Liverpool. From the beginning, his plan included a town for his workers and their families. He called the town Port Sunlight, and literally buttressed it against the walls of his factory. By 1907, it was home to nearly four thousand people.

Port Sunlight was hardly the first architecturally ambitious company town. In the 1850s, the remarkably named Sir Titus Salt, an industrialist and Liberal MP, founded the village of Saltaire in West Yorkshire, which was intended as an improved environment for the workers at his textile mills.[20] The picturesque stone houses that he built remained in the gift of Salts Mill well into the 1930s (today, the mill itself is a rather spectacular shopping centre and art gallery, the latter much associated with the work of David Hockney, who was born nearby). In the early 1800s, the radical social reformer Robert Owen, having married into a cotton-milling family in New Lanark on the River Clyde, began to plan improvements to the dire living conditions of the workers who lived next to the mill. By the 1820s, Owen's model town was attracting thousands of curious visitors from all over Europe, while Owen himself spent much of the rest of his life founding rather beautiful-looking but generally disastrous utopian communities in the US. Indeed, as early as the 1760s, the potter Josiah Wedgwood's model town Etruria – named rather fancifully for the home of the ancient Etruscans, a pre-Roman

An engraving by F. Bates of Robert Owen's proposal
for New Harmony, Indiana, 1838.

civilisation noted for their terracotta pots – began to fan out
from his rapidly growing pottery in Stoke-on-Trent.

But Port Sunlight was something distinctive – not only
for its size and success, but also because of how it worked
as a material elaboration of its founder's social and moral
philosophy. This wasn't exactly the same as Howard's, but it
shared the vision of making a new kind of urban space, and
a new kind of urban person, through a mix of architecture,
natural materials and social order.

To be honest, the reason Lever's name stood out to me was
because I had a personal interest in his legacy. The research
that I was carrying out, and which resulted in this book, was
being funded by the Leverhulme Trust, which had gener-
ously given me a prize, and a significant amount of money
for research expenses, in 2017. The trust had been formed
from a bequest in William Lever's will in 1925, and today it

funds a wide range of academic research. It's an independent charity, and yet, as its website puts it, it 'continues to own Unilever stock and, as per the terms of Lever's will, its Board is largely drawn from Unilever [*sic*] past and current executives'.[21] More pointedly, though, the trust has also recently been questioned by some of its grant-holders and others about how it handles its historical relationship with Lever Brothers' colonial plantations and settlements in the Congo and the Solomon Islands. In 2020, the trust funded a four-month scoping project to sketch out the state of the current knowledge of this history, and says that it is now funding research to further explore these legacies.[22] In the meantime, I decided to do some exploring of my own.

I finally arrived in Port Sunlight, on the banks of the River Mersey, quite late on a cold evening in November 2021, after a disturbingly long and creaky train ride from my home in south-west England. I had spent the journey, and its many stops, with Jules Marchal's extraordinarily grim book, *Lord Leverhulme's Ghost*, in which Marchal, a historian and former Belgian diplomat (the book was originally published in French, and only recently translated into English by a small left-wing press), doggedly traces out the details of Lever's activities in the Congo. On first glance, as the train nears its destination, the location of Port Sunlight seems kind of inauspicious for an experiment in urban living. This is, after all, the marshy edge of a peninsula in England's unglamorous north-west. But as soon as you see the wide expanse of the Mersey, as well as the monumental financial and trading buildings that still line it on the Liverpool side of the river, you get it instantly: this had, after all, been, the historian Amy Sergeant reminds us, the second-most-important port in the British empire.[23] Port Sunlight might have been designed as a sedate garden village, but Lever placed it quite precisely. The town and its factory are not at all in some bucolic hinterland. Though it hides these qualities well, Port Sunlight was from its inception a cosmopolitan, high-tech, *global* place. As we will see, this would not turn out to be a good thing.

Something that maybe separates Port Sunlight from a lot of other model or company towns, I realised as I walked around, is that it actually *is* quite beautiful and charming. The houses, originally built for workers in the factory (today, anyone can buy one), are mostly arranged in short terraces. But what makes the place attractive is its sheer variety. Lots of different architects were involved in designing the houses in Port Sunlight, including major figures like Edwin Lutyens. And yet there's a family resemblance in the quasi-medieval, William Morris-influenced aesthetic. Though mostly terraced, the houses are still notably cottagey, with large gables and big wooden beams; there are lots of half-timber houses, and Dutch-style ornaments and patterning. Though technically not a 'garden city', as you walk around it's plain that green space is everywhere in Port Sunlight. A proper architectural historian would probably talk about the town's debt to the Arts and Crafts Movement, but a more modest visitor might just think that Port Sunlight has a kind of Bilbo Baggins energy – and why not?

Sometimes, too, it gets a bit monumental. At the centre there are two intersecting expanses of park, which, from overhead, form something like a crucifix. If you stand at the war memorial at one end of town, with the Union Jack fluttering plaintively over your head, you can look straight down, past a long expanse of flower beds, to the neoclassical art gallery that Lever commissioned for his own collection in 1922. Directly to its left is the memorial erected after his death just three years later: an expressionist figure with her arms up stands on top of a 60-foot pillar; at her feet, there's a set of full-size human figures representing Lever's preferred virtues – industry, education and (this last symbolised, for some reason, by a woman suckling an infant) charity. Okay, at this point it's maybe all gone a bit Albert Speer. But still. There's a charm.

Port Sunlight is supposed to look like a picturesque garden. But it's also a place of business. Across the town's southern edge, a redbrick factory wall still runs for some distance, its carefully sealed doorways reminding you that Unilever, the successor to Lever's soap company, still manufactures bathroom-adjacent products here. These include the shower gel Dove and also a bleach called Domestos, which is generally used to clean toilets. This association of the town with cleanliness and hygiene is not accidental. As you walk through the neat rows of modest houses, set respectfully back from the place of busy manufacture, the shared desire for a certain kind of physical as well as moral purity is palpable. This is, in many ways, not a bad thing. Without question, Port Sunlight offered significant material improvement for the factory workers who once lived here, not only in terms of working and living conditions, but also in general health outcomes, as well as education.[24] There was firm discipline, it's true – for the worker who stepped out of line, not only their job but their home was at stake – but for those willing to play by Lever's rules, a level of social and physical comfort was available in Port Sunlight, well beyond what was offered elsewhere. This included facilities for recreation, for self-improvement, even for growing your own vegetables, if you really wanted to. Such was his pride in it, Lever even used images of the town in his soap adverts. They captured the clean, healthy, morally good life he wanted both his customers and his employees to imagine for themselves. Indeed, his goal, says the historian Amanda Rees, was to 'produce a distinctive visual ideology to shape the behaviour and attitudes of factory workers and their families'.[25] The idea was to provide a healthy environment for workers, with not just pretty houses, but also good, temperate, bourgeois activities – gardening, communal dining, debate, and so on.

As you walk around, there is something extraordinarily peaceful about Port Sunlight – but something kind of jarring too. At one point, not long after I arrived, and with the evening closing in on the mostly empty streets, I took a wrong turn and ended up in a kind of hollowed dip in a no man's land that was still filled with crisp autumn leaves; a stream* ran through it, arched at the end by a very small, cute stone bridge. I took a bunch of photos but, honestly, it was too much. There's a point in landscaping where things take on the uncanny quality of a Thomas Kinkade painting or start to look like something generated by artificial intelligence. You get the feeling that if you look too hard, you might spot a computer-rendering error – a disembodied hand, say, or half

---

* As I write this, I wouldn't actually swear to there having been a stream. But the fact that there definitely is one in my mind's eye is at least some kind of data point about the atmosphere of the place.

a human face, hovering glitchy and ghost-like in the background. That faintly sinister sense of glitch – the feeling that at any moment the scene might break, a curtain might drop – never went away for me. I came to be grateful that the only hotel I could find, which was really more of a pub with rooms, was just outside the town's boundaries. As I passed through a set of hedges and onto a main road to get to it, there was an *instant* and really kind of welcome transportation back to the everyday ugliness of provincial modernity. That evening, not wanting to sit in the pub, and looking for some supermarket wine, I trudged a couple of miles down a barely lit path, in the opposite direction from Port Sunlight itself, until I came to an anonymous strip mall on the Wirral peninsula, with a cinema, and some fast food places, and teenagers in cars, and a branch of the slightly upmarket British chain store Waitrose. It could have been anywhere, and I could have died from happiness. Port Sunlight isn't gated, certainly. But its symbolic and moral edges are clear. The town wouldn't be more tightly closed off from the petty bourgeois everyday of the Wirral if Unilever's factory wall simply curled itself around the place entirely, pulling the residents gently away from the hustle, strife, uncertainty and low-key alienation of twenty-first-century capitalism.

Walking out the next morning, I realised that, in daylight, you get a sense of the specificity and deliberation of Lever's plan for his people-shaping environment. He had delineated ten to twelve houses per acre, and the road to be at least 45 feet in width, with a strip in its centre paved for cars; around this, Lever imagined a gravel pathway, then grass, and 'if possible', an avenue of trees. Houses should be minimally 15 feet back

Factory wall, Port Sunlight.

from the road, with space for a vegetable garden behind and open space for recreation within easy reach. There is no room for extravagance here – or, at least, this is a vision in which extravagance is produced not by elaborate decoration or style, but by the simple provision of open space and nature. 'A few sprays of ivy,' said Lever, 'and a greensward in front of the house, a shrub here and there, and the plainest and most economical cottage, architecturally, becomes more beautiful than a more costly and elaborate one, built right on the edge of the footpath without any intervening fringe of greensward.'[26]

Throughout his writing, it becomes clear that Lever's urban vision has two central themes: race and nation. The cottage home, he told a visiting housing conference in 1907, is 'the unit of a nation'. The more comfortable and happy the home, the healthier its inhabitants, and in turn, the more efficiently productive the nation. The early twentieth century, Lever argued, was a period of competition between nations, governed not by armies of soldiers, but rather by armies of industrial workers. The nation that will be declared 'the fittest to survive' will be the one that best prevents the 'deterioration of the race' through 'physical fitness'. And it is the home and its surrounding environment that play the determining role. Even if 'the strain of modern life is ever increasing', Lever went on, 'this should not necessarily tend to the deterioration of the race'. A 'healthy home life and environment', he declared, will 'produce a healthier, stronger, and more virile race'.[27]

But look, strip away the eugenics, which was broadly characteristic of people of Lever's class and background; ignore, if you can, the fantasy of imperial domination lurking in the background of his anxious paean to vigour and virility; and honestly, it's hard to object to many of the specifics of his urban vision. Lever wants 'proper air space and good planning', as well as 'the provision of large open spaces and recreation grounds outside the home'. For adults, he wants 'healthy relaxation from toil when strenuous work is done'; and for children, a careful calculation of residents per hectare so as to reduce infant mortality. He even showed that the average height and weight of a child in a Port Sunlight school were higher than in an equivalent council school. All of this proved that (and I will quote this at length, because it captures a vision of the relationship between life and environment that came to the fore in Lever's own day and remains deeply influential in our own):

> Given regularity and permanency of employment to the parents, and consequently also of feeding and clothing of the children, reasonable and proper housing conditions, plenty of surrounding land for healthy, open-air recreation, provision of Parks, Swimming Baths, Gymnasia, Football Field, Cricket Field, Clubs, and all that makes for healthy out-door life, and the children of our artisans and labouring people became equal in physique to those of the better classes.

Port Sunlight was a machine for producing the future of the imperial nation. Drawing on the statistics of a Mr Fraser from his firm, Lever goes into quite weird, exhaustive detail about the number of children born to the different grades of employee at his company, before concluding, with great satisfaction, that by far the largest families are those of the higher-grade workmen, 'the most intelligent of the working classes', as Lever approvingly notes, and thus 'Port Sunlight shows the way to the rest of England'.

Lever is often read as a somewhat benign paternalist of his age. Sure, his ideas were odd and a bit patronising, goes the thinking, but there is at least a concrete vision for making a better life for his employees and their families. All of this is true enough. But it's also the case that for Lever, a better life for his own employees, in the form of a healthy town, was not an end in itself; it was part of a competitive, colonial endeavour, a white supremacist strategy to maintain British domination. As the historian David Jeremy points out, Port

Sunlight was an attempt to demonstrate that sharing prosperity, and not profit, was the path to social peace.[28] The planned town, in this sense, is an engine of social harmony at home and imperialism abroad. Its hastily planted greenswards were spaces for the production of good, docile British workers – and, if need be, good, violent British soldiers.

The main ingredient in William Lever's soaps was vegetable oil, chiefly palm oil. Palm oil, in turn, is extracted from the oil palm tree, a species native to West Africa, among other places. To service the needs of his booming soap business, Lever first tried to get exclusive rights to extraction from oil palms in what was then British West Africa – a region that today covers much of Ghana, Nigeria, Sierra Leone and the Gambia. This request was refused by Britain's colonial office, on the basis that such exclusive rights might foment local unrest. Lever began to look elsewhere.

In 1908, the Belgian state took over control of the so-called Congo Free State, a space that had hitherto been a private possession of the country's genocidal King Leopold II. In Leopold's wake – he died the following year, but not before burning all archival evidence of his own atrocities – Belgium tried to promote the newly annexed Belgian Congo as a cleaned-up '*colonie-modèle*', in which, among other advancements, forced labour would be forbidden. With supplies of rubber and ivory exhausted by Leopold, but anything other than continued exploitation seemingly unimaginable to the European authorities, the Belgians turned to the groves of oil palms that made up much of Congo's interior. They actively tried to interest Lever in extracting the oil, and in 1911,

Lever Brothers and the Belgian government finally formed a company, Huileries du Congo Belge (HCB). This company was ceded vast amounts of land in Belgian Congo (more territory than actual Belgium), with the idea that they would build infrastructure, including towns, to house and educate workers, while creating conditions for the exploitation of the palms. The largest such settlement was called Leverville. It was built on the banks of the Kwilu River, across from an existing village called Lusanga.

On the surface, the logic of Leverville was the same as that of Port Sunlight: that humane conditions – decent homes, schools for children, recreation facilities – make for better workers. The town would again be an engine for creating people – in this case, a Congolese middle class – who would share the moral outlook and bearing of their counterparts on the banks of the Mersey. Lever's international reputation as a humane capitalist was a major selling point for the Belgians, who were keen to see the same physical and moral improvements in Africa's interior that Lever's model town for the British working classes had already attempted to produce. In reality, though Lever sunk a great deal of his company's money into developing infrastructure and saw little profit, and though he was undoubtedly driven, at least in the abstract, by the same paternalistic desires as on the banks of the Wirral – which is to say, a desire to extract surplus labour from his workers for his own private benefit, under at least an implicit threat of immiseration, but to do it in a nice way – this never came to pass.

As the historians Reuben Loffman and Benoît Henriet have carefully documented, wages at HCB were bad and forced labour persisted well into Lever's era; there were accusations of corruption by HCB's agents; and there were feeble attempts to inculcate 'European' values among the Congolese workforce (essentially, this meant trying to turn the Congolese into good, desiring consumers through a money economy and a network of company-owned enterprises where they could shop).[29] But really this was all a smokescreen. From the beginning, according to Jules Marchal, who has spent decades excavating Lever's Belgian activities, Leverville was about forced labour, monopoly capital and brutally low wages maintained by coercion, as well as, where necessary, by violence.[30]

One of the major aims of HCB's leaders throughout this period, as carefully documented by Marchal, was to be allowed simply to move the workers – which is to say, move their entire villages – nearer to the place of work. The Belgian Department of Colonies, still at least loosely committed to the *colonie-modèle*, resisted; the Congolese would simply become serfs, they said, essentially the property of the company. In May 1926, Lever's company sent a memorandum in response: if they were allowed to move whole settlements near to the land containing palm groves, these would not be just any new villages, they might even become *garden villages*. Sure, the company wrote, this would make the colonial natives extremely dependent on the company economically, but was this not already the case in many European villages built near large industrial facilities? Was this not, they asked, what they had already achieved in Port Sunlight?

Perhaps the comparison goes too far. But here, in the end, is the only way I can make historical and political sense of

King Charles's idea – and he is far from the only one to hold it – that buildings and cities should grow naturally, as from the soil. The idea is not only to freeze the physical and social form of the city in time; it is to insist, in the same breath, that a particular utopian vision of urban function and shape – a vision of the city as beautiful, ordered, rigidly hierarchical – is the obvious and natural state of things. And the people produced by such an urban space – people who are bright and well rested, people who eat carefully and rest quietly, people who are ready for nearby work, people who keep their bodies and minds scrubbed clean of impurity – are also, in this vision, in their natural condition. Of course, there are critical differences marked by racism and colonialism. But a similar kind of logic holds in England, North America and West Africa. Because the green, living city is not a heterogeneous, unpredictable space of human creativity and culture. It is an organised, well-oiled machine for the production of new kinds of people, people ready to take up the place already assigned to them under conditions of both coloniality and monopoly capitalism.

The garden city, from this perspective, is no benign relic of Victorian reform. It was – and remains – a deeply influential experiment for the transformation of urban space and urban citizens. In the decades after Lever's death, his ideas about town planning fell out of favour and became impossible to realise. However, some of the general principles that guided people in Lever's time – in particular, ideas about how space can shape moral character – were to receive something of a new lease of life from a surprising quarter many years later. Shorn of the racist, imperialist underpinnings of Lever's ideas, this new lease of life came from the natural sciences, and in particular from psychology. If, in Lever's era, the garden city was intended to cultivate people's eternal souls and their moral characters, soon it would have a new, but not wholly different, object. By the end of the twentieth century, we would be focused instead on what the modern city was doing to people's minds and brains.

# 3: Like a Rat in a Maze

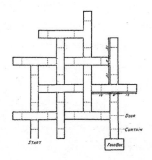

Plan of a rat maze used by Edward C. Tolman, 1948
(originally by M. H. Elliott, 1928).

In the middle decades of the twentieth century, a global polio epidemic that had been simmering for fifty years exploded into one of the century's most devastating outbreaks of infectious disease. The disease we call polio is caused by the poliovirus, which moves from person to person mostly through human faeces, spread around by poor hand hygiene. It affects mainly young children and the effects can range from a short illness lasting a week or so, to life-altering paralysis, and ultimately death by suffocation, as the respiratory muscles cease to function. The historian Dora Vargha records that at the peak of the global polio pandemic in the 1950s, about eighteen per hundred thousand people in England and Wales were infected with it, twenty-four per hundred thousand in Hungary and, by 1952, a devastating thirty-seven for every hundred thousand people in the US. Between 1950 and 1954, about twenty-two thousand people each year were paralysed by polio in the US; in 1950 alone, three thousand children died from it.[1] To most people in the world today, polio is a half-known, ghost-like disease from their parents' or grandparents' era, but its mid-century Euro-American iconography – roomfuls of children encased in iron lungs; starched, matronly nurses; wheelchairs, stiff leg braces, large wooden crutches – still offers a potent visual shorthand for the horrors of pandemic infectious disease.[2]

Jonas Salk was, in the late 1940s, a young virologist working at the University of Pittsburgh. Having moved to Pittsburgh from New York City to start his own laboratory, he was one of the many people working desperately on a vaccine that would prevent infection by the poliovirus. But then something important changed for Salk, which altered the course of both his own life and the pandemic he was immersed in. The story – maybe 'myth' is a better word – goes like this. Salk found Pittsburgh – hard-scrabble, industrial, dirty Pittsburgh – to be not the most conducive environment for the delicate mental labour of vaccinology. So he left and made his way to the small town of Assisi in Umbria, central Italy. Dug into the slopes at the foot of Mount Subasio, Assisi is famous among Christians mostly as the birthplace of St Francis, the medieval ascetic and founder of the Franciscan monastic order. In Francis's wake, and also that of St Clare, Assisi became a centre of medieval monasticism and a site for significant architectural projects. One of the most prominent of these was the Basilica of St Francis, whose distinctive Gothic half (the Basilica actually forms two churches) is lined from floor to ceiling with frescoes by Giotto and members of his school. In fact, today the entire medieval town is a UNESCO world heritage site, including the famous Eremo delle Carceri – a semi-hidden complex of caves and outbuildings located in a forest gorge some distance outside the city, where Francis was said to have come to pray, often staying for some time in the caves. In some versions of the myth, Salk spent his time in Assisi at the Basilica; in others, he even spent significant time in the caves. Either way, he returned to noisy, industrious Pittsburgh not only refreshed and renewed, but having made the crucial intellectual breakthrough that would deliver the world's first successful polio vaccine. Salk intuited that a technique he had already used in developing an influenza vaccine, whereby a dead version of the virus was used to induce an antibody response, might work with polio too. He returned to Pittsburgh, began successful field trials of his dead-virus vaccine in 1952, licensed it in 1955, and a mass vaccination campaign began the same year.[3]

The history of both polio and polio vaccination is, of course, a lot more complex than this. Indeed, despite the myth-making around Salk, an oral vaccine developed by his contemporary, Albert Sabin, which was a good deal easier to administer to children, and which was initially used with great success in the Soviet Union, quickly became the vaccine of choice in many countries.[4] Still, I want to stay with the story for a moment – and I want to stay in Assisi, perhaps sitting contemplatively in one of the shaded quadrangles of the Basilica San Francesco, for just a bit longer. In the 1960s, having finally received funding to establish his own biological institute in La Jolla, California, right on the edge of the Pacific

Ocean, Salk engaged the modernist architect Louis Kahn to design an ideal space for the production of scientific knowledge. The Salk Institute, the complex that Kahn ultimately designed, is a set of strong but modest-looking buildings that appear for all the world like rows of fiercely concreted, monastic caves. Working explicitly with ecclesiastic and contemplative history, as well as the more prosaic demands Salk made on him, Kahn had built a machine for thinking at the edge of the Pacific. 'Its function may be for science,' said the *Los Angeles Times* in 2016, 'but Kahn's structures feel more like a temple to nature.'[5] Another architectural publication wrote that 'Kahn's scheme for the Institute is spatially orchestrated in a similar way to a monastery: a secluded intellectual community.'[6] These connections by Kahn and Salk to nature and monasticism are not incidental. Nor are they – as we may

A view of the Salk Institute for Biological Studies.

be inclined to suspect – an example of California's noted tolerance for airy bullshit about the power of the environment.

These connections reflect, rather, a commitment to a new idea: that the kind of building you are in has a serious bearing on the kind of thinking you can do; that the very structure and content of your thoughts, the function of your brain, is profoundly mediated by the physical environment – natural or built – that you happen to find yourself in. In 1992, speaking at an awards ceremony held by the American Institute of Architects, Salk said that his and Kahn's shared intention was 'to influence in a positive way the conditions and circumstances of the environment for those working within the institute so that they, in turn, might then influence each other in the work they produced and in so doing, extend their influence beyond through the products of their collaboration'.[7] In another speech the same year, attended by President George H. W. Bush, Salk referenced the 'turbulent times' they were all living in – this was less than a year after the end of the first Gulf War – and argued for 'a new way of seeing and a new way of thinking both about nature and the human side of nature'.[8] Science, he said, can only be understood in its relationship to art. He had founded his institute because he had realised that 'all of the problems of man will not be solved in the laboratory'. Indeed, the laboratory style of thought might *itself* become a problem. Humans have become 'pathogens against our planet and pathogens against each other', Salk said. And this tension between human as pathogen and human as cure is what his institute, in its physical form, attempts to resolve. The 'timeless' quality of Louis Kahn's design 'offers inspiration, hope and promise, as we experience both its beauty and the truths that are emerging from it'. This is a design for science that is *not* about the organised production of knowledge, in other words. Rather, it is a design that tries to create the physical, and thereby psychological, conditions for particular *kinds* of knowledge: human, mindful, curative, alive to the limits of science itself.

In 2002, following a meeting in San Diego of the American Institute of Architects, a group of architects, with scientists from the nearby Salk Institute, founded the Academy of Neuroscience for Architecture (ANFA). Its mission, says the academy, is to 'promote and advance knowledge that links neuroscience research to a growing understanding of human responses to the built environment'.[9] Through workshops, conferences and lecture series, the academy is interested in things like how light and sound can be used in healthcare settings, how visual perception of space works and how people respond emotionally to different spaces.[10] The fundamental idea here – and ANFA is just one node in a much larger international scene – is that the work of designing buildings is, at least in part, the work of figuring out how buildings can best meet the psychological and neurobiological needs of the people who inhabit them.

The idea that the mind works differently in different places is extraordinarily powerful. It also feels intuitively right. After all, you wouldn't try to file your tax return from a laptop while seated on a bench in the city centre. You'd seek out a quiet space, with a comfortable chair and enough space to work, somewhere with not much noise, maybe painted in a soothing shade. And you'd do this not simply because this is a nicer place to do the job, but because you have some sense that you'll do the job less well, maybe you won't even be able to do it at all, if the physical surroundings are not properly attuned. Salk takes this idea a bit further. He doesn't just advance the general notion that a person can reason (or love or despair) *better* in places that are more suited to this kind of mental activity. He proposes the more specific theory that particular physical environments have particular psychological effects; that these can be worked out, analysed, manipulated, made use of, with the right know-how. It's the idea that spaces can and should be designed for mental activity – and even if this isn't what medieval monks thought they were doing, it's what they were doing nonetheless.

But two more insidious ideas are implied here. One is so obvious and so ingrained in us that we might simply overlook it. This is the notion that spaces that are good for thinking, and also for mentally resting, are *not* spaces that have the characteristics of urban environments. They are not noisy, bright, smelly, hurried, stimulating, filled with other people. In fact, we might say, even without the melodramatic divide between Pittsburgh on the one hand and an Italian mountain monastery on the other, that the city is the opposite of everything that Salk was looking for in a psychologically optimal environment. Secondly, there is the idea that your surroundings don't simply affect your cognitive abilities or mental activity in the moment, but the actual deep functioning of your mind and brain. In other words, there are physical environments that can, over time, *hurt* your mind or brain: the built environment, purely by virtue of its physical qualities, could induce some of the deeply negative, sometimes even fatal experiences that today we group under the term 'mental illness'.

Today, a lot of anti-urban thinking derives from this notion – that the city is a space that produces mental illness, not only because of its hectic or worrisome social life, but because of its actual physical structure. We have moved from a fairly banal claim – that you can do your best scientific thinking in a nice monastic cave – to a harder, more serious argument: that the urban environment damages your mind. To counter this effect, it is often suggested, we need to radically remake the city into something more psychologically restorative. We need to turn it into something quieter, calmer, *greener*. We need to reshape the city so that, in truth, it no longer looks or feels much like a city at all.

In 2011, in the city of Mannheim, Germany, a group of scientists gave some research volunteers a numerical score based on whether they were living in a city, a town or a rural area.[11] They put the same people in a brain scanner and gave them a stress task (they had to perform some mental arithmetic while receiving negative feedback from the scientists). What the researchers found was striking: the higher the population of the place where the subjects lived, the more likely they were to have increased activity in an area of the brain called the amygdala while under stress. The amygdala, the scientists pointed out, is associated with a sense of environmental threat, and is often involved in anxiety and depression. But they also found something else: if you factored in how many years a person had lived in an urban environment up to the age of fifteen, a whole different region of the brain came into the picture – the perigenual anterior cingulate cortex, a major part of the limbic system, involved in dealing with chronic social stress. What this means, the researchers suggested, is that people process stress differently according to whether they grew up or lived in a city. Growing up in an urban environment, the scientists concluded, has a negative effect on how people deal with stress, and the effects of this experience are clearly visible in the brain.

What might cause this, though? *Why* does growing up in a city affect the brain in this way? In Chapter 1, I mentioned a 2019 study by a group of researchers in Aarhus, Denmark, that tried to answer this question.[12] Denmark has a lot of what are euphemistically called 'population-based registers', though in reality what this refers to is a huge and somewhat creepy state data-gathering exercise that tracks Danes across a range of life events, from birth to death, logging their addresses, employment and so on, along the way. This is highly problematic in various ways, of course, but at least it's good news for Danish scientists, who can access an amazing data set on the whole country. The team in Aarhus were able to use these registers to build their own data set on more than 900,000 people who were born in Denmark between 1985 and 2003, who were living in the country at age ten, and for whom there was data on mental health, social class and where they lived (like I said, creepy). Then they did something really clever: they gave everyone a score based on the amount of vegetation near their house when they were kids, which they determined using old satellite images. Plotting this 'vegetation index' against the medical data, they showed that the more green stuff someone had near their house as a kid, the less likely they were to be diagnosed with a mental illness in adulthood. They were even able to demonstrate a dose–response relationship: in other words, as the amount of green space went up, so the level of apparent protection against mental illness increased in line with it. Not having green space near your house when you're growing up, the authors concluded, is a major risk factor for developing mental illness. In places like cities, where there's less vegetation, there is a specific and urgent need to increase the amount of urban nature in order to reduce rates of mental illness.

Okay, but then another question arises: what is green space actually doing that's so protective? *This* question was addressed in 2015 by researchers in Stanford who sent some volunteers out for a walk in and around Palo Alto, the very small 'urban' area that surrounds Stanford University.[13] Before they went out, the scientists gave the volunteers a 'resting-state' brain scan – an approach to scanning the brain where, unusually, the subject is given no particular task to do, so that the scientist can see how different regions interact with one another when the person is 'at rest' (this is the idea, anyway).[14] The researchers also gave the volunteers a questionnaire to see how prone they were to 'rumination'. This term refers to the kind of pervasive, inward-looking attention people give to why they feel the way they feel – usually why they feel so *bad* a lot of the time. It's a complicated concept. The word 'ruminate', meaning to think or over-think, comes from the Latin *ruminatio*, which means (literally) chewing the cud. We call cows ruminants because they chew, swallow, throw up into their own mouths, then chew it over some more. If you've ever experienced depression, you can probably see the analogy pretty clearly – and in fact, rumination is a style of thought often said to be heavily implicated in depression.

The researchers sent half the volunteers out on a walk around an elevated green path on the Stanford campus, one that regularly featured deer and squirrels, from where you could see nearby Mountain View and, in the distance, the San Francisco Bay. The other half were sent on a looping walk down El Camino Real, the busiest street in downtown Palo Alto; this, the researchers noted, was noisy thanks to three lanes of car traffic and lined mostly with one- or two-storey commercial units. When the two groups came back from their walks, the scientists did *another* brain scan, and then gave them the rumination questionnaire again. The nature group showed less rumination than before they went out on their walk – they weren't turning things over in their minds so obsessively – whereas the urban group showed no change. Rumination has been associated with a brain region called the subgenual prefrontal cortex, which is often implicated in mood and emotional problems. And just as with the rumination score, the people who had been on the nature walk showed less activity in this area of the brain than those who had spent time in Palo Alto. We know, the researchers argued, that urbanisation is associated with mental illness, and we know that being in contact with nature – or the lack of it – has something to do with this. But we don't know *how* this relationship works. Maybe, they suggested, just maybe, rumination is the key. Natural landscapes provide a kind of positive *distraction* that helps people ruminate less. It helps them think less. It helps them let things go.

Well, maybe. But honestly, it's hard to see what a place like Palo Alto or Aarhus tells us about 'urban experience' in, say, Dakar or Manila. The idea that the built environment can be imagined to work more or less the same everywhere, is experienced the same way everywhere, seems to miss the complications of culture and history. So, too, does the idea that 'vegetation' is an obvious or universal category. Rather than there being some kind of unmediated passage point between, say, a random tree and your literal brain function, there is surely an *awful* lot of filtering going on, based on your background, your social class, what literature you've read, what country you grew up in, what you had for breakfast that day. The city might be a physical space, but it's also a social environment. The scientists know this, of course, but I'm not sure their experimental methods are well placed to grasp it. Because this is where things get really messy. To get to the bottom of it, or at least understand what's going on here, we need to move to a different kind of explanation. We need to look at the history of how neuroscientists have to come to think about this problem. And to understand *that* we need to take a crash course in how rats find their way around mazes.

The history of how we have come to understand the modern mind and its relationship to space is, in significant part, as the historian Paul Dudchenko once pointed out, a history of how rats learned to find their way around mazes.[15] In 1900 and 1901, a psychologist called Willard Small, at Clark University in Worcester, Massachusetts, published two papers under the title 'An Experimental Study of the Mental Processes of the Rat'.[16] The hard thing about trying to make general psychological observations in rats, Small noted, was that on the one hand, you want to give the animal as much space for free expression of its own desires as possible, but on the other, you need to control the conditions enough so that you can compare the actions of one rat to another. Small's solution to this dilemma was to build a maze – or actually, several. A maze, he reasoned, was close enough to the rat's preferred environment of underground tunnels. It had enough options, and enough potential for error, for the animal to have to make some decisions and learn to find its own way around; most importantly, the maze was a space that could be observed, top down, from a kind of God-like position, as the unfortunate rat's movements were watched, surveilled and recorded by Small and his assistants. He even modelled his maze on the rectangular labyrinth at Hampton Court Palace in London, constructing a dense network of blind alleys and cul-de-sacs for the (hungry) rats, as they tried to make their way to the edible prize at the centre of the enclosure.

Small's interests were in animal intelligence and learning. He didn't care about space at all really. And yet the maze, an ingenious device for studying rat psychology, almost accidentally established spatial navigation, and the relationship between thinking and the physical environment, at the centre of experimental psychology, in a way that the discipline would never be able to subsequently shake off.

Place some food in the centre of a maze, said the psychologist Edward C. Tolman in a now-canonical 1948 paper, and put a hungry rat at the entrance: the rat's going to make a lot of errors, but eventually it's going to find the food.[17] Keep doing this at twenty-four-hour intervals with the same hungry rat, and over time it'll make fewer and fewer errors and find the food more quickly. There are two ways to explain this phenomenon. One is a stimulus–response explanation. This imagines the rat as a kind of small, furry telephone switch-board, where its sensory system receives a set of inputs from the external world and the animal's muscles a corresponding set of outputs from its nervous system. In this view, in response to specific stimuli (going down a blind alley maybe, or get-ting a strong smell of cheese), the inputs and outputs become better aligned over time, and the signal comes through with more clarity. But Tolman offered an alternative explanation: what if rats aren't like a switchboard at all, but instead like a bunch of people bent over a map, trying to make sense of it. Sure, the rat is clearly receiving sensory information as it works its way around the maze, but what if instead of forming a series of individual learned actions at each decision point, the rat was doing something more intellectually ambitious? What if it was using all this sensory information to build, inside its head, a *map* of the space? What if the rat was hold-ing together, mentally, some kind of general representation, image or understanding of what that physical environment was like, and how one might move around it?

The rat, in Tolman's view, is not a stimulus–response machine; it is instead looking for the best signals with which to build its map. He described a set of experiments carried out by another researcher, who created a maze where, in order to get to the food, the rat had to make a series of choices with many different kinds of options (the correct doors might be light or dark, they might be on the left or right, and so on). If these options are randomised, then the situation for the rat is impossible. In this case, says Tolman, the rat *hypothesises* – it first tries all the right-hand doors, or all the light grey ones, or whatever. It does not blindly try options but instead attempts to get some systematic hold on the space. In one of his own experiments, Tolman trained his rats to follow a single path to a food source, which was across a bridge and at a right angle to where the rat began. Having taught them the path, Tolman then changed the set-up, so that what had been a simple right turn now radiated into a series of ten possible directions. In the majority of cases, the rats chose the path that corresponded most closely to where the food had been the first time around. In other words, they were *not following stimuli*; they were navigating to a specific, mapped-out point in space where they expected to find food. They had a sense of the food not as simply being at the end of a tunnel, but as located somewhere in an abstract space. The rats were making maps, Tolman famously argued – *cognitive maps* of space. And they were building these maps – as well as storing them – in their brains.

Tolman, one of the major psychological experimenters of the twentieth century, then gets a bit weird. Cognitive maps come in two types, he says. They might be like narrow strips, in which an animal has mapped out point A to point B. Sometimes, though, the rats have a more comprehensive map of the wider space, so that when things get moved round, they can adapt more quickly. Rats make bad maps, Tolman says – strip maps that go only from A to B – when their brains are damaged. But sometimes they work in strips because there are just too many motivations or frustrations in the set-up. Consider, he says, a middle-aged woman whose husband has just died; imagine, indeed, a woman who has 'regressed (much to the regret of her growing daughters) into dressing in too youthful a fashion and in competing for their beaux'. The excess of frustration – he presumably means sexual frustration – after the husband's death leads to a regression to the much narrower, strip-like map of her situation. Or consider, he says, the 'poor Southern whites, who take it out on the negroes [*sic*]'. This is also, says Tolman, an example of a 'narrowing of the cognitive map' – an inability, produced by an excess of frustration, to comprehend the wider territory, to abstractly grasp the complex relationships between things, as opposed to a simple focus on A and B. But just look at what motivates the rats to be better mappers and better thinkers, he says. Take away excesses of frustration and motivation – feed everyone enough, keep everyone warm – and people will be able to live (here Tolman slips into Freud's language) in line with the Reality Principle, and not the Pleasure Principle. In other words, in the right circumstances people are able to understand the complexities of how the world holds together, and their internal maps, their frames for making sense of things, become thick, rich, open. We must, Tolman says, 'subject our children and ourselves (as the kindly experimenter would his rats) to the optimal conditions of moderate motivation and of an absence of unnecessary frustrations, whenever we put them and ourselves before that great God-given maze which is our human world'. Rather like the map in the story by Borges, which expands and expands until it grows bigger than the territory it purports to show, Tolman's cognitive map has ceased to be simply a representation and has become, instead, a world-making device in its own right. We have, he says, almost a moral duty to train our brains to make better maps – and thereby, better worlds.

It's worth remembering that with World War II having just ended, and the Cold War just beginning, there was a certain liberal idea that psychology in the post-war era should be a *moral* science, one that would contribute to a global movement of American-led peace and reconciliation by showing how man's wilder urges could be tamed. But in this careful (and scientifically unjustified) turning of the map into something of a metaphor, Tolman makes spatial navigation – human beings' cognitive relationship with space, or our capacity to make our way through our environment in a more or less satisfying and non-frustrating way – into a royal road for human psychology more generally. From now on, environmental navigation was no longer a rodent-laden backwater in experimental psychology. It was the basis for an entirely new structure of psychological thought.

By 1970, a little more than twenty years after Tolman's work, the London-based neuroscientist John O'Keefe had been doing single-unit recording experiments on the brains of rats for some time. In single-unit recording, a micro-electrode is used to record electrical activity in a single neuron. O'Keefe had developed his own head-mounted micro-drive for rats, through which neurons can be isolated and their electrical activity recorded as the animal moves around more or less freely. During a kind of experimental slip-up, O'Keefe started recording cells in the hippocampus and noticed immediately a correlation between the strength of the hippocampal activity and the animal's motor behaviour. This was odd. The hippocampus, as was widely accepted at this point, was involved in memory. In a now very famous paper, O'Keefe and his collaborator Jonathan Dostrovsky described what they did next: they anaesthetised a bunch of rats, attached micro-drives to their heads, drilled holes in their skulls and passed a series of electrodes into their brains to see what the neurons were doing.[18] Some of these neurons, they realised, responded when the rat was on a specific part of the platform and facing in a particular direction. One of them fired only when the animal was being restrained and facing in a particular direction; another responded to a moving visual stimulus, but again *only* when the rat was on a particular corner of the platform. The experimenters tried moving the platform around, turning on and off various bits of nearby machinery, adding and removing a curtain around the platform, and so on. None of these did much, except for the removal of the curtain, at which point the animal behaved as if the environment had totally changed. What they had perhaps found here, O'Keefe and Dostrovsky suggested, was a 'spatial reference map' in the hippocampus of the rat. The hippocampus, in this interpretation, is wired to help you find your way through space. There might be cells, in other words, that fire when you're facing in a particular direction. O'Keefe referred to these cells as 'place cells' and argued that the hippocampus must be the home of the cognitive mapping system that Tolman had proposed a quarter of a century previously. In a book a few years later, O'Keefe and Lynn Nagel argued that 'the hippocampus is the core of a neural memory system providing an *objective* spatial framework within which the items and events of an organism's experience are located and interrelated' (my emphasis).[19] In other words, this framework doesn't simply locate objects relative to an organism's own position, but maps an absolute, objective space, independent of the things in it. In the decades that followed, the branch of neuroscience known today as 'spatial cognition' grew into an enormous area of research.[20]

Jonas Salk's vague intuition about why some places are better to think in than others; scientists in Stanford sending students for a walk down a congested street in Palo Alto; John O'Keefe on a platform in London in 1969, clutching a rat with a hole in its head – these may seem like disparate events. But to understand so many of the taken-for-granted ideas in our own time, we need to engage in what the philosopher Michel Foucault called 'the history of the present'. To understand our current ideas about how buildings and brains might respond to one another, to grasp how the brain has become understood as an organ that is deeply affected by the space it happens to be in – and what it can see in that space, and what direction it is facing within it – we need to follow the trail backwards until what strikes us *right now* as so obvious, clear and true, seems, once again, very weird, disjointed and new.

'Hugo,' I said to neuroscientist Hugo Spiers, 'tell me about London taxi drivers having unusual brains.' We were in Hugo's surprisingly poky office in central London, from which he leads the Spatial Cognition Group at University College London (UCL), setting forth on the path established by figures like John O'Keefe. We were talking about work by another UCL neuroscientist, Eleanor Maguire, and her collaborators, which has shown that London's black-cab drivers, who have to show that they can navigate the city's multilayered tangle from memory, have on average bigger hippocampi than other people.[21]

'What I think was really important in that study', said Hugo, 'is that when Eleanor Maguire, who had the idea, went and did it, she'd read about the fact that certain birds, the ones that store nuts, have a bigger equivalent of the same brain area than the ones that don't store nuts. So there was a kind of story there, that this bit of the brain was specialised. But more importantly, squirrels changed the size of the hippocampus with the seasons. So in winter it's bigger – they need to remember where the nuts are – and then it shrinks in summer, when they don't. So there's a real sense in which, if that's true, then when a human has to learn and remember fifty-eight thousand streets [as London's black-cab drivers do], surely that should have an effect on your brain.'

I asked Hugo what, in his view, a good city would look like, based on what we know about how people navigate and spatially locate themselves in urban areas.

'Well, one option', he said, 'would be to create an entire grid like Manhattan, and then people just go, "I'm on First Street. I want to go to 56th Street." You just go there, but the problem with that sort of thing is the sense of place gets kind of a little bit less . . . you know? Manhattan has got this wonderful uniqueness to it, but in places where it is highly grid-like there is a kind of monotony to it.'

I silently agreed with this. New York has always struck me as weirdly dull for a city of its size.

'It doesn't feel particularly positive for cities that are built on a literal grid,' Hugo continued, 'and designing like that isn't something you'd want to do. You need a break from the grid to help people get a sense of space, and the way I would have developers do that is by looking at data on the cities that have the best outcomes. Somewhere like Lisbon might be good.'

Later, he said: 'If you're trying to think about how you're designing a city, the question is: is this just a generic city, or is it going to be a very corporate, business-oriented city, or is it going to be a garden city? One thing we know now that you'd certainly want is green space. So London actually does quite well on this. There is a lot of green space here that makes London liveable. But there are cities in the world where it's not so good.'

We talked about this a lot, and about how 'green space' might be a more diffuse category than people want to imagine. You can add a wood to an area, Hugo agreed, and some people will love it. You'll see all sorts of benefits from people having access to green space. But if something like, say, knife crime goes up in that area, then that would quickly override any positive effects. Also, if there's no one paid to watch or maintain the wood, it'll quickly become an unwelcome or unpleasant space. The simple presence of a wood in itself isn't what matters.

'There are so many variables', Hugo said, 'that you could easily give up and say, "What's the damn point in looking at the environment and people's psychology?" And I think some people certainly *did* think like that. The field [of environmental psychology] didn't get funding. It was an area of psychology that really dropped away because it wasn't fundable.'

We talked a lot about social factors and how the various cities we both knew well felt very different and distinctive, in ways that were not always easy to figure out. 'Most neuroscientists don't get into these kinds of things,' he said. 'Certainly, in my lab we don't do the kind of questions you're asking. It's hard to get funding for that.'

I remember at the time being very struck by this: by the contrast between what were clearly brilliant, even ingenious, experimental designs for thinking about how humans experience urban environments at the neurobiological level and, in spite of these incredibly smart, thoughtful people applying themselves to the complexity of it all, the sense that, still, *there were so many variables*. That when you actually thought about it, all the city really is, from a scientific perspective, is variables upon variables; variables all the way down. How could we ever truly hope to understand, except in the crudest way, the relationship between our minds and our physical environments? How could we even begin to make sense of urban culture and feeling, those often intangible, even inexpressible qualities that are at the heart of any serious psychic connection between a person and a place?

A few months after speaking to Hugo, I was back in London for a conference on healthy urban design that was being held at the Royal College of Physicians. Unexpectedly, for the home of a centuries-old institution housed in Regent's Park, among some of London's most stereotypically grand and 'traditional' terraces, the Royal College of Physicians is based in a very beautiful, modernist, concrete building. Designed by Denys Lasdun, perhaps British architecture's most important modernist, the building is composed of a series of large concrete rectangles, increasing in size and overhanging one another as they extend upwards – like 'an inverted pale ziggurat', as one journalist put it[22] – held up

The Royal College of Physicians, London.

by sometimes alarmingly thin, unadorned, square concrete pillars.

I walked through the enormous atrium and up the beautiful wooden staircase that dominates the interior of the building, straight into a talk by Jeremy Myerson, an academic and designer who specialises in inclusive design, especially in how design can meet the health needs of older people. City dwellers, Myerson was saying, tend to enjoy a health advantage over others, but this is not evenly distributed.[23] In my notebook, I carefully wrote down words like RESILIENCE and FAIRNESS. The city, said the next speaker, the physician Howard Frumkin, is a prototypical urban habitat – I wrote down URBANISATION – produced by the extraction of fossil fuels and population growth. But today, cities are increasingly challenging for human health. We need to prepare, Frumkin said, for flooding, heatwaves and water shortages. We need to think seriously about migration and the need to evacuate cities in the future. We need to think about physical activity, but also about *happiness*. Here I sat up a bit. What if cities were designed for happiness? Frumkin asked. There is converging evidence, he went on, that promoting happiness means promoting health. And poverty is bad for happiness; in fact, there is a clear connection between happiness, social capital, poverty and health that could and should be integrated into urban design. Physical activity and contact with nature, he said, are major factors affecting health and happiness in the city. BEHAVIOURAL ECONOMICS went into my notebook, along with SYSTEMS THINKING.

I was taken, though, with the notion that happiness, an emotional state, might be the key to urban health – that it might be the true goal of good urban design. Could this straightforward desire for happiness, the capacity of our built environment to simply make us feel good, be at the heart of the relationship between mental health and the city? The idea that cities are bad for mental health is not a new one. Ever since the first era of widespread asylum-building, on the cusp between the eighteenth and nineteenth centuries, it was noted that a disproportionate number of asylum inmates were urban dwellers and, indeed, that activities like farming, walking in the countryside – what we would today call 'nature contact' – offered these patients potent curative resources. In 1939, two University of Chicago sociologists, Robert Faris and Warren Dunham, argued that if you think of the city as an ecological space – like a duck pond, say, or the soil beneath a tree – then you can see how different kinds of mental illness map onto its different zones; different forms of schizophrenia, for example, are visible in 'disorganised' parts of the city centre, where men live alone, where they drink, and so on.[24] These two ideas – first, that the city is an ecology; second, that the ecological study of the city is a critical starting point for studying mental illness in urban areas – would go on to become enormously influential across a wide range of academic disciplines. Still today, the relationship between mental illness and city life is a vexing, unresolved question.[25] But the counter-idea I was facing here – that if bad urban design makes people ill, then good design must surely have the opposite effect – was something new.

These issues are, of course, similar to the problems explored by people like Ebenezer Howard and William Lever in the previous chapter – and indeed, people in this world sometimes build on the work of those figures quite self-consciously. But the explicit focus on mental health, and especially on happiness, was nonetheless something different. I had been reading a book by the Canadian urban thinker and writer Charles Montgomery, who argues that the problem of how to achieve happiness has guided urban thought at least since Socrates dominated the Athenian agora.[26] Happiness and urban form go together, says Montgomery, whether in the public baths of ancient Rome or the private pleasure gardens of eighteenth-century London. Today, though, he goes on, the most important thing we know about the interaction of happiness with urban design is the extent to which the city connects people – or keeps them apart. 'Even though the modern cosmopolitan city makes it easier than ever for individuals to retreat from neighbours and strangers,' he writes, citing neuroscientific research and studies of the hormone oxytocin, 'the greatest of human satisfactions lie in working and playing cooperatively with other people.' And the city is our most important machine for accomplishing this.

By now it was nearly lunchtime, and bucking the trend, as I do, for seeking co-operation or even conversation with others at these kinds of events, I went out to the park to eat my lunch alone. Out of nowhere, a fox approached me, like a dog, clearly looking for some of my sandwich.

'Okay,' I said, tearing off a bit, 'you can have some, but I'm not counting this as either nature contact *or* mutual co-operation.'

Back inside, a slightly wearisome parade of policy wonks, property developers and messianic architects was under way.

The fox in question.

There was a lot of talk about human connection, and positive behaviour, and nudging. I went to a session on health in the workplace, sponsored by a manufacturer of office furniture, during which we were encouraged to get our colleagues involved in their own wellbeing story. There was a general concern about the effects of loneliness on health, and in truth I had begun to feel somewhat lonely myself. HEALTHY PLACEMAKING, I wrote in my notebook, and PARTNERSHIP WORKING – though I didn't really know what this meant. At one point, someone said, 'Sitting is the new smoking.' Lots of people talked admiringly about Copenhagen, which I found weird, because I had been to Copenhagen several times and thought it was just about the most miserable and isolating place I had been to in my entire life.

Finally, a medical doctor called Jacob King came on to talk about urban space and mental health, and in particular the need for design interventions that could be measured, clinically, in terms of their mental health outcomes. He referred to recent clinical trials of nature-based psychotherapy, which suggested that 'the more natural an environment, the more attention is restored, and the more stress is reduced'. King caveated this by saying that it might not translate everywhere, however; maybe what we call green space is not good for everyone or wanted in all places – perceptions matter. This question of perception and difference was nagging at me.

The last speaker I saw was a landscape architect called Bridget Snaith, who talked about racism in parks and park design. She pointed out that when we talk about 'green space', we often mean 'white space'. In fact, she said, there's a lot of cultural difference in terms of landscape preferences;

not everyone has the same fantasy of rolling hills. This was surely true, I thought. I had long believed that the idea we all have the same low-key, fascist desire for some kind of beaux arts City Beautiful was deeply strange. There is a real absence of ethnic minority representation in urban parks discourse, Snaith went on, as well as a weird, Eurocentric idea that nature is a particular kind of thing, and that loving it is a universal affect.

I'll return to this idea – that green urbanism, whatever else it is, is sometimes also a deliberate strategy of exclusion. But what Snaith was pointing to here was something that had been troubling me for some time: that what I sometimes saw as a weirdly anti-urban tendency in urban design – the sense that the city is a space of threat, and stress, and illness; a space that needs to be controlled or repaired – was only partially about the physical environment. Never mentioned explicitly but, it seemed to me, sometimes in the background nonetheless were the very diverse kinds of *people* you find in cities – people, that is, who don't always fit a white, hetero-normative, suburban ideal of trust and civic virtue.

During my research for this book, I spent a lot of time attending workshops and conferences that were broadly about how the physical environment affects mental health. At some point during every one of these events, usually quite early on, someone – often a civil servant or a policy person – would talk very earnestly about the work of Roger Ulrich. In 1979, Ulrich wrote a paper pointing out that a general assumption we have – that nature is psychologically good for us – was basically untested; everyone was just taking Frederick Law Olmsted's word for it. So Ulrich set out to test it for himself.[27] In fine psychological tradition, he took a bunch of students from his own department who had just sat an exam – he took this, perhaps optimistically, as a sign that the students would be stressed or alert – and gave them an anxiety test before showing them some images he'd had made. Half the students were shown pictures of green, natural, vegetative landscapes, while the other half got images featuring only urban scenes. The subjects were asked to rate how much they liked each image, then Ulrich did the anxiety test *again*, and asked the students what kind of place they'd grown up in. If you know the genre, there's not going to be much surprise about how this turns out, but remember that Ulrich was swimming then in fairly untested waters. After looking at the images, the urban group reported worsening scores across a range of psychological states, such as sadness, fear and aggression, and attentiveness. In other words, they were angrier and more frightened after looking at images of cities than they were before. For the nature group, Ulrich got the entirely opposite pattern: these people felt more affectionate and carefree; they reported that both their breathing and heart rates had gone down. 'In contrast to the nature scenes,' Ulrich concluded, 'the urban views tended to work against emotional wellbeing.'

At the end of his paper, Ulrich speculated on some of the possible lessons. Planners, he said, may want to think about adding some green space to urban areas. But also, he said, maybe those in charge of places where lots of people are *already* pretty stressed – hospitals, for example – should think about how much contact with nature they provide. 'Does a pre-operative hospital patient', he asked, 'experience less anxiety if his window overlooks a park rather than, say, a motorway or vegetationless parking lot?' Ulrich's subsequent attempt to answer that question produced perhaps the most influential environmental psychology paper ever published. In it, he described how he had collected the medical records of surgical patients who had been assigned to rooms on two different floors in a hospital in Pennsylvania, over a ten-year period. On these floors, as it happened, patients were randomly assigned to rooms that had one of two views: from some you could see a nice clump of deciduous trees out of the window; from others all you got was a bare brick wall.

Ulrich took the records of all the patients who had had gall bladder surgery *and* been assigned to a room on one of these two floors. He then looked at how long each patient had been in hospital, how much pain relief they asked for, whether they asked for tranquillisers for their anxiety, and whatever else the nurses wrote down about them. The results were remarkable. Patients who could see trees spent fewer days in hospital, received fewer notes on their charts describing them as 'upset and crying', asked much less frequently for potent painkilling drugs and had fewer post-surgical complications.

In the decades that followed, Ulrich developed a large and influential body of research on the relationship between looking at representations of natural (mostly vegetal) objects, and human wellbeing, especially in relation to health outcomes. This ranges from research on hospital gardens, to people's passive experiences of plants, to the relationship between interior design and wellbeing, to the effect of putting up landscape posters in your office, and the benefits of a hospital garden for people visiting relatives in the ICU.[28] And yet every time

114

I hear someone reverently cite this work, two things immediately strike me – and more generally, they seem relevant to how we think about the traffic between space and the mind. One is about context and time, the other about nature. First, context and *time*. The 1970s and 1980s, in North America, form an era that we have come to associate with so-called 'urban decay'. Whether we take this as a real thing or just a collective moral panic, it's certainly the case that a prominent cultural trope at the time of Ulrich's research was that the city was a dystopian place, a centre of danger, crime and decay, a historical form of human habitat that was by then in steep and likely terminal decline.[29] The 1970s is the decade of New York City's seemingly endless 'fiscal crisis', with rubbish piling up in the streets and whole city blocks becoming derelict. It's the era of *Taxi Driver* and *Death Wish*. I'm not arguing that Ulrich or any other researcher is promoting or interested in these kinds of ideas about the city. My point is that this, nonetheless, is the unavoidable cultural context in which these scientific ideas are emerging; this is the precise moment, as the urban historian Otto Saumarez Smith puts it, when 'modernist orthodoxies in approaches to cities began to unravel'.[30]

What was at stake here was a larger crisis in twentieth-century urban planning, whose tools had been applied – often in quite an unthinking and arrogant way, it's true – to a great many cities in the three decades since World War II. It's the moment when Jane Jacobs's anti-modernist 1961 tract, *The Death and Life of Great American Cities*,[31] was becoming ubiquitous among urban intellectuals; when Robert Caro's *The Power Broker* – an unflattering biography of Robert

Moses, the New York City urban planner and great adversary of Jacobs – won the Pulitzer Prize.[32] In other words, it's the moment when the utopian assumptions of twentieth-century architecture and urban planning, at least when applied to any kind of collective organisation, started to sink, quite palpably, into the ground.

This isn't to say that all that's happening here is cultural. It's important to note that these findings about nature scenes and wellbeing do seem to hold up over time, even though that era of imagined decline, in most Euro-American cities at least, has long since ended, and indeed been reversed. But I do think it's worth noting that the highly influential literature on how images of urban landscapes make people afraid, sad, stressed, or whatever, comes from an era in which the slow death of the city, and a kind of generalised, even *libidinal*, interest in the submission of entire urban districts to crime, dereliction, etc., was a major part of everyday popular culture. It doesn't seem like too much of a leap to wonder how any other idea of the city might have prevailed in the places these studies were being carried out, or among the populations being studied (i.e. psychology undergraduates), the majority of whom had likely transferred directly from their suburban home to some self-regarding nowheresville of a college town – Amherst, let's say – without pausing much along the way to question any of their own assumptions about life, or the physical spaces that produce and contain it.

Second, *nature*. It is 'a clear-cut finding in this research', Roger Ulrich wrote in a 1997 contribution to a volume on 'biophilia', that there is 'a strong tendency for diverse European, North American and Asian groups to prefer natural landscapes over urban or built views, especially when the latter lack natural content such as vegetation and water'.[33] The term 'biophilia' is often associated with Edward O. Wilson, who published a deeply silly book under that title in 1984.[34] The term describes the idea that human beings have an evolved need to be around natural, living things, like plants and animals, and that if this need is not fulfilled, they will quickly become quite ill. As the philosopher Lauren Greyson puts it, biophilia, or at least this version of the concept, 'resembles, in suspicious ways, the theories of disenchantment that trace nearly every conceivable ill plaguing the individual and society to the nomad's fall from grace and the rise of civilization'.[35] This evolutionary account of humankind's deep need for nature has nonetheless been widely influential in scientific studies of the relationship between psychology and the environment. It has given weight, for example, to concepts like 'attention restoration theory', which suggests that gazing into nature improves concentration.[36] The latter term is widely used within the world of landscape architecture, and in studies of the relationship between mental health and place, though meta-analyses of its effects are not exactly overwhelming.[37]

Either way, all of this rests on some clear-cut notion of what 'nature' actually is. Rachel and Stephen Kaplan are clear in their landmark 1989 text on attention restoration theory that they intend the term 'nature' to be understood pretty broadly and inclusively. And yet some studies, Roger Ulrich pointed out in a 1997 paper, suggest that this positive effect of natural scenes deteriorates when artificial elements are introduced: 'electrical transmission towers and power lines, large advertising signs or billboards, and prominent concrete or asphalt road surfaces' have a 'strongly detrimental effect' on the preference for pastoral landscapes. This is where things get tricky. In the 1980s, the environmental writer Bill McKibben famously argued that because there is now no place or object on the planet that doesn't bear the stamp of humanity in one way or another, we have actually lost the idea of nature altogether.[38] Such a strict separation between the artificial world of humans and the organic realm of nature has a long pedigree, but I don't think it stands up to much scrutiny. A scene doesn't become unnatural just because JCDecaux starts to advertise cars in the corner of it. Research in environmental psychology consistently shows a preference for vegetation and water, certainly. But much vegetation, of course, is where it is, and looks how it looks, due to quite brutal and highly industrial human manipulation of the soil. Forests grow and regrow in line with the agricultural and economic needs of humans in the vicinity. Water often moves in the direction that humans have made it move. The beautiful rolling landscapes of the English countryside, so-called, are actually the product of industrial-scale and human-driven deforestation; your average Cotswold hillside, which wealthy Londoners pay a fortune to visit so they can commune with nature, is, alas, as brute and scarred a scene as any factory floor.

So, people can perfectly well have a preference for green fields and rows of vegetation – each to their own in such matters is my policy – but they cannot so easily claim, I think, that what they are preferring here is *nature*.[39] I don't deny that Ulrich and his many collaborators are measuring something useful; nor do I want to slip into the boring fallacy, exhibited by many writers on this topic, of imagining that anything shown to be not quite 100 per cent natural must, therefore, be social all the way down. But throughout this book I *do* want to poke at the idea that what people find restful in vegetative scenery is the presence or suggestion of *nature*. I'm not at all won over by the idea that the city unsettles because it is an unnatural place – as opposed to the idea that it unsettles because, collectively, we have spent a number of decades telling young, mostly white college students, and their parents, that the city is, somehow, a dangerous place, a dying place and, sotto voce, perhaps also, increasingly, an excessively diverse place.

This was all getting kind of heavy, so I decided to go and see Dr Eleanor Ratcliffe, an environmental psychologist whom I'd got to know a little in the early stages of doing research for this book. We had once gone on the same urban nature walk, around some of the more industrial parts of east London, and at one point I'd looked back and seen Ellie, quite alone and entirely unselfconsciously, hugging a tree. 'This,' I thought, in a dull world of statistics and outcomes, 'is my kind of psychologist.' Ellie does research on how green environments can be 'restorative' for people – in other words, how they can help us recover when super-stressed or overwhelmed. In contrast to some of the experimental work using dodgy mobile brain devices, her way of thinking about these topics had always struck me as especially nuanced and alive to complexity.

It's definitely the case, she told me, 'that a lot of the environments that are quite stressful, that tax us mentally, have a lot of distractions in them. So, an example I often give in my lectures is being at Waterloo train station in London. There are so *many* stimuli going on: there are tannoys and people, and you're trying to find out what time a train is leaving and where the ticket machine is. So there's this hectic auditory and spatial information that's overloading you. Whereas, very often, restorative environments, like nature, have rather little going on, or what's going on is doing so in quite a slow, measured way. Maybe the leaves are moving or there's a pattern of light on water or birds singing. But these stimuli, these properties in the environment, are not too demanding. And that gives people an opportunity to rest mentally.'

We talked a bit about urban versus rural environments, and what it might mean not just to compare the two, but to compare, say, an urban scene and a hillside that were both considered beautiful. The thing is, though, said Ellie, it's not really *nature* that matters. 'Nature has certain positive properties', she went on, 'that in some circumstances can help people recover cognitively. Nature isn't cognitively demanding. And very often the kind of nature that people go to is calming, so it's not threatening. It's very beautiful and it's quiet, so all of these things are conducive to relaxation and stress recovery.'

But there's also a cultural element to it, she pointed out, in that 'people associate nature with feeling good'. She said: 'We're told so much, "Oh, you know, go outside." It's almost like the fetishisation of nature, in my opinion. I'm not trying to say that nature isn't good for people, but I think perhaps the claim that there's something magical or special about nature might be a bit overblown. It's just another type of environment. It just so happens that it's a lot more calming.'

What are you saying, I asked – that it's more of a cultural thing that we find green spaces calming?

'It's not that the effect isn't real,' she said, 'but we have all learned that, you know, nature is good for you and makes you feel calm, so *of course*, when you go into nature, yes, you really do feel calm.'

Then she said: 'No one just sits and is exposed to an environment. I mean, I'm sitting in my flat at the moment, and one of the reasons I decided to rent this flat is that it has a really long garden, which reminds me of my childhood garden. So, when I saw this garden, I wasn't just being "exposed" to it; I had these memories of other gardens that I'd known, and I felt good about it because I was thinking about these past memories. And I believe that there is this role of people constructing their experience of what might be a restorative environment using their expectations, their memories and their past experiences.'

This example really struck me. To be slightly simplistic about it, the question I had been turning over in my mind for some time was whether the supposed calming effect of nature – which *I* had never felt, at least – was real. Maybe it was a simple prejudice, but I wasn't at all convinced that the mere presence of grass and trees could have what sounds like, in all truth, a quasi-religious, even transcendental effect on nearby humans. My suspicions were at least partly because I found the most common explanation for why this might be – that humans evolved in the African savannah and are naturally driven to seek out environments that somehow reproduce this early experience – kind of laughable, a child's fairy story for weak-minded evolutionary psychologists who believe in 'biophilia'. But speaking to Ellie reminded me that this was the wrong way to think about it. The issue isn't whether or not the effect is real – if enough people say they feel the effect, it's real, and that's the end of it. The issue is whether the effect is caused by some *inherent* quality of natural materials, some physical property of trees and grass that just makes people feel good, or if instead it's a result of cultural expectation. The physical places we find relaxing turn out to be exactly the physical places that we've been told, for our entire lives, *should* relax us.

In the same way, the spaces that *don't* relax us and that we often find stressful, that can sometimes even stress us so much that we become ill, are those that our culture has long held up as being threatening and scary. Of course, it's true that cities actually are cognitively demanding in some way – they really are often noisy and filled with distracting stuff. But it's also true that we experience these spaces after a lifetime spent being bombarded by what the historian William Cronon calls 'the symbolic conventions of the dark city'; we are primed for that stress because we are surrounded by simple-minded cultural narratives about the terrible things that might befall us in urban space.[40] This is a scientific problem – how can you control for such cultural priming when you design an experiment? – but it's a political and moral one too. At a certain point, rather than simply planting trees and bushes everywhere, we might need to confront the prejudices and fantasies that have rendered the city such an object of fascinated horror. These are racialised fantasies, certainly; but they are also fantasies of class, the product of a repressed disgust at having to encounter visibly unwell or unhoused people; they are also the product of plain old free-floating xenophobia and nativism. Maybe it's not 'the city' that's making us ill after all.

Perhaps, instead of trying to fix the city, we could try to fix ourselves and the weird and actually kind of racist, anti-urban public culture that we've allowed to flourish, unchecked, since the last few decades of the twentieth century. In particular, we might learn to think a bit more critically about that great symbol of anti-urbanism whose presence now marks all kinds of strange hopes and desires for better city-making. I am talking, of course, about the urban tree.

# 4: The Conquered City

The Marble Arch Mound.

In the autumn of 2020, as the UK emerged from Covid-driven public health restrictions that had seen most shops closed for some time, Westminster City Council – the authority responsible for London's retail-led West End – figured they needed to do something. They wanted to entice people back to the shops and let it be known that the city was open again. What they needed, they decided, was a bold new visitor attraction at the less used, slightly grimier end of Oxford Street, near Marble Arch. So they hired a Dutch architecture firm, MVRDV, who had recently built a giant stairway in their home city, Rotterdam. For London, MVRDV came up with a 'hollowed-out mountain', a temporary green structure that would loom over Oxford Street's crappy chain stores and restaurants and 'demonstrate the need to add nature to cities'. There would be plants, soil, sedum, and forty-five trees across the top of the new construction. Inside, there was to be a 'dancing light show that simulates the interconnected root structure of a birch tree forest'.[1] The idea was that people would pay to walk up this temporary urban hill, take in the view, and then come back down through a forest experience in the interior. The Mound, said MVRDV – this was the structure's unhappy name – would 'encourage Londoners to rethink the area and question why they allowed a former green spot became [sic] surrounded by traffic'.[2]

In February 2021, the project was announced to the public, with an artist's impression showing a small grassy hill, near the actual Marble Arch. Designed by the Regency architect John Nash in 1827, and once the triumphal entrance to Buckingham Palace, today the Arch is just another sad imperial relic on a traffic island. The Mound tried to rectify this indignity somewhat by connecting the Arch to nearby Hyde Park. It would create a 'grassy knoll', said the London *Evening Standard* approvingly, 'with mature trees and a walkway to a viewing gallery'.[3] In July, the Mound opened to visitors. Almost immediately, a Twitter user called Dan Barker[4] posted a long, detailed thread of his visit, for which he had paid £6.50. Barker described the Mound as like being in 'the inside of a 25m enormous scaffold, dotted with a few trees'. There was an 'emptyish storage area', he said, as well as 'rubble' and 'random cables scattered about'. His thread, carefully dotted with photos of what really did look like a forlorn building site, went viral. Other damning images of a weirdly brown and treeless fake hillock quickly appeared on social media. Within days, Westminster City Council offered refunds to anyone who had paid to visit the Mound and announced that the attraction would be free until it got up to scratch.[5] In August, with the Mound still not complete, it was revealed that its reported cost of £2 million had risen to £6 million. The deputy leader of the council resigned.[6] By September, the *Guardian* was reporting that the Mound was 'drawing crowds keen to see how bad it is'.[7] One news outlet called it 'London's worst ever tourist attraction' and 'a literal mound of dirt'.[8]

Finally, in January 2022, bowing to the inevitable, Westminster City Council announced the Mound's hasty closure. An internal report described the episode as 'devastating'.[9] On their own website, MVRDV said that the Mound 'had been left to rot' in the middle of Oxford Street. 'As a practice,' they said, 'we have rarely seen such a loveless execution of our designs.' In a final indignity, the art magazine *Frieze* published an 'interview' with the Mound by the writer Huw Lemmey, who depicted his subject as crying self-pityingly into a tissue. 'I thought I could have meant something,' Lemmey ventriloquised the Mound. 'Originally, I was supposed to consume the Marble Arch, smothering a symbol of petty human triumphalism. Nature is Healing, you see.'[10]

'Nature is healing' was indeed a phrase that had become popular with a certain kind of environmentally minded commentator during the Covid pandemic. It captured an idea that with urban centres temporarily abandoned, the natural, non-human world might take the opportunity to 'heal' itself – and thus, implicitly, heal us too, physically and morally. Social media was flooded with fake images of dolphins and swans reclaiming the canals of Venice as humans were corralled indoors. At best, this idea represents a very naive brand of environmentalism and forms a neat vehicle for the low-budget moral goods (city bad; nature good) in which a lot of popular environmental thinking trades. At worst, it revives the idea most famously associated with the Georgian-era economist Thomas Malthus: that for an overpopulated human world to achieve its natural equilibrium, a lot of people are simply going to have to die – that, indeed, it might be better if they got on with their dying sooner rather than later. This is, perhaps, a lot to burden the poor Marble Arch Mound with. But the monument was, quite explicitly, in its own terms, an imposition of 'nature' on the city. It was an attempt to somehow fix urban space by turning at least a part of one iconic commercial street into a forest. The Mound's decrepitude is, in this sense, oddly instructive: in its physical and ideological abjection, in literally showing us the crudely scaffolded dirt that undergirds so much 'urban nature', the Mound offered an unusually naked, unflattering glimpse of a set of ideas and intuitions – about nature, and trees, and parks, and cities, and humans – that have become incredibly powerful in urban planning and architecture.

One of these intuitions is that human society is somehow not well – literally and figuratively. We are overproducing and over-consuming; we are becoming fat, hateful and immoral. We eat too many snacks, use too many plastics, and spend too much time online, burning up the ever more scarce resources of our precious, mossy glebe – so goes the familiar lament. But the suggestion is also that we are not well in the sense of physical disease. Our bad lifestyles, our distance from traditional modes of production, our up-close, jangly mode of urban living, our shopping and our discarding, our ill treatment of chickens and cows, all of it creates illness – not only the so-called 'lifestyle diseases' of modern living, like diabetes, but infectious diseases too, as new viral pathogens breed and spread across an ever more intensely industrialised, tightly connected world. And finally, so this thinking goes, we are not well in the sense of mental distress: all this making and consuming, the buying and the throwing away, far from being a joyful act of wilful destruction is actually really *stressful*; the work we have to do to keep it all going is miserable; the artificial cities we have to live in to contain it are noisy, smelly, forbidding. We live in 'an age of excess', says the Indian writer and scholar Sumana Roy, in *How I Became a Tree*, 'more food and clothes and houses and things than we needed, an extravagant show of wealth and emotions'. The trees, by contrast, have things figured out. 'Who has ever seen a tree', Roy says, 'and exclaimed, "Such a jealous tree!" the way we do about children in the playground and adults in the auction hall.' This produces, for Roy, a fantasy of transformation: 'I wanted that confidence of the tree, the complete rejection of all that made humans feel inferior or superior.'[11]

This fantasy, though expressed with unusual craft by Roy, is common enough. Trees are widely imagined as an ideal solution to the cultural, psychological and moral degeneracy of the city. Trees can *heal* modern and urban life – or so it is thought. They can heal in a scientific sense, but also in a spiritual one. They can help resolve our internal anxieties as individual people, but they can also intervene in our collective failures as a society. You can, then, see how one very compelling solution to the multiple urban crises of our times arises: plant more trees. Doing so – if we are to believe a UK government press release celebrating 'Tree Week' in 2021 – will in one swoop make 'our towns and cities safer, healthier and more pleasant places to be, helping boost people's wellbeing as well as contributing towards efforts to tackle climate change'.[12] Planting trees would transform the spaces we live in. It would give more room to nature and improve the earth's atmosphere. It would cool cities down and increase biodiversity. People could get out to visit the trees, and this would relax them a lot. Spending time planting trees and tending to them would also mean less time buying stuff, or watching pornography. And people *like* trees. They're big and charismatic. They're shady. They make humans feel good about themselves. Even as pitiless and desiccated a figure as Donald Trump has been seduced, having announced, in 2020, that the US was going to plant a trillion trees.[13] 'Nobody's against trees,' Marc Benioff, the internet billionaire behind this scheme, told an audience in Davos, Switzerland. 'The tree', he said, is 'a bipartisan issue'.[14] A year before, the esteemed academic journal *Science* had published a paper that showed there was room on the earth for another 0.9 billion hectares of tree canopy, which could store 205 gigatonnes of carbon.[15] People went crazy. Companies started buying up farmland in all kinds of random places to plant trees. It got so bad that the lead scientist on the paper had to go on the news to tell them to stop – such fevered tree planting risked damaging biodiversity, as well as reducing the space for farmland.[16]

The Torre Guinigi, Lucca.

So this is the context in which Westminster City Council – whose beat, I stress, is the most built up and commercial part of the largest, busiest city in Europe – wanted to spend £6 million on a hill and put a bunch of trees on top. This, truly, would be an act of collective healing. The Mound, said the *Guardian*'s architecture critic, much like New York's High Line or the oak-topped Torre Guinigi in Tuscany, was an attempt 'to harness the charm and power of the elevated tree'.[17] In fact, as Ali Karimi pointed out in the *Architectural Review*, it was just one of several tree-related public installations in European cities that year. These included a temporary forest in the courtyard of London's Somerset House and another planted in the centre of a football stadium, originally built by the far-right leader Jörg Haider, in the unhappy Austrian city of Klagenfurt. The problem, said Karimi, is that in a temporary installation, 'the tree is inevitably objectified and performative, able to raise questions but unable to be a tree'.[18] This seems to me not quite right. Because to be a tree today surely *is*, quite precisely, to be a performer. The urban tree is *not* an unfortunate natural object placed in an unforgiving new context, torn from its innocent state and made to dance for pennies in the big city, like a country rube from some bad nineteenth-century novel. In fact, the Mound, insofar as it accidentally revealed the urban forest to be a kind of construction site, as something built out of rubble, electrical wiring and metal poles, was maybe more accurate than it knew. Objectification of the tree is not an unfortunate side effect of these projects. Objectification, as far as urban trees are concerned, is the whole point.

Because the tree is, as much as it is anything else, a cultural object. It helps us to tell stories about ourselves and the world we think we're creating. One useful way to think about trees is to focus not so much on their ecology or environmental role, but instead on why they're suddenly so visible everywhere – in literature, election campaigns, architecture, visual arts, health, and so on. Maybe this sounds melodramatic, but I've been struck by a kind of *treeification* of wider culture over the last few years, especially in relation to our ideas about the urban environment, and more especially still in relation to our ongoing desire for collective and individual repair in and through that environment. It's as if, all of a sudden, there is no problem in the built or physical or social environment that might not be solved by a well-planted oak; no personal crisis that could not be fixed by leaning into a sturdy yew or beech. The trouble is that, like all cultural objects, trees are complicated – they tell more than one story. Trees can represent a certain naive idea of healing and connection with nature. But they can also stand in for something harder: they can represent a nostalgia for some more avowedly primitive age; they can make petty human feelings and hopes secondary to the timeless processes of nature; they can represent a world, ultimately, that is not only 'more than human', as my unfortunate colleagues in the geography department sometimes like to say, but that is distinctly *anti*-human too.

Consider the sheer number of ways in which trees are imagined to fix modern life – and, in particular, modern urban life. In 2021, the UK government sought applications for its Urban

Tree Challenge Fund, a £10 million scheme to plant 130,000 new trees in towns and cities across England.* In a press release, the government said that the trees would be focused on deprived areas, with someone from Slough council effusing that the fund would allow them to 'focus on upskilling for employment, active lifestyles, citizen science and volunteering'. It's hard to know what a tree has to do with 'upskilling for employment', but then that's the point: there is nothing a tree can't do. In Wales, the government has planted a tree for every child born in the country since 1 January 2008, and – somewhat randomly and maybe problematically – since April 2014 has planted another in Uganda as well. The aim of this, they say, 'is to create publicly accessible woodland, build a stronger connection between children, families and their natural environment and engage with local communities'.†

It gets worse: in late 2021, an eccentric initiative called the Queen's Green Canopy surfaced, which urged people to 'plant a tree' to mark Queen Elizabeth II's diamond jubilee; plans were also announced to 'identify 70 Ancient Trees to celebrate Her Majesty's 70 years of service'. The patron of this strikingly feudal initiative was the Queen's eldest son, Prince Charles (as he was then). The campaign partnered with the Department for Environment, Food and Rural Affairs, as well as the Royal Horticultural Society. Its 'platinum sponsors' included noted environmental leaders such as McDonald's, Coutts bank and Rentokil.

---

* That's about £77 per tree – which seems expensive.
† Though, charmingly, the Welsh-language word for 'children' is *plant*, which shares a Latin root (*planta*, meaning something like 'offshoot') with the quite different English word 'plant'.

On Sundays, I sometimes go into my local chain bookshop and take surreptitious photographs of the latest non-fiction books about trees. There's *The Wood* by John Lewis-Stempel, *Wildwood* by Roger Deakin, *The Wood for the Trees* by Richard Fortey, *The Hidden Life of Trees* by Peter Wohlleben, and its follow-up, *The Heartbeat of Trees* – neither of which is to be confused with either Colin Tudge's book, *The Secret Life of Trees*, or Thomas Pakenham's *The Company of Trees*. For children there's *The Tree: An Environmental Fable* by Neal Layton. For lovers of adult fiction, there's Richard Powers's Pulitzer Prize-winning *The Overstory*, a novel about lots of different people whose lives are inextricably bound up with trees ('a big novel that tells us as much about trees as *Moby-Dick* does about whales', says *The Times* – though it's unclear whether this is intended as recommendation or warning[19]). For those who prefer audio, there's the BBC's big-budget podcast eco-thriller *Forest 404*, the story of a treeless future dystopia where human beings' awareness of their unconscious arboreal nature gets triggered by an illicit recording of the Amazon rainforest.

In 2019, Singapore's Changi airport opened Jewel, a four-storey indoor forest, complete with a waterfall, hotel, 3,000 trees and early check-in facilities.[20] In the same year, Stefano Boeri, an Italian architect already famous for his Bosco Verticale in Milan – two residential towers lined up and down with more than nine hundred trees – proposed a new 'Forest Stadium' to replace the dilapidated San Siro football ground, 'in which trees surround the field and the stands and living nature becomes the protagonist of the football experience and a new urban landscape, for all citizens'.[21]

Also in 2019, in the middle of a bruising election campaign and keen to distract voters from a growing scandal about his youthful enthusiasm for blackface, Justin Trudeau tweeted: 'We'll plant 2 billion trees over the next ten years. That's it. That's the tweet.'[22] In 2018, a student campaign began at the University of Sussex to switch the institution's default internet search engine to Ecosia, a Germany-based business that donates 80 per cent of its profits to reforestation organisations. 'You search. We plant' is their slogan.[23] In November 2021, a green fintech firm called Tred launched a Mastercard debit card made from recycled ocean plastic that allows the user to 'plant trees as you spend'.[24] I could keep going.

All of this cultural attention to trees as objects of collective rehabilitation, meanwhile, seems somehow linked to a political and economic period in which the environmental activists, Extinction Rebellion, staged a surprisingly successful intervention in a range of global cities; in which reassembled far-right organisations are suddenly very interested in their respective nations' natural ecological heritage;[25] in which Amazon founder, Jeff Bezos, an almost-too-cartoonish idea of a corporate villain, is retooling his Blue Origin aerospace company to advance a very real scheme to abandon the earth for a wooded simulacrum in outer space.[26]

It's certainly understandable, as the spectre of climate disaster comes ever nearer, as the looming obliteration of much that currently exists on this planet becomes less deniable, how a certain lament for the tree, a kind of libidinal, woody *desire*, might seep into the wider culture. And with this fear, sure, there might come a growing suspicion of industrial and urban life and the destructive economic logic of capitalist growth, whose major piece of supporting infrastructure is, it's true, *the city*.[27] You could, on this basis, interpret the cultural pre-eminence of trees as simply a rational response to climate change and the economic model that produces it. And yet the London Mound was, as various commentators have noted, at best an *idea* of a woodland – it was foresting as plaintive artistic gesture rather than tree planting as serious ecological action. Maybe this was intended in a pedagogical way. One can imagine, perhaps, busy shoppers near Marble Arch, clutching their Primark and Zara bags, being brought up short, suddenly reminded of some other, less consumption-oriented life, as Westminster City Council's dirty mound loomed on the horizon. I don't find this plausible, but I can see how other people might – not least the Mound's designers and funders.

But I can't stop myself wondering if there isn't also something less obvious, something perhaps more *psychological*, going on in this sudden, intense, collective attention to trees and green spaces. Maybe it's simply guilt about deforestation and an attempt to expiate our past sins. But I'm inclined to think of it instead as a form of transference: how else can you explain the fact that the thing we're wantonly destroying, and destroying to the point of our own ecological crisis, is somehow imagined as the very source of our cultural and psychic salvation? Something is happening in the woods, and it's not simply healing. 'The city is our superego,' says the writer Luke Turner, in his memoir of cottaging in Epping Forest, 'rendered in bricks and mortar, concrete and glass. In the forest the id cavorts under the pollards.'[28]

Let's take this metaphor one step further and do what any good therapist would do. Let's go back to the beginning of things, to where the trouble with trees first started.

In 1607, an uprising against the practice of enclosure blew up in Northamptonshire and quickly spread to the neighbouring counties of Warwickshire and Leicestershire.[29] Initially, a landlord called Thomas Tresham erected a series of fences and borders around what had been common grazing land. A crowd of a thousand people descended on the land, dug the fences up and camped there, in what became the first of a series of uprisings against enclosure across the three counties. Among the leaders of this short movement was one 'Captain Pouch' (real name John Reynolds), who claimed to derive supernatural powers from a pouch he kept at his side. Eventually, the uprising was put down in bloody fashion by the local gentry's private army; various leaders of the rebellion were hung, drawn and quartered, with pieces of their dismembered bodies displayed around nearby towns. When Reynolds himself was executed, his famous pouch was found to contain only a small lump of local cheese.

In the wake of these grim events, an agricultural writer called Arthur Standish, much disturbed by what had taken place, spent some years travelling around the affected areas, speaking to people about what had led to the uprising. In the larger sense, what was going on here was the emergence of agricultural capitalism: the gradual move away from a communal, if somewhat inefficient, feudal 'open field system' towards the development of land into a more intensive, private factory for the production of animal protein and grain, which could then be sold on the open market. A major additional cause of the disturbances, according to Standish, was, however, the high price of fuel, brought on by the excessive felling of trees. This, in turn, was at least partly motivated by the needs of the growing glass and iron industries (both of which require very high temperatures, making them extremely wood-intensive).[30] In 1613, Standish published his *New Directions of Experience . . . for the Planting of Timber and Fire-Wood*, setting out 'some projects for the increasing of Woods, the decay whereof in this Realme is universally complained of'.[31] In his book, addressed to the King, Standish provides an ecological solution to a political crisis: he proposes growing more trees to bring fuel prices down, as well as to provide food for the peasantry, in the form of fruit.[32] Enclosure was certainly a kind of political violence, but in making sense of this violence, the historian Joan Thirsk points out, Standish calls the reader's attention to a different set of environmental things and practices: to soil, and the use of lime, and the proper distance between trees.

Maybe, then, our own interest in trees isn't just some recent development. Maybe there are long-forgotten events, buried deep in the political and ecological history of the planet, arguments and visions that can be traced back to specific cultural and scientific projects, that connect us, anxiously, to trees and to forests. Maybe, indeed, there really are good, long-standing reasons for why we simply find the increasingly treeless city to be an alienating, frightening place.

Certainly, fear of tree scarcity was a perennial issue in many European countries up until the nineteenth century. As early as 1534, the English jurist Sir Anthony Fitzherbert published his *Boke of Husbandrie*,[33] an agricultural text that issues various stern lectures on the proper management of wood in and around the manorial farm, including how to carefully cut timber from trees without killing them or doing them great damage. Centuries later, Karl Marx devoted several newspaper columns to a new German law that overrode common rights to wood-gathering and treated the taking of wood as a felony.[34] Indeed, Marx's very first example of commodity fetishism in *Capital* is the production of a table from wood 'furnished by nature'.[35] Perhaps, though, the single most influential arboricultural text from across these centuries is John Evelyn's *Sylva*, a work first delivered to the Royal Society – Evelyn was one of the society's founders – in 1662. As might perhaps be expected from one of the age's foremost diarists, *Sylva* is still strikingly readable today. The text mixes pastoral dreaminess and hard-nosed husbandry; as well as serious advice on the growth and management of specific tree varieties, Evelyn provides lines of poetry, moments of whimsy and frequent literary and philosophical allusions. At one point, he breaks off to consider what wood Christ's cross would have been made from, and having considered the various sources and claims, concludes that – surely – only English oak would have been able to constrain a dying god.[36]

At the heart of the book, though, is a species-by-species account of the trees of England – their physical description and taxonomy, their growth and development, the soils they prefer, how best to lop them, whether and how they might be transplanted, and what their timber might be good for. Evelyn, a committed royalist, was writing amid the restoration of the English monarchy in 1660, and he emphasised the need to replant woods and forests that had been destroyed during the Civil War. Just as, for Standish, forest depletion marks the social and economic decay of early capitalism, so tree planting, for Evelyn, is the mark of England's revival – specifically, the revival of its king – in the wake of internal conflict. In both cases, amid the political tumult of early modernity, the tree is imagined as a *restorative* object; its serene and regal branches signify social harmony, monarchy, order.

Indeed, as the literary scholar James C. McKusick points out, though Evelyn had a serious, utilitarian purpose in his concern for the military consequences of so much forest depletion, his project also had an imaginative – perhaps, one might say, *ideological* – bent.[37] What he was creating was nothing less than a new vision of the woods, in which trees are not only natural objects, but political and moral figures too. Evelyn, says McKusick, gave the English 'a new way of seeing forests': not only as economic assets, but as aesthetic markers of the nation, as the bearers of an 'intrinsic sacred character' that needs to be preserved. Here is the nation, then, made sturdy by its canopy of mighty oaks; and here, too, its grateful subjects, made secure, like the small creatures of the forest floor, in the shelter of these great, regal plants. Here, too, it seems to me, is how we should read the tree: as a morality tale that offsets the shock and violence of a modern, capitalist, republican and increasingly *urban* world.

In one sense, then, you could read the Mound, and the Queen's Green Canopy, and Donald Trump's trillion trees, and idiot venture capitalists buying farmland in various rural parts of the globe, and all the rest of it, as – okay – stupid, but also unremarkable. Nonsense as it is, this is simply the continuation of a centuries-old tradition of lamenting the loss of trees, and in particular lamenting their loss to creeping industrialisation, urbanisation and colonisation. '*Cad a dhéanfaimid feasta gan adhmad?*' goes a famous Irish-language lament from the late eighteenth century, as English landlords, with no interest in the ecology of their own landholdings, stripped the woods from their ill-gotten estates. '*Tá deireadh na gcoillte ar lár.*' ('What will we do now for timber,' in Eiléan Ní Chuilleanáin's translation, 'with the last of the woods laid low.'[38]) Deforestation, we might say, is a kind of anxious underbelly of modernity; the tree is the absent presence through which the costs and ambivalences of 'progress' get registered.

This isn't quite right, though, because something changes in the nineteenth and twentieth centuries. Partly, this has to do with the scale of deforestation. In his field-defining 1975 book *Trees and Woodland in the British Landscape*, the ecologist Oliver Rackham points out that while up to 1945 there had been a sustained but gentle growth in tree loss, thereafter things go off a cliff. 'The next thirty years', he writes, 'were a time of unprecedented destruction of ancient woodland.'[39] In this period alone, in fact, about half of Britain's woodland simply ceased to exist. This was a different order of problem, but also a different *kind* of problem, to that faced by people like Arthur Standish and John Evelyn. For them, anxiety about tree loss was in large part a question of economic and military sustainability: in an early modern economy heavily reliant on timber for fuel, no longer having access to trees might prove grievous indeed. What haunts *us*, though, are not so much economic but rather atmospheric and geological forces: climate change, and that wider epochal set of human effects on the planet which we have come to understand as a new geological period, the Anthropocene. Certainly, the relationship between trees and cities, or between forests and industries, once operated within a broad sphere of economic rationality; there were costs and benefits to tree loss, after all. In more recent centuries, however, as the trees become scarcer, the cities wider, the economies larger and the planet warmer, things take a more historical, psychological and even metaphysical turn.

This way of thinking has many roots. But one of the thicker ones leads to the American environmentalist and polymath George Perkins Marsh, and his magnum opus, *Man and Nature*, first published in 1864.[40] 'There is good reason to believe', Marsh wrote, 'that the surface of the habitable earth, in all the climates and regions which have been the abodes of dense and civilized populations, was, with few exceptions, already covered with a forest growth when it first became the home of man.' Marsh was not only convinced of the earth's secret history as a forest, he also advanced an account of how we might understand a new kind of historical relationship between politics and ecology, between depleted forest environments and urban civilisations long since gone; in his view the fall of the Roman Empire, for example, was in good part due to the Romans' destruction of their surrounding woodlands.[41]

*Man and Nature* was, in its day, an enormously influential account of how humans have impacted the earth and the consequences this has had for society. The story of 'man and nature', for Marsh, was in large part a story of deforestation. Working with the evidence he had to hand – the deep presence of forests in ancient writings and 'primitive art', the remains of trees in soil – he concluded that extensive tree cover had to be the earth's original, natural state. It was only when early humans started to exhaust the sparse tracts of plain and savannah in their immediate environment that they began to expand into the forested areas and cut the trees. 'The destruction of the woods', says Marsh, 'was man's first geographical conquest, his first violation of the harmonies of inanimate nature.' The need to create space for agriculture – and the happy coincidence that a burned-down forest provided not only space, but also excellent soil for agricultural production – was the first disaster. Later came the lumber trade, and sea navigation, and the need for wood for ships; then came population growth and the need to burn more wood to keep more people warm and fed. Cutting down trees, indeed, became a symbol of progress and modernity: in France and other European countries, says Marsh, the forest – originally a space demarcated for the King to hunt in – became a site of gleeful destruction in revolutionary times.

Marsh was far from the first person to note the geographical and environmental importance of the forest. Nonetheless, he formalised and systematised that knowledge in a way that made forest ecology a central subject in the new science of geography (the American Geographical Society had been founded a decade earlier, in 1851). More importantly, though, in Marsh's work we find not only an early version of forest science, but also the awakening of a modern forest *ideology*: the sense that the planet was forest *first*; that everything after has been a process of geological and moral diminution; that, in the end, all of human society might amount to little more than a small, short-lived incursion on the planet of trees. For

Marsh and his contemporaries – this was also the era of figures like Thoreau and Emerson – trees, as nature, represent an age of innocence, an era of 'semi-primitive' goodness, as the literary critic Leo Marx would later put it.[42] And this historical perspective came laden with a future promise: that in spite of the world we have made for ourselves, we might yet reclaim that innocence through the planting and cultivation of the forest.

This idea relies on a view of nature – awesome, inhuman, increasingly under threat – that had become widespread and mainstream only with the emergence of the Romantic movement at the tail end of the century that preceded Marsh. That movement, as it found itself (quite literally) overrun by the outgrowth and effluvia of the nineteenth century's exploding industrial cities, created, for the first time, something approaching a shared environmental consciousness. Campaigns and protests sprang up. Quite suddenly, a new moral and aesthetic vision was available, a vision that, as the environmental historian Harriet Ritvo points out, could claim a global human stake in the care and protection of the natural environment.[43] Nature – that wet, leafy stuff outside the city – had become not only a scientific category, as it had been for the Romantics, it was now a *political* thing too. Nature was something to be argued over, defended, legislated.

This cultural and political vision was also bolstered, finally, by a new kind of biological thinking. As the nineteenth century turned into the twentieth, a range of different disciplines – botany, anatomy and agricultural science among them – started to come together under a new master term, 'ecology'. In the work, first, of the German naturalist (and proto-Nazi)

Ernst Haeckel,[44] and then later in the writings of the British zoologist Charles Elton and his contemporaries, a new science of plants' and animals' 'physiological responses to the physical properties of [their] surroundings'[45] made it possible to understand humans and their environments as, now, deeply intertwined. The question of living in the countryside or living in the city had become both serious and anxious. It *mattered*, suddenly – it mattered philosophically, and it mattered scientifically – whether you made your life among trees or among chimney stacks. And it had begun to matter, finally, and more than a century later, to me.

'We evolved', said our guide, 'for, some say, up to two million years living in the forest. And then, for the last three hundred years, we've moved to these urban cities. And then everybody's health deteriorated.' It was early November, and my research assistant, Ruth Sharman, and I were in the middle of a wood near the picturesque village of Tintern, in the Wye Valley, South Wales. It was a cold, wet morning, and I don't know about Ruth, but in that moment I felt, if anything, rather keen on the benefits of urban modernity and its various comforts. I kept this opinion to myself. We had come to Wales to meet Tom Court, a forest-bathing guide who operates out of a small farmhouse in a wooded hillside, not far from the town of Chepstow. Tom had agreed to take me and Ruth on a meditative, sensory walk through the forest – an experience that included, to our shared alarm, encouragement to walk barefoot along the wet forest floor. As thick, leafy mulch squeezed in between our toes, Tom told us that we were actually on an old Roman path through the woods that led to the ruined ancient city of Trellech, and eventually, via a pilgrimage route, to St David's – once Wales's ancient capital, now a tiny, forgotten city at the edge of a faraway peninsula, jutting forlornly into the Irish Sea. 'This sensory connection', Tom said, walking nimbly ahead in his own bare feet, 'helps us to trigger our sixth sense: our whole self, our electrical connections, our inner savage, as we call it in Wales. We're trying to activate that animal instinct. We're trying to become more animalistic, because we then stop using our thinking brain, where we store all the stress and mental problems.' We had walked for some hours through the woods, occasionally stopping to rub ferns or yew leaves between our fingers, breathing deep from our hands to take in the surprisingly sharp, bright smell of the forest. We stopped to look at blown-over pine trees, bright red, arsenic-laden yew berries, small rows of yellow coral mushrooms and, just once – Ruth found this – a tiny germinating acorn, lying wet and silent, not far from its presumably hopeful mother.

I had contacted Tom because I wanted to get close to something I had first heard about a couple of years previously, when I saw Dr Qing Li speak in Athens, and which I thought might help me understand the widespread desire to have more trees in urban space: *shinrin-yoku*, or forest bathing. These were terms I had started to come across more and more as I moved around events on urban greening, spoke to more planners and architects, and read through research on stressed and anxious urban humans. Forest bathing, though it had initially sounded to me like a sort of benignly new age, if slightly bourgeois, practice – to be put in the same box as reflexology or 'wild swimming', maybe – actually

My feet in the woods, Wye Valley.

loomed large in the world of people who were trying, in all seriousness, to make contemporary cities less bad for their inhabitants. And their vision wasn't just of a nice, pretty, crowd-pleasing practice (who doesn't like a nice walk among the trees?). Rather, their claim is that forest bathing is a major intervention in how we could actually inhabit the city of the future. If *economic* anxieties about urbanisation and tree loss had dominated the early modern world, to be replaced by a more geological and ecological view of the disappearing forest that emerged in the nineteenth century, I was interested, now, in how a distinctively *psychological* relationship to trees, both inside and outside cities, might carry this story into the present. There is, of course, nothing new in the idea that nature soothes the troubled mind; this has been a central claim of the various mental health sciences since their foundation.[46]

And yet there was something novel, I thought, in the more recent and much more general claim that we modern urbanites could *all* do with a regular dose of forested nature; that, indeed, the future of urban living probably meant keeping yourself well and stable by getting out among the trees once a month or so; that living well in the twenty-first century meant finding your pre-industrial, pre-urban self wandering somewhere deep in the forest.

In practice, forest bathing can take a few different forms, but it usually means being led quite slowly and mindfully by a guide through the forest, not necessarily over very great distances, doing different kinds of sensory or meditative practices as you go. Simply being in the forest has a therapeutic effect, Stefan Batorijs, a leading trainer of forest-bathing guides, told me when I first started investigating it, 'because it accesses a part of our innate survival system that is pre-industrial and unaffected by the neuroses that afflict modern human beings'. Stefan's work draws on a distinctive mix of philosophical, literary and scientific research; he's as happy talking about phenomenology and Goethe as he is about the evolution of the vagus nerve and the Moro reflex. There's nothing especially romantic about forest bathing, Stefan insisted, when I brought this up. 'The point is that spending time in the forest triggers access to ancient survival mechanisms, which in turn can help us to make more authentic choices in our lives.'

I also spoke to a scientist called Kirsten McEwan, who had carried out a successful trial of a forest-bathing intervention.[47] She told me that as someone who was convinced of the benefits of nature, but who was driven by hard evidence, she was keen to collect physiological data on people undertaking forest bathing (things like their heart rate), as opposed to conducting surveys or asking people about their experiences. 'There's really good evidence from Japan', she told me, 'that just breathing in those chemicals [emitted by trees in the forest] gives us a massive immune boost, which can last for a month.' Kirsten's own research, meanwhile, has shown a positive relationship between heart rate variability – a measure of heart health – and spending time in nature.

There was no doubt that walking through the forest with Tom felt *good*. I even got used to the barefoot walking after a while – and it's true, it did alter my sensory experience in quite a profound way. I didn't measure my heart rate or check on my vagus nerve, but it seems like you'd have to try really hard to claim that spending a few hours walking through a broad-leaf forest, with your usual world of work and family suddenly invisible, silenced, even temporarily suspended, *wasn't* at least a bit restorative.

Forest bathing feels like getting in touch with something ancient – and in one sense, that's true. A certain kind of relationship between some aspects of Japanese culture and trees has been remarked upon by outside visitors ever since they were first allowed into Japan, beginning in the mid-nineteenth century.[48] The sensory practices that are often at the heart of forest bathing, meanwhile, including the meditative inward focus on bodily sensations, are indebted to a range of what many today call 'mindfulness' practices. These have diverse histories, but at least some are entangled in the Buddhist traditions that took root in Japan and neighbouring countries from around the sixth century AD.[49] And yet, as Tom explained to us, the practice of *shinrin-yoku* is also thoroughly modern. 'After World War II', he told us, as we walked through the damp Wye Valley, 'and mass bombings of the agricultural land in Japan, everybody moved to these mega-cities, ten to twenty million people living in a big urban space. Then the government sat back and watched the cost of keeping people alive rise. There were people dying at their desks from stress. There were people committing suicide on unprecedented levels.' It was only in the early 1980s that Japan's Forestry Agency began a programme of investigation into what is today known as 'forest medicine', and only since the early 2000s that scientists have been researching the connection in earnest.[50]

As they got taken up in Europe and the US, these practices also slotted comfortably into a range of existing traditions. The literary scholar Samantha Walton notes that a wide set of 'naturopathic' healing practices have been popular in spas throughout Europe since the 1850s; in the US, around the same time, various gurus built on the ideas promoted by transcendentalist writers by offering hearty mountain retreats for – in Walton's words – 'nerve-shattered and exhausted intellectuals'.[51] This was also, of course, the age of neurasthenia, that mysterious nervous malady of late-nineteenth-century urban life, a diagnosis, the historian Mark Jackson points out, that 'revealed a profound and widespread ambivalence about modern civilisation'.[52] On the one hand, then, forest bathing is a practice that sometimes trades in images of timeless connection to nature, and yet it is roughly the same age as the Nintendo Entertainment System, another deeply influential product of 1980s Japanese urban culture. On the other, a practice that gains a lot of cultural currency from a sense of novelty and distinction is at least partly based on nature-based solutions to the stress of industrial life that have been with us for some hundreds of years.

'It's exploded,' Shirley Gleeson, a forest therapy practitioner and trainer, told me later. 'When I became interested in this work originally, fifteen years ago, nobody really knew what I was talking about.' I'd been keen to speak to Shirley ever since I saw her give a talk at a conference on forest therapy, where I'd been struck by her super-affirmative energy (and also because I realised that her accent, like my own, was from Ireland's boggy and unglamorous Midlands). A former social worker, today Shirley runs a successful eco-wellness consultancy near Dublin, offering training for forest therapy practitioners and guides, sessions for individuals and events for spas and hotels. 'People used to say to me, "Oh, you're doing that nature stuff,"' Shirley said. 'They didn't really understand it, you know? And I mean, now there's this *huge* explosion: ecotourism, nature-based workplace well-being, mental health interventions, green prescriptions . . . It's everywhere.'

'What changed?' I asked.

'There's more research,' said Shirley. 'I think the pandemic has been major in terms of really bringing people's awareness to the importance of nature and their local places. I think the health professionals are becoming more open to it. The health systems are under pressure. They need new, innovative ways of working. There's the whole social prescribing movement.' She drew a distinction between forest *bathing*, a kind of eco-tourism activity lasting a few hours, and forest *therapy*, a more rigorous, mindfulness-based intervention, usually going on over some weeks with a trained practitioner and aimed at helping people with chronic mental health conditions. 'The more stress that somebody's under,' Shirley said, 'the likelier they are to develop mental health problems or have a relapse . . . A lot of people that have experienced trauma are in fight or flight. So this . . . *soothing* is vital in terms of reducing that kind of trauma.'

This distinction is critical, I think, in terms of how we should think about the burgeoning popularity of forest bathing, not only as a health or wellbeing practice, but also as a kind of commentary on modern urban life. On the one hand, there's the idea of forest *therapy*, as Shirley distinguishes it. Here, the claim is essentially that being in the forest, and especially being there in a mindful, structured, guided way, has a measurable effect on people's stress levels – which is positive in terms of a whole range of chronic mental health conditions, among other things. This claim is well placed to meet a growing interest in what's called 'green social prescribing' among clinicians and health policy people. This is the idea that a physician can direct a patient to a trained link person, who in turn might send them on to a club or an event that might be good for them, like a community gardening project or a forest walking group.* In this sense, there are

* At the time of writing, the Department for Environment, Food and Rural Affairs, supported by the Department of Health and Social Care and the NHS, has funded a large, two-year formal evaluation of green social prescribing across seven test sites in the UK. As one psychiatrist put it to me, this might simply mean asking a patient what role nature has had in their life – and if it's been a source of security or comfort, then seeing what's out there to help them access it.

good reasons to clearly position forest *therapy* as a (this is my own word, not Shirley's) 'mainstream' or conventional health practice, which can be aligned with existing public health systems, such as the NHS in the UK, or insurance-based ones in the US and other countries. There's nothing wrong with any of that, of course – and indeed, there is increasingly good evidence to support it.[53]

But the story doesn't end there. Because within the forest bathing community, there is also, I think, another, more philosophical and perhaps more (again, this is my own term) 'political' set of ideas about the relationship between humans and the environment and where this has gone askew – which maybe aligns less well with conventional medicine and, indeed, conventional society. Near the end of our walk with Tom, Ruth asked him what he understood by 'nature connection', a term she had kept stumbling upon while writing her Master's thesis on urban foraging. 'It's not about connecting with nature, for me,' said Tom, after a thoughtful pause. 'It's about realising that we *are* nature. But we're disconnected from that notion. We think, as humans, we're the most knowledgeable and advanced species, potentially, in the universe. But the reality is, we're part of this ecosystem, and at the moment we're not living in this ecosystem. We're living outside it. And at the same time we're destroying it.'

He thought some more for a minute. '"Nature connection" is this term that gets bandied about,' he said eventually. 'It's like people just want to go and touch that world. It's still them versus us. But *this* is where we've evolved. This is our natural habitat. This is where our health is the best. It's not that going to the forest makes your immune system stronger.

It's that leaving the forest makes your immune system weaker. This is where we *should* be. We should be out here, foraging berries, and David Attenborough should go' – Tom adopted a plummy English voice here – '"Look at the humans in their natural habitat."'

Ruth and I laughed, but he went on, quite seriously, 'We *are* nature. And that's why we need to "connect" with it. But we actually feel like our natural habitat is watching *I'm a Celebrity* . . . in a concrete house, full of electrical wiring. That's not our natural habitat. Sure, I think you can connect with nature in an urban environment. Will it have the same benefits as coming to a deep, ancient forest? No. But it's better than walking the concrete streets.'

I really enjoyed walking with Tom. And even I, a committed forest sceptic, found that if I wasn't *soothed* exactly, then it had nonetheless become clear to me – I could feel it under my skin – that something experientially distinctive *is* happening, and starts happening quite quickly, when the sound of the modern world fades away and there's nothing around you except steep grey pillars of birch and pine, a layer of dying leaves on the now-vanished ground, and the daylight, such as it is, flickering in and out, as if the sun is playing a cruel game with a small child. As a resolutely urban animal, and despite sincere efforts to be otherwise, I find the forest to be a deeply sinister, even frightening space. And yet I can nonetheless acknowledge an attraction, even a kind of *compulsion*, buried deep at the heart of my own fear. If the forest is not always good, it is always different.

'We've become so numb and so soft,' Stefan Batorijs, who is also the founder of Nature and Therapy UK, said to me, while walking through some woods in the Dartington Estate, South Devon. 'We've lost touch with the raw animal faculties that we have within us. We're encouraged to suppress those parts of ourselves in order to fit in socially. But when we go into wilderness areas, it brings us back into touch with something that's primal and eternal within us. It allows us to access all of the accumulated wisdom that precedes a lot of that conditioning that we're subjected to now.' Stefan's is not some atavistic attraction; though he reads widely in philosophy, he is clear that his sense of an ancient self is part of our genetic inheritance that we need to rediscover. 'People like flowers', he said to me during an email exchange, 'because their ancient selves knew that flowers meant fruit. Not being able to detect vegetation in an urban area causes the body to assume drought conditions and respond accordingly. Spending time in the forest triggers access to these ancient survival mechanisms.'

Whether or not you agree with this view – I don't, but I find it interesting – it's an argument that is more complicated, I think, than the straightforward empirical view that being in the forest lowers your stress levels, and this is good for your mental health, and so on. What I think is at stake here, rather, is a serious philosophical critique of urban modernity as such. As Samantha Walton points out, neither the nature cure itself nor the wider cultural diagnosis that gives the cure its energy – the idea that we are made mad and bad by being out of ecological step with the natural world – are new. The Romantics, the transcendentalists, the first outdoor explorers and forest bathers: none of these were into nature simply because the evidence showed that it was good for our health.[54] Or maybe it would be better to say that for them, the moral domain of human health was much wider than it is for us, because they had a sense that nature could make humans great again – that wilderness experience can repair a moral edifice much bruised by industrial civilisation and urban life. Green social prescribing might not see itself as continuous with these movements, but it is clear that these histories are still very much present; that even in our resolutely empirical age, when the deathly rhetoric of 'what works' governs clinical decision-making, this much deeper sense, that the forest corrects a larger historical error, is not so very far below the surface.

In his memoir *Nature Cure*, the celebrated British nature writer Richard Mabey describes an encounter with a young swift in the attic of a house he was occupying with friends.[55] The fledgling had fallen from its nest and lay with its new wings stretched out, unable to take off or move. 'We could see', says Mabey, 'the price it paid for being so exquisitely adapted to a life that would be spent almost entirely in the air.' The image stayed with Mabey as he began his own sideways tumble into a deep depression, pitched from a life to which his body was no less minutely attuned. 'I had become', he says, 'the incomprehensible creature adrift in some substantial medium, out of kilter with the rest of creation.' Mabey interprets this as a collective rather than individual problem. 'Maybe', he says, 'that is the way our whole species is moving . . . we're becoming unearthly.' He describes how neither pharmaceuticals nor talk therapy, nor even a stay in hospital, could get at what was ailing him, until eventually, in a very bad state, he was sent to the countryside to stay with friends.

Once there, he moved into a house that seemed like it was hewn directly from the forest: there was an oak door and an oak desk; oak windows from which he could see, in the distance, the oak woods. And over time, within the 'woody intricacy' of this new habitat, Mabey began to heal. He is much too acute a thinker, of course, to imagine that simply being surrounded by wood can resolve such a deep malaise, but Mabey is clear that he attributes his illness at least partly to his distance from nature, and his recovery to a process of (this is, to say the least, a striking metaphor) 'nature entering me'. He does not see this as a problem peculiar to him; rather, he reads his own depression as just one story within a wider, *collective* denial of nature.

In the same move, we can read his reshaping of his own life as a more ecologically attuned creature in a new kind of vegetal habitus as an example of how we are all going to have to learn to live in the future. Mabey is a famous nature writer for a reason: with great subtlety, he draws together the two different but intertwined ideas that animate this vision of a planet of trees. On the one hand, the world of mental health, of depression and anxiety, of diagnoses, and clinicians, and therapies, and pills. And on the other, an older and stranger *geological* story of how the planet has changed, how we have changed it, and how, in the changing, our attunement to our physical surroundings has slipped – until we have found ourselves in cities filled with concrete houses, laced with electrical wiring, watching bad TV and eating worse food. This is, unquestionably, a powerful story of individual and collective redemption; and sure, sometimes it ends up with a benighted municipal bureaucrat putting a tree on a traffic island, like that's going to solve something. But still, its cultural force remains undimin-ished. The dream of the tree is as powerful as ever.

There are three major sources of human unhappiness, wrote Sigmund Freud in *Civilization and Its Discontents*.[56] There are our own bodies, which sicken, wither and cause us pain. There's the world around us, which can burn our homes down, release a new virus into the human population, wash a tsunami onto the shore with just thirty minutes' notice. And then there's other humans – the source of that endless, shifting constellation of collective achievements and inventions that we call society. Why does this last one, asks Freud, strike so many people as the *true* source of their unhappiness? How has it come to pass that for so many of us, 'what we call our civilization is largely responsible for our misery . . . that we would be much hap-pier if we gave it up and returned to primitive conditions'? The answer, he says, is that civilisation replaced individual power with collective power. Just as in our psychological develop-ment as individuals we gain mechanisms to overcome our base instincts, so in our *collective* process of civilisation we develop social tools to block those dark urges – like violence, or incest – still lurking within us; forces whose unleashing might still, if we are really honest about it, make us *truly* happy.

Maybe this goes too far. But just as we have Eros, says Freud, the desire to make life, so too we have its opposite: an instinct for death, a drive towards aggression and destruction. Civilisation grips this instinct and holds it down, 'like a gar-rison in a conquered city'. In this process, a person is made to feel bad about not only things they have done or might do, but also things *they will never do*. The external constraint becomes internalised, and the sense of guilt is born. 'The price we pay for our advance in civilization', says Freud, 'is a loss of happiness through the heightening of the sense of guilt.' Freud, by this time one of Europe's most famous and controversial Jewish intellectuals, was writing in Vienna between the wars, and revising his text as the Nazis were becoming a major force in Germany. It is surely no surprise, as the Freud scholar Matt Ffytche points out, that he had come to see humans as 'ultimately predatory, and only slightly evolved from an underlying animal condition'.[57] Freud's lifelong belief in scientific progress, says Ffytche, is here quite absent. Misery, aggression and death, at the endpoint of European modernity, are what preoccupy Freud in the last decade of his life. 'Men have gained control over the forces of nature,' he says finally, 'to such an extent that with their help they would have no difficulty in exterminating one another to the last man. They know this, and hence comes a large part of their current unrest, their unhappiness, and their mood of anxiety.'

What are we actually talking about when we talk about nature, and its suppression, and how human happiness is affected by the shifts between these two poles? It is convention by now, in a book like this, to say that perhaps there is truly no 'forest' and no 'city', no external 'nature' that is clearly distinct from human 'culture'. Rather, there is an endless world of hybridity and mixture, where the green field is in reality a kind of factory, where the barren car park, if you look closely enough, is teeming with entire planets of vegetation and microbiota. In the pine forest, Tom showed us how nineteenth-century speculators had planted the trees at a slant to the sun, so they would grow quick and tall, all the better for speedy cultivating and chopping. But it turned out that pine was structurally problematic, and so the thin, slanted pines stay where they are; a forest, yes, but also a factory in ruins. I take all of this very seriously. But I take seriously, too, the idea that nature and wilderness are real things; I am willing to entertain the conceit that they only really exist outside the city, which is indeed hostile to them; I am inclined even to agree that it really *has* been the work of urban modernity to cast them off, indeed to do violence to them, and not only symbolically or ideologically, but as real things in the world. I think I agree with the forest bathers that nature is real and distinctive, and modernity hostile to it. My question is, though: what makes us so sure that modernity isn't right?

If nature is restorative, what exactly is it restoring? When we go to the woods as a kind of escape, what are we actually trying to escape from? This idea that the woods are where you go for rest and relaxation – I actually have a growing suspicion that not only might it be wrong, it might even be the inverse of the truth. Forests, for our ancestors, says the author Sara Maitland, 'were dangerous and generous, domestic and wild, beautiful and terrible'.[58] After all, this is the terrain, she points out, of that strange, morally ambiguous form, the fairy tale, where you are just as likely to be boiled and eaten in a stranger's house as you are to make it home safely. 'Coming to terms with the forest,' Maitland says, 'surviving its terrors, utilizing its gifts, and gaining its help is the way to "happy ever after."'

What if it's the *city*, then – that milquetoast territory of fine-grained human regulation and fey politesse, that carefully balanced choreography of desires thwarted and excesses tamed – that represents peace and calm? And what if it's the forest – the ungoverned place at the edge of civilisation, a grim landscape, one that refuses the artifice and restraint of urban modernity – that is truly the space of tumult, excess and anxiety? Maybe this reflects only my own lack of faith in my fellow humans, but still . . . I remember too well that feeling of the cold sun flickering in and out of the branches in the Wye Valley like it was playing a game with me, as if it was reminding me that, in the end, I was just another creature on the forest floor; just another frightened animal, out there, quite alone, on the fringes of an indifferent and uncaring planet of trees.

# 5: Save Me

A tree on Rivelin Valley Road, Sheffield.

In 2011, following an unprecedented decade of drought, the authorities in Melbourne, Australia, commissioned a survey on the state of their city's trees. The results were even worse than expected. Melbourne's tree cover, which the city relies on for keeping itself shady and cool, as well as for reducing pollution and managing storm water, was in a truly desperate state: without intervention, half of the city's trees would be dead within twenty years.

This would be bad news anywhere. But it was devastating for Melbourne, a city whose implicit self-image as a genteel outpost of European colonialism is very much bound up with its rich, extensive tree cover, as well as its more general botanical excesses.* This was, understandably, a topic of significant public concern. So the city organised some workshops to get locals involved in solving it, using printed maps of the city's tree network that, perhaps inevitably, people really wanted to take home.[1] To help, Yvonne Lynch, a city government employee, came up with the idea of instead making a single 'digital urban forest'. For some weeks, Lynch and her team worked with a local digital designer on making a publicly available online map that showed, at a click, every tree in the city – each individually marked, categorised by species and given an identification number and health status. You can still look at the map today: tree number 1063779 is a sadly dying plane tree in Bourke Street; tree number 1041057 is a surprisingly healthy young eucalyptus on Rebecca Walk. The idea was that citizens would use the map to identify trees that looked unhealthy or that had maintenance problems, and then click a link to email the municipal authorities about it.

That link, though, didn't say, '*Send an email about this tree.*' It said: '*Email this tree.*'

* If you ever want to know about the surprisingly extensive relationship between colonialism and plants, visit the Royal Botanic Gardens in Melbourne, founded in 1846. Take in the rolling, lush greens of the European and Australian trees; if you're feeling lucky, go into the herbarium and ask them to show you some of the specimens collected in the 1770s by Joseph Banks, which they still store there. Banks was the botanist who travelled on Cook's first voyage to Australia. Later, he became president of the Royal Society in London and helped set up Kew Gardens with George III. It was Banks's plant-collecting enthusiasm that prompted Cook to give the harbour where they had first anchored the name that we still know it by today: Botany Bay.

And that slight shift in imperative turned out to be crucial. For the drought-ridden citizens of Melbourne, suddenly confronted with the digital manifestation of their own dying eco-scape, the invitation to email a tree directly was an opportunity for arboreal encounter that proved impossible to resist. People began to email the trees. But they didn't write in with bureaucratic maintenance concerns so much; instead, they started to offer a far wider set of their own tree-related thoughts and desires.

'*Dear Algerian Oak,*' wrote one user to tree number 1032705. '*Thank you for giving us oxygen. Thank you for being so pretty. I don't know where I'd be without you to extract my carbon dioxide. (I would probably be in heaven.) Stay strong, stand tall amongst the crowd. You are the gift that keeps on giving.*'[2]

'*Dear Green Leaf Elm,*' goes another, to tree number 1026655. '*I hope you like living at St. Mary's. Most of the time I like it too. I have exams coming up and I should be busy studying. You do not have exams because you are a tree. I don't think that there is much more to talk about as we don't have a lot in common, you being a tree and such. But I'm glad we're in this together.*'

I first heard about these emails during a conference on green roofing infrastructure, held in one of the vast, deeply weird 'co-working' buildings that now occupy the former Olympic site at Stratford in east London.[3] These are basically like aircraft hangars, only they don't make planes there, they make apps for phones instead. As a worker whizzed past me on his electric scooter, en route to buy his coffee from a van that said it was staffed by unhoused people, it struck me that here was maybe a contrivance of work and economy that all the green roofs in the world weren't going to fix.

At the time, I had been thinking a lot about how trees might not be innocent bystanders on city streets; how they might play a more direct, instrumental role in how cities are governed, how they are imagined as very particular kinds of modern places. You can see, from this perspective, how saving Melbourne's urban forest might be a big deal for the people in charge: lose the trees, and you lose your claim to good, modern, *scientific* management of urban space. But even in a wider sense, an online urban forest acts as a powerful symbol of how a city has claimed and even tamed nature. The city's trees are a potent, living representation of how, in the process of urbanisation, we took unruly nature and we *organised* it. We made it submit to the city's strict grid lines, its rational and hierarchical ordering of buildings, its immovable commuting and delivery schedules. Saving Melbourne's urban forest really matters, then, because if we're no longer able to manage the trees, a big part of what a city is, or what it sometimes claims to be – a well-ordered space of rational human industry on an otherwise inhospitable planet – is suddenly, quite radically, in question.

When I actually spoke to Yvonne Lynch about it a few months later, however, she described how, for months, she would come into her office in Melbourne and begin her day by reading the emails people had sent to the trees. 'The stories were so poignant that you would just not forget them,' she said. 'Some of them brought me to tears.' She told me about receiving messages from all over the world: from someone emailing a particular tree to say that its presence had protected them from suicide during a dark period; or a mother writing to a tree that had given her strength when her baby twins were dangerously ill, to say that today, her favourite thing to do was to drive past this same tree, with her mercifully healthy children sleeping in the back seat. 'An emotional tapestry of the city has been revealed,' Yvonne said, referring to the emails. 'I have been privileged and honoured to be the recipient, on behalf of those trees, of some of those deep thoughts and emotions.'

In the last chapter, I talked about trees in cities, and about people in cities trying to get out of cities to see trees, as part of a wider turn away from urban modernity. I said that the tree in this sense plays a symbolic and ideological role, representing a growing anxiety about how our mode of life (physical, economic, even moral) sometimes feels like it's coming apart at the seams. In this chapter, I want to hold on to that idea and extend it into thinking about the concept of an 'urban forest' more specifically. After all, if you think about how many trees the typical city is home to, then it's not hard to imagine it as something like a forest. At least, that's what some people think. Others argue more forcefully that by cultivating trees and planting more of them, cities should strive to *become* forests. I think this is weird. And I was poised to write a chapter about it in the spirit of the philosopher Michel Foucault, focusing on urban bureaucracy and city management, arguing that seeing the city as a forest was a way of seeing it as a potentially unruly and wild place that could – if we are careful to use the right tools and don't spare the axe – be brought under rational, bureaucratic organisation. Control the plants, and you control the people too. But my interview with Yvonne was an early clue that these terms were too reductive. This is partly because the complex, multifaceted people who work in urban governance around the world simply resist this kind of easy analysis. But our conversation was also an early sign of something else: as I would come to realise, the attachments that people in cities make to trees can't be reduced to a bureaucratic ruse. Trees really *do something* for people in cities. They have psychological importance for urban residents. And, as I was to learn, political importance too.

When I first started attending events about healthy cities, green cities, future cities, and so on, a term I often heard was 'ecosystem services'. I wrote it in my research journal several times, all in caps. I didn't really know what it meant, and I guessed it was something pretty gross, but still there was a kind of bureaucratic poetry to the conjunction that attracted me in spite of myself. What could it mean to reimagine a city's river, or a bank of street trees somewhere, or an urban park that soaked up excess rain, as a *service* – like a railway or an electricity pylon or a food-delivery app? What strange magic allowed the shifting lines of a local government employee's spreadsheet to redefine scrappy bits of nature as urban infrastructure, with no less dignity than the most finely engineered bridge?

The notion of 'ecosystem services' comes, perhaps predictably, from that most accidentally poetic of the management sciences: economics. The idea is that there are natural ecosystems in cities, and these ecosystems do things for the people who live there. Most of these things are loosely related to health and wellbeing, or to the improvement of the urban atmosphere. Trees, for example, cool people down and make them less stressed. Vegetation filters the air. The soft, leafy surfaces of plants help to reduce noise levels. You can drink water from a lake, and after that water comes back out of you again, you can treat the sewage in a wetland.[4] 'Trees in particular,' say the geographers Catherine Phillips and Jennifer Atchison, 'are increasingly valued as contributing to solutions for contemporary urban challenges including climate change, urban heating, air quality, and disconnection with nature.'[5] And all of this can be quantified too – even turned into a cash benefit. We know, for example, that excess noise is bad for mental health. If you can figure out, say, how much one square metre of leaf cover reduces the overall noise level in your city on average, then you can figure out how much the total urban leaf cover is saving you in terms of hours of clinician time, or pharmaceutical prescriptions, or whatever.[6] This is, of course, exactly what environmental economics does, putting an unexpected and maybe idiosyncratic monetary value on something whose value is not obviously monetary. The same trick operates in the closely related term 'natural capital', whereby, for example, all the 'nature' within a certain territory is given a nominal monetary value and then categorised as a kind of *capital*, which is to say as an economic asset (and of course, like all assets, it can be cut up, privatised, sold off). In the UK, the Treasury's 'Green Book' – its technical advice on how to apply cost–benefit analysis to a policy proposal – encourages a natural capital approach to decision-making. Natural capital, the Treasury says, is a store containing 'certain stocks of the elements of nature' which delivers benefits to society through ecosystem services.[7] In other words, ecosystem services are benefits we can acquire through our stock of natural capital. This stuff is catnip to council bureaucrats* and local politicians who manage city budgets. The dominant ideology among city managers, whatever their political views, is that good city management is rational, *scientific* city management. And whatever else you might say about it, the ecosystem services framework at least has the air of science, reason and control about it. 'Look,' it says, 'not even the merest leaf, not even the most miserable shrub, is outside our purview.' And while it's true that, like most concepts that come from mainstream economics, ecosystem services and natural capital are broadly evil, they're used by people who are generally trying to do good. After all, if you want to justify the existence of a park, or if you're trying to save a small woodland from the developer's axe, then demonstrating the economic value of that woodland as a vital ecosystem service, part of the city's wellbeing infrastructure, sounds a lot more convincing to developers, council scrutiny committees and secretaries of state than wanting to save a woodland because kids play in it, or dogs piss in it, or whatever the reality of the situation is.

But concepts like ecosystem services and natural capital are doing something else too. The practice of urban greening, says the sociologist Hillary Angelo, isn't really about ecology. It isn't so much about providing shade or lowering temperature. Rather, it's about creating what she calls 'social imaginaries' – or 'cultural understanding of the moral order of a social world'.[8] These kinds of shared understandings, our background sense of what the social world is like and *should* be like, have very real effects, according to Angelo. They

---

* I say this as a former council bureaucrat.

shape and structure the societies we make for ourselves; they give rise to rules and laws; they govern our sense of what's good, and they guide our actions in trying to reach that good.

One such shared understanding, it seems to me, one that was very powerful until quite recently, is that the city can, for good or ill, be thought of as a kind of human boot-print on the surface of an otherwise hostile planet. In an unpredictable, scary global environment, the city can be made to feel like a space of reassuringly human order, calculation and modernity – a predictable, regulated, managed sphere of economic and cultural activity. The city, in this account, is essentially a technology for making the natural environment manageable, or at least for making us *think* the environment is manageable. That's what the idea of 'ecosystem services' does. It takes, say, a little stream, or even a giant lake, and it *manages* it – it declares, 'Nature is manageable!' – and in so doing turns it into just another piece of rationalised infrastructure within the city's ever-growing boundaries.

This managerial logic extends quickly to humans. The science and practice of tree management in the nineteenth century, says the environmental historian Sonja Dümpelmann, as it learned to prune the unruly and the unexpected and deployed new techniques for creating order out of potential chaos, was in the vanguard of the 'Taylorization' of the American city.[9] 'Taylorism' was a quasi-scientific management philosophy, popular in the early twentieth century, which tried to make spaces like factories more efficient by doing things like analysing workflows really closely and cutting out unnecessary actions. The urban tree, similarly managed according to a system of close observation and rational calculation, thus creates an image of the city as a space under firmly scientific management, subsumed to the demands of productivity and efficiency.

This is surely correct, but what happened in Melbourne reminds us that it isn't the whole story. Or, maybe, that this story isn't as powerful as it once was. That something else – some weirder psychic connection between people and trees – is pushing its way through the dull sheen of this managerial logic, like an unruly root or branch suddenly cracking the top of a well-ordered pavement.

In Paris a few years ago, the mayor, Anne Hidalgo, announced plans to create a new 'urban forest' by planting trees and gardens around four of the city's most famous landmarks. Paris not only aims to be carbon neutral by 2050, but also has a stranger and more ambitious goal, which is to make 50 per cent of the city's surface vegetative by the same date.[10] Ms Hidalgo, the *New York Times* reported, 'has positioned herself prominently among the mayors of the world's premier capitals as an advocate for what she bills as a new, and necessary, kind of urban landscape'.[11] The people in charge of Madrid, not to be outdone, are planning to build a 'green wall' around the city, with 75 kilometres of forest and half a million new trees.[12] In New York City, an environmental non-profit called the Nature Conservancy has made a first-of-its-kind assessment of the city's tree cover across public and private land, treating New York's seven million trees as a single forest system. This new 'urban forest', they argued, 'should be treated as a whole system of critical natural infrastructure to sustain New York City for decades to come'.[13]

None of this is new, exactly. As Sonja Dümpelmann points out, tree planting has been central to urbanisation in Europe and North America since at least the nineteenth century. In an earlier era of rapid urbanisation, trees were a way of creating identities and forming boundaries, both physical and ideological. In Berlin before World War II, Dümpelmann notes, 'Many conservatives believed that urbanization threatened the superior Germanic race, which was considered to have evolved in the wooded areas of the temperate zone now deforested and threatened by desertification. Tree planting was therefore perceived as salvation.' Washington DC, she goes on to say, used tree planting, and its self-proclaimed status as the 'city of trees', as a way to position itself among – and ultimately supersede – the imperial European capitals such as Paris and Berlin, each famous for its carefully tended trees, parks and gardens.

Urban trees have always been political, but their politics are not straightforward. Initiatives like Brooklyn's Neighbourhood Tree Planting Corps in the early 1970s, says Dümpelmann, in which mostly African American residents self-organised to plant trees in their heavily stigmatised Bedford-Stuyvesant neighbourhood, became an act of defiant community-building, and an important story of the civil rights movement in New York City. On the one hand, this represents a bottom-up desire to make a claim on space, and indeed the status of full humanity in that space, through an organised aesthetic and environmental action. On the other, as Dümpelmann notes, there is a longstanding top-down interest in deploying urban nature as a 'civilizing device for citizens deemed unruly; the well-meaning desire to spread green space more evenly between urban space is also legible as an anxiety about those people not (yet) made subject to nature's civilizing influence'. When a neighbourhood organises itself to plant some trees, we might read this as an empowering act of taking ownership of space. But we might also see this action as a claim about who is deemed worthy enough to share in the goods of urban civilisation. When we plant a tree, we do so partly for our individual pleasure, I am sure. But we do it, too, to make a statement about what kind of person we are – virtuous, decent and worthy of respect; someone who cares about their environment; someone who is in and *of* nature; someone who, like all natural beings, is willing to submit themselves to a well-ordered and functional hierarchy.

These tricky relationships between nature, governance and design are perhaps nowhere more visible than in the City Beautiful movement, the more or less fascist school of urban design that radiated outwards from Pierre Charles L'Enfant's 1791 plan for Washington DC and Baron Haussmann's remaking of Paris in the 1850s and 1860s. The City Beautiful movement emphasised aesthetics in urban form, with a certain kind of monumental classicism at its centre, working within a hazy assumption that the good city, in terms of governance, virtue, power, civic feeling, etc., is not only encapsulated but *produced* by these qualities.

What distinguished the City Beautiful was not simply a foregrounding of aesthetic effect, but a calculated disinterest in anything else. The City Beautiful designers, says the writer and town planner Peter Hall, accepted no brief for the social life of the city; they had no interest in things like urban justice or equality, and even such pragmatic concerns as commerce and health came some distance behind the column's fascist thrill (the ultimate City Beautiful, Hall points out, would have been Albert Speer's design for Nazi Berlin).[14] Still, as the geographer Nikolas Heynen argues, in North America the City Beautiful is the reason why so many urban trees still exist today.[15] At the height of North American urbanisation, Heynen says, there was an attempt to import a kind of nineteenth-century European nature ideology, an idea of rugged, dominant man as both in and astride nature, and then to reproduce that ideology within a new, colonial context, one in which control of territory, of nature, of other humans, was very centrally and explicitly at stake. It's also worth remembering that many of today's most beloved City Beautiful remnants came out of acts of violent displacement, as in the case of the 1857 destruction of Seneca Village in New York, a settlement of free Black landowners that was razed to enable the building of Central Park.[16]

So there's nothing new, especially, about the political functions of urban tree management. As a coherent *scientific* object, however, the 'urban forest' is much more recent. Some accounts credit it to the Toronto-based forestry researcher Erik Jorgensen in the 1960s. When Dutch elm disease, an infectious, tree-killing fungus, reached that city, Jorgensen and his colleagues realised that tackling it meant adopting not only new scientific tools and resources, but also, says the historian Joanna Dean, 'a new way of thinking about city trees' entirely. The 'urban forest', which for the first time treated a city's trees as a single, unified organism, was Jorgensen's solution.[17]

Around the same time, the Connecticut Agricultural Experiment Station, a public site for agricultural research that has been in place since the late nineteenth century, held a conference on what it called 'the suburban forest'.[18] In his introductory address, the organiser, Paul E. Waggoner, located his interest in the subject in a moment of mid-twentieth-century abundance and moral generosity. 'Today,' said Waggoner, 'with oil to warm us and power our mechanical muscles, with bins bulging with plenty to feed us, with electricity to light our way, we can and will restore trees to the land.' The suburban forest, he said, is made up of that skein of greenery that suburbanites in places like post-war Connecticut see knit between their homes. It's the patch of tended lawn around the power plant; the verge on the turnpike; the abandoned farm where a row of neat new bungalows comes to an end. Waggoner, like Jorgensen, wanted to aggregate this messy tangle into a new scientific object that could be properly utilised and studied: the (sub)urban forest. Indeed, as soon as it had a coherent object to look at, the new field of urban forestry began to branch out and specialise, including, for example, work on the flora of bombed-out German cities.[19] The first US National Urban Forestry Conference took place in 1979, and scientific journals and handbooks followed. Older publications renamed themselves to fit in with the new zeitgeist. By the 1970s, the study of the urban forest had developed into a major scientific field.[20]

Today's city mayors and urban planners, then, when they talk about growing or protecting the urban forest, are building on some very specific histories from the late nineteenth and twentieth centuries – histories that are in one sense not really about trees at all, but rather about the everyday politics of urban space and a longstanding desire to remake the city as a safe, efficient territory where unruly objects and bodies are kept firmly under control.

And yet, underneath all of this attention to urban forests, there is also a sense of anxiety, I think – an anxiety about the process of urbanisation itself, and about the planet that it has wrapped itself around. This is an anxiety about the moral and ecological consequences of human progress and the emergence of the modern industrial world. But it's also about whether that world is quite as secure as we thought. It's an anxiety about whether all those things that we call 'nature' are truly as manageable, or as governable, as modern humans have allowed themselves to imagine. This anxiety, too, has a history. To understand it, we need to stay in the middle decades of the twentieth century and turn to a series of then-growing concerns over territory, ecology and urbanisation.

On 16 June 1955, seventy researchers from around the world arrived at a lecture room in Princeton University, New Jersey, where they would remain for the next five days. These scholars were all experts in human beings' habitats, and how these had changed over time. They had been brought to Princeton by the Wenner-Gren Foundation (an independent organisation that supports anthropological research) and by four core organisers: William L. Thomas, then an assistant director at Wenner-Gren; Carl O. Sauer, a prominent geographer and landscape theorist, well known as an opponent of environmental determinism; Marston Bates, a zoologist from Michigan who was working on 'human ecology' under the auspices of the Rockefeller Foundation; and Lewis Mumford, whom we have met already, a sociologist, historian and, by then, very famous writer on cities. At the time, Mumford had just published *The Transformation of Man*, a sweeping study of epochal change and the development of what people could still without blushing call 'civilisation'. The meeting was an attempt to think, on a grand and global scale, about the transformations in human ecology, and what these meant for the future of the planet. But it was also marked by the emergence of a newer anxiety, one focused on the state of the natural environment and the growing evidence of its degradation, marked by a distinctively Cold War sense of the now very real possibility of planet-level disaster.[21]

The meeting was called 'Man's Role in Changing the Face of the Earth', and its stated aim was to explore 'what has been, and is, happening to the earth's surface as a result of man's having been on it for a long time, increasing in numbers and skills unevenly, at different places and times'.[22] Fifty-three papers were presented and two volumes published, running to well over a thousand pages. The meeting found that 'man' had originated more than a million years ago, had largely stayed put in Central Africa and South-East Asia for the first 950,000 years, but then, rather suddenly, had spread out across the globe. Along the way, humans learned to plant crops, make use of animals, burn things (mainly forests) and build cities. The planet's once-natural habitat was, in the process, radically transformed, a development that accelerated rapidly during the Industrial Revolution. 'Man . . . changed the surface features,' one reviewer of this exhaustive text observed, 'the soils, the water, the cover of vegetation, the supply of resources, and even to a certain extent the climate.' Recognition of this development, this reviewer went on, had given human geography a certain kind of moral force – a mission to figure out how to damage less, perhaps even to repair some of the damage already done.[23]

And nowhere more so than in relation to trees. If one thing distinguishes man's history on the earth, argued Sir Clifford Darby, the Welsh historical geographer and one of the meeting's most celebrated attendees, it is his attempt to subdue the woodland: 'The attack, begun in prehistoric times, has continued for innumerable centuries, and, little by little, as population has grown, the wood has given way.'[24] Wood was everywhere in antiquity, he points out, physically and morally. It was simply *there*, the stuff of everyday life and culture. Homer compares a stricken soldier to a fallen oak and says that the sound of battle is like nothing so much as 'the din of woodcutters'. Pollen analysis, Darby goes on, shows us just how much of Europe was originally wooded. And in England, certain metropolitan place names encode the history of medieval wood-cutting. Settlements south of London, for example, often have names (ending with suffixes like 'ham') that don't indicate wood. These were the sites of early Anglo-Saxon settlement, where the trees fell first. Places to the *north* of the city, however, more commonly feature endings like 'hurst' or 'weld', indicating the belated presence of woodlands. Here, Darby suggested, the trees survived much longer. Only in the coniferous belt of the far north, where the soil is less fertile and the system of agriculture meant that woods were partially replenished over time, did anything much survive beyond the early modern period.

And yet the history of deforestation, Lewis Mumford reminded Darby, is also the history of the city. The natural

history of urban life, Mumford argued, begins with ceremonies performed in caves; then comes the cultivation of
hard grains, and food storage; populations grow, and so do
their settlements.[25] With more people comes the elaboration of administration and trade; life gets larger and more
complex. The city grows outwards, its overlapping layers of
defensive wall marking its age, says Mumford, like the rings
of a tree. But then something changes. What distinguishes
the city from the village is not size or complexity. It is, rather,
'a tendency to loosen the bonds that connect its inhabitants with nature, and to transform, eliminate, or replace
its earth-bound aspects, covering the natural site with an
artificial environment that enhances the dominance of man
and encourages an illusion of complete independence from
nature'. In Mumford's view, the city becomes an *emancipa-
tion* from nature. But this was still something of an illusion:
the truth was that the city at this stage in history was still
largely dependent on the surrounding countryside for its
survival. Until suddenly it wasn't. With the arrival of the
industrial age, Mumford writes, natural limits on growth,
such as water supply or walls needed for defence, fell away or
were superseded. Exponential population growth took place.
Now entire districts were urbanised. Urban areas began to
reach out to each other like tendrils across the countryside.
The city became *counter-organic*. Conurbations appeared,
and any land left in between, unwanted by the city, became
desert. 'The city,' Mumford concluded, 'by its incontinent
and uncontrolled growth, not merely sterilizes the land it
immediately needs but vastly increases the total area of ster-
ilization far beyond its boundaries.' The city surrounds the

country like an amoeba surrounds its food, quietly breaking it down, absorbing it and finally taking it in.

This idea – that the city is a kind of *anti*-nature – is really pervasive, whether people are celebrating that fact, lamenting it, making use of it or trying to fix it. It unites well-meaning mayors, desperately trying to tend their own depleted urban forests, and less well-meaning officials and economists, sweating the local ecosystem services to improve the city's bottom line.

It's a popular idea; I just don't know if it's very true. I'm writing this at my kitchen table in Bristol, a medium-sized ex-industrial British city, almost three-quarters of a century after Lewis Mumford's rather dire diagnosis. When I look immediately to my left, out into our small yard – even the agent who sold us the house didn't dare call it a garden – I can see two decent-sized trees, an untamed wall of hedge and several overgrown planters, bought and left by my mother after we moved in and not touched by us since. On the table in front of me there is a strange little plant in a pot, really more of a leaf, that my wife found in the street and took home, and in the next room is an overgrown and neglected *Monstera deliciosa* that we were given as a wedding present and now can't bring ourselves to throw out. On the street outside, the walls of our small front garden are lined on both sides by weeds – through laziness on our own side and, I think, a vague gesture at 'rewilding' on the part of the local council on the other. Ten minutes' walk down the road is a large park, which, like much of the city, is topographically strange and features a long slope of trees as you walk in, dotted with thoughtfully placed benches that are much loved by both parents of toddlers and teenagers drinking cider. Of course, this is in some way the story of living in a bourgeois neighbourhood, where the bountiful presence of trees is at least partly a class signifier. There's an old Marxist debate about whether this kind of commodified nature – what Marx calls 'second nature', like my poor lifestyle signifier *Monstera* in its fancy little pot – even counts as nature at all. But I want to leave that to one side. The truth is that urban spaces are festooned with vegetation, wanted and unwanted, useful and annoying, pretty and ugly. Once you start looking, there's green stuff everywhere in cities – and much of it not obviously under any kind of authority or control.

Partly with this in mind, and directly in opposition to their mid-twentieth-century ancestors, many geographers today argue for seeing the city as an 'urban ecology'.[26] The idea that the city is a uniquely *human* space, these geographers point out, that it excludes non-human nature, even to the extent that things like trees have to somehow be *brought back in* – well, this has always been a bit of a fantasy. And usually, as in Mumford's natural history, a negative fantasy at that. People imagine a sprawling dystopia of clean, man-made, high-tech futurity. But that city simply doesn't exist. Even in the most hyper-modern urban spaces, mould creeps down the walls; rain pools in small divots and becomes a home for algae; birds drop seeds and acorns; insects, somehow, incessantly, always find a way inside. 'Beneath the street, the beach', went the famous Situationist slogan of Paris 1968, but 'Beneath the street, the dirt' is the more salient reality. And in your average badly maintained British or North American city, not even very far beneath.

The city, say Matthew Gandy and Sandra Jasper, two writers working in this tradition, whatever science-fiction images we have of it, has never been absent of vegetation. The very earliest cities often prominently featured gardens and planting as expressions of imperial and territorial power. And people in cities have always set aside space for the cultivation of plants, whether for food, medicine or simply the pleasure of being among them.[27] But also, Gandy and Jasper point out, plants have always simply grown, unplanned, often little regarded, in urban spaces. This is especially the case around sites of ruin or destruction – like the 420 different species of plant that the Victorian botanist Richard Deakin counted growing on the walls of the Colosseum, then a neglected and rather wild place, in 1850s Rome.[28]

The city, then, has never not been a botanical place, whether we are talking (this is Gandy and Jasper's typology) about remnant plants (which were basically there before

*C. Spinosa*, from Deakin's *Flora of the Colosseum of Rome* (1855).

humans transformed the landscape, and are still there now), constructed plants (which have been specially selected and planted in particular urban spaces, for whatever effect) or adaptive plants (which weren't there before the city but have arrived now, albeit without deliberate human intervention or cultivation, and have found the city a congenial enough place to stay).

What's important about this perspective is that it isn't centrally about 'greening' urban space or 'rewilding' the city or whatever. To want to 'rewild' the city, after all, is to start from the position that 'the city' and 'wildness' are two different kinds of thing; that 'man' and 'the environment' stand in some kind of formal opposition to one another; indeed, that urbanisation can largely be defined as a site of struggle between them. This is the central assumption that the Princeton conference started with. It then found its way into growing fields of research, like geography and ecology, which for a long time never much questioned it. But it's also an assumption that drives so much of the worlds of 'ecosystem services' and 'nature-based solutions' and 'urban forestry' today; a weird, almost *psychic* separation between nature and the city that underpins a good deal of the obsession with trees and other green things that we see in so much contemporary urban thinking.

I realised, while reading Gandy and Jasper's book, that in trying to understand the role of trees in urban space, I had been looking in the wrong place – or at least, I had been looking in a very limited kind of place. I had spent my time at conferences for planners and urban policy-makers, reading pronouncements by ambitious city mayors, texts about the history of forestry and urban landscaping, and so on. Maybe, instead, I needed to speak to some people who had *always* thought that cities were natural spaces as much as anything else; people who, a bit like the emailers in Melbourne, had a deep connection to the urban tree landscape and a vision of how trees might really be at the centre of a good city, in a way that wasn't at all about control or utility; people for whom the unruly, wayward, sometimes politically awkward aspects of city trees were not only entirely okay, but were maybe even the whole reason for cherishing them in the first place.

'Here's one,' said Christine. We all stopped and looked.

'This is a tree,' I said.

'This tree', said Christine, standing protectively against the trunk, 'was condemned for having caused damage to the pavement that was impossible to fix.' I looked down. The pavement looked totally fine. 'As you can see,' said Christine, pointedly.

It was spring 2022. I had come to Sheffield, in northern England, to meet some of the people involved in the city's extraordinary tree protests, which had ended only a few years earlier. In 2012, Sheffield City Council signed an enormous contract with a private company, Amey plc, for managing and renewing highways in the city, including its highway trees. A survey suggested that around a thousand trees were in such bad shape that they'd need to be felled. Notices started to appear on trees, and quite quickly neighbourhood groups sprang up to oppose the programme. These eventually coalesced into STAG – the Sheffield Tree Action Group. Letters were written and petitions delivered, to no avail. By the end of 2015, more than three thousand trees were gone.[29] Then things got heated.

'This stuff around trees damaging pavements,' I said to Christine, 'did people ever really find it credible?' Secretly, I was thinking about wheeling a pram on some of the pavements near my home in Bristol, where tree roots really did sometimes make it impossible to pass.

'It became clear', said Mark, who along with Christine was the co-chair of STAG, 'that they were using excuses to fell the trees. All the experts we spoke to said, "This isn't a reason to fell a tree."' Christine joined in: 'None of the arguments stacked up,' she said, suddenly very passionately, 'because this is a £2.2 billion contract where they have money to do various things, and it was obvious that a lot of the trees were just being felled because they had chosen to fell half the street trees. It was a policy decision to do it. Then, when people protested, they started saying, "Oh, they're damaging the pavement, disabled people can't negotiate the street." Not that they'd been able to for the last twenty years anyway because of the state of pavements everywhere.'

'Let's take a picture,' I said, and pointed my phone at the roots.

In the middle of a campaign to protect the trees on one particular road, several protesters were arrested. The council got court injunctions to stop people from entering zones near trees. Protesters began jumping the barriers or finding other ways to circumvent the rules.[30] Threatening legal notices were sent out; private security staff were brought in, with an instruction to use 'reasonable force' to get the protesters away from the trees. And then, quite suddenly, in January 2018, with more than

Some tree roots in Sheffield.

five thousand trees gone, the council 'paused' the programme, citing health and safety concerns. During the pause, which was not initially meant to be long term, the council finally changed tack and entered into mediation with the protesters. There was a joint statement on a new approach, an apology from one of the leading councillors, and eventually an entirely new partnership and approach to managing the street trees, which included expert groups from outside, as well as STAG. In 2023, a damning independent report said that during the dispute, the council seemed motivated largely by a desire to simply get its own way. It said that the councillors had used disproportionate measures, including asking the police to be tougher with protesters, as well as pursuing people through the courts. 'Some of the things the Council did were, in the view of the Inquiry, unacceptable,' the report's summary noted, drily. 'Some of the ideas it flirted with, but did not pursue, were worse.'[31]

I had met Mark Brown and Christine King on Rivelin Valley Road, in Sheffield's northern suburbs, the site of some of the most contentious tree protests in the city. Honestly, it wasn't the loveliest place I had ever been and certainly didn't match the image in my head of a leafy area threatened by finger-jabbing council bureaucrats. When I got off the tram, right at the end of the line, I saw a big sign advertising 'real pet grub'. That was the vibe. Rivelin Valley Road itself struck me as a rather boring, tree-lined street. 'It's apparently one of the longest avenues of lime trees in Britain,' said Mark, 'so it's quite an iconic thing. And the council wants to fell quite a lot of the trees.' We were joined by Siobhan O'Malley, a resident who had also got involved in the protests. I liked all three immediately. They struck me as extremely nice, thoughtful and – for want of a better word – absolutely regular people. They were passionate and knowledgeable, but reasonable and pragmatic too. They seemed exactly like the kind of people you'd *want* to be involved in local politics in your city.

We walked up Rivelin Valley Road, where, thanks to the campaign, most of the trees had been saved. It was quiet, and we were right by a nature reserve with a small stream running through it. Really, it no longer felt like we were in the city. 'It started off as thirty-five trees that they were going to fell,' said Christine, 'but the council took some of them off, and it went down to twenty-one. I think they've taken twelve.'

'In isolation,' Mark chimed in, 'removing twenty-odd out of hundreds along this road, you might say . . .' I was kind of thinking that didn't sound so bad. 'But when it was tied into the city-wide campaign,' he went on, 'where thousands were being taken down in a very short time, it was the same objection. We started protesting all the trees, really, because the council just doubled down.'

The plan to cut the trees did seem crazy. As we walked up the road, Christine pointed out individual trees that had been saved. Some of them had been pinned with little hand-drawn love hearts. 'I think initially', said Mark, 'I became vaguely aware of the campaign, and I just thought, "Oh well, the council know what they're doing; it's just residents worried about their house prices."' I was glad he'd said that, because the thought was in the back of my mind too. 'And then they did this Rustlings Road raid,' Mark went on, 'where they arrested some pensioners, and I thought, "This is really not right," and I looked into it a bit more, and the more I looked into it, the more I thought, "There's some real bad stuff going on here," and I wanted to get involved.' He paused. 'This thing about house prices didn't ring true for me. I could never afford a house. I can only afford to rent one. But one of the first things I remembered about Sheffield [when I moved there first] was walking through some of the suburbs, through these lovely avenues of big trees, and I thought, "These are for everybody."'

We went into the nature reserve and walked by a small brook. There was the faint sound of cars on the road, and it started to rain a little. 'At the time,' said Siobhan, 'I was having a work-related issue, and I was out a lot, because staying indoors is no good for you mentally and I love nature. I'm a forager, that's what I do now: I teach foraging instruction, and about wildlife, biodiversity and habitat. At the time, I was doing it for myself, my son and my mental health, just to get outdoors, see nature, see the wild birds and to know it's all going on around you. It's so helpful when . . . almost the meaningless stresses of society sometimes get too much. It becomes a confused jumble, whereas nature is a beautiful, meaningful thing that we can all access. It's what supports us; it's all around us, it cradles us in times of need.'

We talked about how frightening the campaign to save the trees had been, and how heavy-handed the official response. Campaigners would get local intelligence on where felling crews were going to turn up and then race to get there first, to get close enough to the tree so that it couldn't be pulled down safely. This often meant physical confrontations with private security guards. But more sinister, Mark said, was the wider threat of legal action, huge court costs and criminalisation. Christine said that she and another protester had been dragged away from one protest by their arms and dumped face first onto the ground in front of a police officer, who denied seeing anything. 'I had to sleep on my right side for a couple of months,' she said. 'I think I bruised the bone.' I started to realise, as we talked, that the campaign was not just about the trees, it was about other things too – trust in public officials, some sense of fairness and decency, but also really personal experiences of the city. 'There was this one tree,' said Christine. 'The Independent Tree Panel said it was worthy of special consideration because it was such a fine tree, but they didn't care, they felled it, and it's the psychological violence of that that really sticks with you. It makes you angrier.'

There is something about trees, I thought, as we were talking, that seems absolutely central to a lot of people's ideas of what a good city – a good society – is like. When the trees come down, an awful lot of other things come down with them. 'Trees are a world unto themselves, aren't they?' said Siobhan, somewhat wistfully. 'Every tree is a world, and for a lot of street trees, that is somebody's world. One of the trees that got chopped down, this little girl used to go past and pet this tree and had a name for it, and it's gone now. It was a massive tree that the crows and the rooks and the pigeons . . . there must have been ten or fifteen species that would roost in this tree every night, and we would see them in the morning, when we'd do our little vigil when they were coming to take it away, and you'd see this little world of all the different species chattering to life. And insects and lichens and flowers, the things that trees support, you can't replace that. No baby tree is going to replace that.'

We went to a café. I was still trying to wrap my head around how things had got so out of hand. 'There was a certain amount of aggression that never turned into violence,' said Mark. 'We always made a point of passively protesting, and one or two people got pushed around when they brought out the security guards. I got pushed to the ground a couple of times, but the point was always to be passive and not fight back because, well, one thing, it's not in my nature, but also you lose the argument, because they'll say, "Oh, look at these violent protesters."'

We got to talking about some of the local residents' reactions – not all of them positive.

'One of the protesters had a hosepipe turned on her,' said Christine.

'That *is* unpleasant,' I said.

'People who didn't like trees were pretty aggressive,' she went on.

'Very loud about it, yeah,' said Siobhan.

'And they'd say,' Christine said, '"Don't get me wrong, I love trees, but that one's got to go."'

'Yeah,' said Siobhan. '"I just don't want them outside my house," was what my neighbours said.'

Christine sipped her tea, and we all paused.

'You could get the wrong impression, though,' said Mark, 'if you just listened to the loud people, because quite often, when things had settled down, we'd get someone coming out of the house next door, saying, "I'm really grateful for you being here. I don't feel brave enough to stand up to my neighbour, but you're able to come and do that."'

'From what I saw,' said Siobhan, 'for every one angry person screaming their head off, there were three people sat in a house, going, "Thank God somebody's said something."'

'There was somebody who would walk past and whisper, "Thank you,"' Christine said. 'Even though there was nobody in earshot, she still didn't feel brave enough to say it out loud.'

'Because if anyone was looking out their window', said Siobhan, 'and saw them talking to you, that was it, their neighbours would be . . .' She trailed off.

'Yeah, there was a bit of friction between neighbours,' Mark said.

'My neighbour still likes to give me digs about how much she hates the trees outside,' said Siobhan, 'every so often, if I happen to mention them.'

'Why does she hate the trees?' I asked.

'Because they make the moss fall onto the brickwork in her yard and make the birds poo in her garden. The leaves have to be swept up, and the petals from the beautiful cherry tree next to her house make everything sticky. I think that's the extent of her issues with them.'

'There's this obsession with neat and tidy that's quite prevalent these days,' Mark said.

'They're the sort of people who bleach their yards,' Siobhan added.

'Yeah,' Mark replied, 'people who can't control the world, but they control their garden. They pick up every last leaf, and nature doesn't fit into that.'

'We've lost our connection to nature somehow,' Christine said, 'but that's the thing about street trees: street trees bring nature into the city, and they bring seasons into the city. If you think of a street, it'll get hotter and it'll get colder, but a tree gives you the seasons.'

It was becoming late now, and I was getting ready to wind things up. 'There's definitely a psychogeography,' said Mark, 'where certain streets, we go back there, and it will trigger extreme emotions because it was such a powerful thing that happened there.'

'It must really change your relationship with the city,' I said.

'I still haven't driven down the Chatsworth Road,' he replied. 'It's a beautiful line of lime trees, nowhere near where I live, but they took them all.'

There was a pause.

'Three years of felling, lies, insulting people,' said Christine, looking down at the table. 'Three years of creating division in the community. I'm furiously angry about that.' She talked about some war memorial trees that had been threatened. A very elderly man, she said, would sit on the council steps to

protest against it. At the time, Christine was involved in con-
fidential negotiations between the council and the protesters.
She knew the council intended to scale back, but wasn't per-
mitted to say anything. 'I wasn't allowed to say, "Go home,
mate, you don't need to be here, you've won," and it got
leaked by somebody, because it was obvious what the council
was going to do: they were going to wait until Armistice Day,
they were going to walk past this bloke in his mid-eighties
and go, "Aren't we brilliant? We've saved these trees."'

Christine paused for some time. We were all silent.

'It was all about PR,' she said. 'There was nothing about
individual people or how people felt.' She was talking to herself now, I thought, more than to us. 'Because the council
has never acknowledged the damage they did, they've never
given us an apology. They just said, "Move on, we're not felling now, so everything's different. Forget it now." If we could
do that, there'd be no PTSD. There'd be no counselling. But
there's a massive well of pain and anger. You think you're all
right. And then it just comes out.'

I was on a tram back to the train station, trying to make sense
of this conversation and looking at the map on my phone,
anxious, as usual, to make sure I got off at the right stop,
when the name of a building on the map, right by the station,
leapt out at me: Béton House. Béton, I thought, surely had
to be a reference to *béton brut* – or raw concrete, the material
that gives 'brutalism' its unfortunate name. What modernist
marvel could this be? The tram stopped, and taking a chance,
I turned right, away from the station. I climbed up a steep set
of landscaped steps, past a group of bored-looking workmen

and a small clump of teenagers getting weakly high, until I reached the top of a hill. The city of Sheffield was spread out in front of me, into the west and south, and fading into the Peak District in the distance. 'I'll bet you'll say you love Sheffield city centre,' my friend Eva had said to me over dinner the previous night, 'just to be contrary.' And it was true, I did. But from up here, you didn't have to *try* to find the city beautiful. Then I saw, right behind me, a group of huge, post-war housing blocks. Suddenly, I knew exactly where I was: the Park Hill estate.

Park Hill was built in the late 1950s, to replace a notorious area of back-to-back houses that had been hastily established to provide homes for workers who had come in from the surrounding countryside seeking work in the city's developing heavy industries. It was part of a piecemeal, nationwide

A view of Sheffield from the steps at the bottom of the Park Hill estate.

project of 'slum' clearance, which had been taken up with renewed energy after World War II. For this sprawling site, two Architectural Association graduates, Jack Lynn and Ivor Smith, under the direction of city architect John Lewis Womersley, were selected to design a complex of interlaced concrete blocks, linked by walkways – the famous 'streets in the sky' – all of it quite directly quoting Le Corbusier's then recently completed Cité radieuse at Marseilles. Built across a sloping hill, the flats were designed to maintain a steady horizontal facing out into the city, with thirteen storeys at the longest end and four at the shortest.[32] The project was, said one commentator, 'testament to an era when young British architects were revolutionizing the field of residential architecture with radical housing programs'.[33] The buildings were wrapped by wide outdoor decks, big enough to get a milk float around. At the estate's high point, there were nearly a thousand flats, four pubs, schools, shops and doctors' surgeries.[34] The space around the buildings was largely pedestrianised, 'with the ground between the buildings laid out as a park space threaded with a system of footpaths including several small play areas'.[35]

Park Hill's story was more or less that of all ambitious urban social housing in England in this period: a grand 1960s project, followed by a kind of studied neglect and managed decline, as successive Conservative governments began to redirect the state away from any responsibility for providing housing, selling off what they could and carefully neglecting what they couldn't.[36] Park Hill was also badly affected by the collapse of heavy manufacturing in Sheffield, and especially the steel industry. Many residents lost their jobs, and the estate quickly got a reputation for deprivation, crime and social problems. One of the blocks was demolished by the council, and it seemed like the rest would quickly follow. Park Hill's 'status has changed gradually', wrote the architecture critic Owen Hatherley, 'from a source of intense municipal socialist pride to dilapidated sink estate'.[37]

But then something surprising happened: in 1998, Park Hill was given a Grade II listing, a formal classification marking buildings of special interest that should be preserved, if at all possible. Now there was no way the remaining blocks could be demolished.

In 2004, the developers Urban Splash were contracted by Sheffield City Council to redevelop the site. Urban Splash had made their name in warehouse developments in Manchester and Liverpool in the 1990s, and have since become a go-to company for eye-catching 'regeneration' projects throughout England. At Park Hill, they added colour panels to what had been brick infill and built a big open gateway to the estate. They shortened the decks and landscaped the grounds. The flats themselves were enlarged, made open plan and 'modern'. About six hundred were to be sold on the open market, their council tenants having been largely moved on, with just two hundred available for 'social rent'.[38] A book on modernist estates interviewed two of the new residents, both university lecturers. 'We are both big fans of modernist architecture,' one explained. 'It is incredibly convenient for work, and it gives us an opportunity to live in a different way – our other house is a 1903 terrace house.'[39] In some of the undeveloped low-rise blocks, a small hub of original tenants still remained.

All of this is objectively sort of terrible. It represents the collapse of a certain kind of urban utopianism, which had been borne along by ambitious, resolutely modern design, and its replacement by a cheesy gentrification project for middle-class professionals. It means the removal of another large swathe of public housing and the reimagination of modernist design, from *trying* to be – even if it was always kind of an elitist project – a democratic, even socialist, practice; and its transformation, instead, into a kind of lame lifestyle signifier for people with good salaries but unsatisfying lives, who probably use terms like 'mid-century', and buy Ercol chairs on eBay.

But it's also very beautiful, as capitalism's excesses so often are. I actually gasped when I turned a corner and was confronted by the blocks. This might be, I thought, a feeling similar to what it would have been like to see those buildings for the first time – even if back then they must have looked truly futuristic, whereas now they code as a familiar piece of hipster nostalgia. But still. The blocks have been washed back to a kind of pink hue, and the coloured panels really work. The whole thing has the weird feeling of a kind of municipal Legoland, but in a good sense. I took some pictures of one of the blocks from in front of a tree whose branches were bent almost as if to grandly present the wonder behind it, and sent one to my friend Rod. 'I see,' he wrote back, 'so trees are good when they're in front of modernist buildings.' This was a familiar tease from my friends, who were convinced I was writing a book about how trees were bad. But I wasn't, I would insist. I was writing a book about how trees were *complicated*. And it was true, sometimes I did think that people who went on a lot about trees in cities or the state of the urban forest were really talking about how much they didn't like a place like Park Hill, a place that still had that twentieth-century confidence that Lewis Mumford was starting to get nervous about as far back as 1955, a place that would gladly cut the hill into a straight line and load it with spacious new homes and doctors' surgeries and playgrounds and pubs, for thousands and thousands of people who could otherwise never have afforded any of it. But that thesis was incomplete, I realised. I was thinking about Christine then, and the man on the council steps, and all the other tree protesters, and what they had been through in defence of their own idea of a forested urban utopia – one that included the lime trees on Rivelin Valley Road *and* a place like Park Hill.

Around the buildings, Urban Splash had erected panels etched with people's memories of the place in its pre-gentrification phase, memories that were powerful enough to still be moving, even if you thought there was something faintly grotesque about someone's literal memory being materialised as a memorial to – even a kind of recuperation of – its own evisceration. 'We were not guinea pigs in our eyes,' said one, 'it wasn't brutalist, it was new and clean and exciting. There were playgrounds and grass to play on yet the city was only a short bus ride or a gentle stroll away.' The words were in gold, etched onto a free-standing blank slate slab. It looked like a tombstone. I took out my phone to check the time. Ten minutes till the train back to Bristol. I looked back over the city one last time. Then I went back down the hill, got on my train and went home.

# 6: The Twentieth Century Did Not Take Place

Church of Christ the King, Turner's Cross, Cork.

In July 2019, *Time* magazine reported that Barcelona's most famous church, the Sagrada Família, had announced a completion date, more than 130 years after its construction began. 'Thanks to an influx of funding,' the magazine noted, 'some striking innovations and a lot of old-fashioned craftsmanship, the famously unfinished church is now on schedule to be completed in 2026, the 100th anniversary of the death of its architect, Antoni Gaudí.'[1] The euphoria was short-lived. Just two years later, reporting on ongoing attempts to put a giant twelve-point star on top of one of the cathedral's main towers, the *Guardian* informed readers that due to Covid-related delays, the latest completion date had been shelved, with no new one announced.[2] People were up in arms. Questions were asked about what exactly was being done with all the income from visitors, while locals protested about a plan to attach a huge stairway to the main entrance, which would involve knocking down three city blocks. It wasn't even clear, people said, that the stairs had anything to do with Gaudí's original plans.

I've always felt a strange sense of attachment to the Sagrada Família. It was, I think, the first properly famous building I ever visited, part of a brief stop-off on an unusually adventurous school tour in the mid-1990s. I wish I could say that its weird, bulging spires and polychrome-forest interior were imprinted on my small provincial mind, thereby seeding an abiding fascination with nineteenth- and twentieth-century architecture. But the truth is that my only memories of that trip are that it was too hot, that we spent most of our time on a bus, and that we discovered the exotic Continental pastime of roller-blading. I have no idea what any of us made of arguably the most famous piece of ecclesiastical architecture in Europe.

Still, we would have been a good audience for it. Just a few years earlier, most of us had undergone the Catholic coming-of-age sacrament, Confirmation,* in a rather less famous modern building: the Church of Christ the King, in Turner's Cross, a small working-class suburb just south of Cork city centre. Christ the King is an exceptionally strange religious building to find in Cork, or anywhere else in Ireland really, where church design tends to be as grimly unimaginative as

---

* In which one is publicly *confirmed* as a follower of Christ; in most of our cases, this would turn out to be an optimistic declaration.

the practice it encloses. Christ the King, though, is different. It's built entirely from concrete – the first such church in Ireland – and composed of a series of thin, rectangular, pillars that move up and out from a central hexagon, then around the sides of the building, before meeting at the front, to form an almost incidental spire. This gives the church a strikingly narrow, high, rectangular front elevation, which is then dominated by a nineteen-foot high-modernist statue of Christ himself, radiating serenely between a set of zigzag concrete reliefs.

The Church of Christ the King was designed by a Chicago architect, Barry Byrne, who had been commissioned by the Bishop of Cork after he had read an article about Byrne – written by Lewis Mumford, of all people – in the lay Catholic magazine *Commonweal*. 'Here is an architect', Mumford enthused, 'who has reconciled tradition and innovation; here is an artist who expresses the continuity of the church with its own past, without attempting to stereotype its present activities.'[3] Byrne had been trained by Frank Lloyd Wright and was associated with Wright's 'prairie school' of architecture, but he got his major break by taking over the practice of Walter Burley Griffin, when Griffin won the commission to do the master plan for the new garden city of Canberra, Australia, in 1913.[4] This all makes for a very beautiful, very strange and very incongruous architectural inheritance in a Cork suburb, one lying completely at the other end of the scale from Gaudi's weird, bulbous construction. If Turner's Cross has the clean hexagonal shape of a modern steamship, the Sagrada Família is more like a wreck dredged from the bottom of the ocean, swollen with water and time, cankerous with shells and buboes, a thick brown mess of blobs, trunks, spires, turrets.

Barry Byrne is recognisably a twentieth-century modernist, but Gaudí is much harder to pin down. On the one hand, the methods he used to design the Sagrada Família – famously, he hung a model of the church on weighted strings, upside down, and let gravity arrange the spires into their final form[5] – are often taken as forerunners of the 'parametric' or 'form-finding' approach championed by many of today's self-consciously avant-garde computational architects.[6] Forget human design, says this school of thought; let the earth's physical parameters, like gravity or the flow of water or the way bubbles form, decide how a design plays out. At the same time, Gaudí's relationship to Gothic style could easily place him among those who, today, understand themselves as 'traditionalists' in matters of architecture and design. Indeed, for all its oddities, the thick-turreted Sagrada Família is recognisably a piece of nineteenth-century Gothic revival, an attempt to establish its author's own speculative continuity with centuries of European church-building.

How does Gaudí produce this strange simultaneity between the old and the new, such that his most famous building seems almost to stand outside time and history altogether? The answer, I think, has something to do with his work's relationship to *nature*. The spires of the Sagrada Família swell and gather like living things; they look encrusted and aged; indeed, the experience of the interior of the church is often compared to the experience of being in a forest, with the ceiling propped up by a thick phalanx of columns 'shaped like tree trunks'.[7] Gaudí, says the Mexican architect Javier

Senosiain, 'took nature – "the work of the supreme architect" as he called it – as his model and archetype'.[8]

Christ the King in Turner's Cross, the church that I more or less grew up around, is an unambiguously twentieth-century, modernist construction. With its use of new materials, its straight lines and its open spaces, with its explicit break from its surroundings and its hint at a broader social transform-ation in the offing, the church occupies a very specific, defined period in architectural history. The Sagrada Família, however, is very different. Here is a church that began its life in the nineteenth century – and is, somehow, still under con-struction in the twenty-first. It's almost as if it missed the twentieth century altogether, straddling the periods directly before and after modernism, without ever touching down in that remarkable, debased, often very violent period.

This play with time is worth paying attention to, I think. When I began doing the research for this book, when I started reading and talking to people who were interested in the relationship between architecture, cities and nature, who were interested in neuroscience, and human-scale plan-ning, and the benefits of trees, I was struck by how often they linked what they were doing *today* with work that preceded the twentieth century. So often, it seemed, not only were con-temporary ideas about cities, buildings and nature at odds with the 'modern' or 'modernist' architecture of the twentieth century, but people concerned with these issues were actually looking back beyond that period altogether, as if it had never happened, rather as one might awkwardly glance over the shoulder of an unwanted guest at a party. This seemed to be something that united people who otherwise, in terms of their architectural notions, looked like they had nothing much to do with one another at all. It was the case for conservative 'traditionalists' who enthused about conventionally beautiful Georgian squares in otherwise dank English provinces; but it also held for future-oriented experimentalists, the kinds of people who talk in suspiciously vague terms about genetics, and code, and get commissioned to design swishy museums in sad, post-industrial cities.

For Gaudí, the use of natural forms seems to make the Sagrada Família both very contemporary, a building truly of the twenty-first century, and very old, a building that stretches back into the Middle Ages. In the same way, for contemporary architects working with nature, whether they are traditionalists trying to recreate beautiful, naturally soothing olde-time squares, or parametricists (I'll come back to this word) reimagining design as if it were a kind of biological or geological blueprint, it's almost as if modernism, with its synthetic materials, its hard right angles, its human-centredness, its willingness to stamp its mark very explicitly on the environment – *it's almost as if this movement never happened.* It's almost as if there is a desire on the part of people who are very invested in nature, and biology, and how the two might relate to architecture and design today, to simply act like the twentieth century never happened in the first place.

So I was interested – and concerned. Here, after all, are groups of people who have otherwise nothing to do with one another, are indeed often very opposed to one another, but who share one huge, dominant and, to me, very troubling idea. On the one hand, there are self-consciously avant-garde people using new computational methods, advancing strange ideas about buildings and genetics, who are deeply concerned with ecology and the environment and are often attached to the most prestigious architectural academies. On the other, there is a large contingent of rather fogeyish people, often working in regional architectural practices, who are committed to reproducing forms that have traditionally and somewhat conservatively been imagined as beautiful, restful and well ordered for many centuries.

But the idea that unites these two groups, whether they love classical porticos or computer-coded curves, the idea that disturbs me, is that the human being, whatever else it is, is a natural and biological creature first of all; that the great mistake of the century that ended a couple of decades ago – and it is, now, very firmly ended – was that we tried to build a new world from scratch; that the *real* disaster in modern planning and design, the foolish notion that we're still paying for, was that we allowed ourselves to imagine we could actually transcend our pitiful, wretched, earthly, irretrievably *natural* state.


Downing College, Cambridge, is probably the most grimly traditional and backward-looking part of the UK's most grimly traditional and backward-looking city. The main bit is conceived as a kind of eighteenth-century arcadia, with grand but still rather self-effacing, low-rise classical facades, gathered around an unmoving, dead-looking lawn. There are some embarrassed-looking trees, and here and there you can find students sitting on a bench or at the foot of a column, like well-placed statues in some mad aristocrat's idea of Georgian picturesque. In May 2022, I was there, nonetheless,

Downing College, Cambridge.

trying to find the college's much newer convention centre, built in the 1980s thanks to a gift from a prominent graduate, the multi-millionaire low-calorie-diet guru Dr Alan Howard. But even this had been designed by the architect, Quinlan Terry, to blend into the dull, landscapey classicism that marked the rest of the scene. Here, it seemed, was Cambridge in miniature: on the surface, an ersatz recreation of classical antiquity, timeless, traditional, sedately unmoving; but hiding in plain sight was the only thing making this limp charade even half possible in the twenty-first century, viz. the city's real existence as an eager catalyst and shiny death-node of high-tech bioscience, rich people's bodily anxieties, and venture capitalism.

I was there for an event on architecture and health, hosted by Cambridge's Centre for the Study of Classical Architecture as part of a wider attempt to understand how buildings affect human biology and psychology. Put simply, classical or some-times 'traditional' architecture is an approach to architecture that's a bit backwards-looking, self-consciously rooted in history, not favoured at all by architecture's academic estab-lishment, kind of right-wing – but in a low-key way – and very much not cool. It isn't a unified or coherent movement ('traditional' cottages in, say, Shropshire are not in the least bit classical, for instance*), but it nonetheless captures a general way of thinking about architecture that harks unashamedly back to ancient Greece and Rome, often also to the fantasised neatness of Georgian England's urban squares, and some-times to an interest in a kind of crafty, bustling idea of the medieval city. It emphasises, typically, some combination of civic grandeur and pride, but also modesty and knowing one's place; an attention to neatness, order and symmetry, but also allowing space for something quirky and individual; an inter-est in decorative elements, but from a fairly defined list; and a concern with building to a 'human scale', or at least in a way that is recognisably *for* human beings, their everyday lives and what is imagined to be their natural conviviality. It splits the history of architecture in two, with the advent of the twenti-eth century as the breaking point at which these longstanding

---

* I am using 'classical' and 'traditional' somewhat interchangeably in this chapter – though, as this example already makes clear, something can be 'traditional' and very much not 'classical'. Nonetheless, the two approaches share a common relationship to time, and to how we value the styles of previous eras, thus forming a sharp contrast with modernism, where, ideologically at least, there has often been a willingness to do away with older styles altogether. It's this contrast that really interests me in this chapter, which is why I will sometimes bundle 'classical' and 'traditional' together.

ancient principles were abandoned and a radical, terrible rupture took place.[9]

What's crucial is that this way of thinking about architecture doesn't see itself as a historical style or a preference like any other – in the way that we might say, I don't know, I like the Parthenon, you love the Guggenheim, tomayto, tomahto. Instead, traditional and classical architects see themselves as operating within a set of traditions that celebrate everything obviously and eternally good in built form. This means they sometimes see our relationship to architecture and the buildings we like not as a product of taste, or culture, or a random outcome of the historical period or place you happened to be born in, but rather as something governed by timeless and, indeed, biological principles of how buildings and humans naturally go together. You can like the Guggenheim, if you want – good for you. Just be aware that you're wrong, immoral, maybe even a bit sick. Though there is nothing inherently right-wing about all of this, classical and traditional architectures are often associated with the political right – indeed, sometimes the far right, who have lately made 'modern architecture' a symbol of all they find wrong and degenerate about the contemporary world. Not for nothing did Donald Trump, in a parting shot of characteristically impotent spite, issue an order mandating that all new federal buildings must follow 'classical and traditional architecture' styles.[10]

As I arrived at Downing College, though, quite in contrast to Trump's bumptious inanity, I found tweed, and bonhomie, and genteel pastries on the lawn, before the small assembly was redirected into Quinlan Terry's rather grand auditorium to think about how classical architecture and health might go together. Modern 'hospital cities', the handout declared, 'are seen as dystopian worlds full of frightening technicality'. This seemed weird to me, as I settled into my seat in a corner of the room. I was no fan of the typical concrete hospital campus, but 'frightening' seemed a bit much. 'How we shape the interior and exterior environments of buildings that provide healthcare', the handout continued, 'are questions of high currency.' This is 'not just about how we manage health, but . . . how we manage public policy and improve society itself'.

The star attraction was John Simpson, a well-known classical architect who had recently worked on the Defence and National Rehabilitation Centre, expanding a facility for injured servicemen and -women into something for the wider population. Due to 'increasing neurological evidence of the benefits of traditional architecture to wellbeing', the centre's website notes, 'Stanford Hall, a Grade II*-listed country house in the heart of the Leicestershire [sic] was chosen for the project'.[11] The idea had come from Gerald Grosvenor, the sixth Duke of Westminster, who convinced the then defence secretary to back the project. The refurbished hall was formally handed over by the duke's son, Hugh Grosvenor – at the time a twenty-six-year-old aristocrat with about £10 billion to his name following the death of his father – as a gift to the nation in 2018.[12] I was still struggling to make sense of this distinctly British melange of aristocracy, violence, and patronage, as Simpson flashed up images of eighteenth-century hospitals. Look, call this a post-colonial chip on the shoulder as much as you like, but it seemed to me the object being stapled together in this weird matrix of aesthetics and healing was not the injured serviceman or -woman. It was, in fact, the United Kingdom itself, a nation which, underneath its picturesque charms, remains thoroughly in hock to its aristocratic class; an exhausted intellectual and aesthetic production whose misplaced sense of global import is (barely) held together by the shattered bodies of mostly working-class soldiers. Here, I thought, maybe a little self-righteously, was what a dystopian world full of frightening technicality sounded like to me – *not* a 1960s hospital stuck on the edges of some provincial town.

Anyway, I hadn't come to hear John Simpson, but rather an architect called Donald Ruggles, whose book, *Beauty, Neuroscience & Architecture*, I had recently been engrossed in while trying to make sense of what, exactly, being in touch with nature might mean for architectural style.[13] What we call beauty, Ruggles argues in his book, is something like an evolved neurological capacity for recognising visual patterns that are likely to produce pleasure. When we see a pattern we like, the ancient, emotional part of the brain triggers an endorphin release that the more recent *thinking* bit of the brain registers as a feeling of pleasure. So when we say of a building or work of art that 'it's beautiful', what we're really doing is giving voice to this sense of chemical pleasure. Some natural patterns, such as fractals, produce these effects. But Ruggles's particular interest is in a pattern that he calls the 'nine square': an intersection of two vertical lines and two horizontal lines to form nine boxes (like a tic-tac-toe board). This, Ruggles argues, is the visual basis of most of mankind's most famous structures, from the Parthenon to the US Capitol. The nine square, he says, is in any event 'one of the root patterns provided by nature'. It is recognised by tiny infants in human faces and is the basis of parental bonding.

In his Cambridge talk, Ruggles described how, as organisms, we need beauty to achieve homeostasis (a term for good biological regulation). We have a drive to seek out 'beauty–pleasure events': moments when we see beautiful things and experience pleasure as a result. Such beautiful things, he said, are non-threatening, coherent and recognisable. Beauty is what a baby sees in its mother's face, and so, I guess, when we look at a beautiful building and take pleasure in it, we are really gazing on the face of a kind of giant collective mother figure. But the critical thing is that beauty is not some aesthetic frippery; it's a natural thing, an evolutionary need. In its absence – for example, when confronted by contemporary architecture that does *not* use these kinds of patterns and is, therefore, ugly – we become stressed, even unwell. And this is why classical architecture matters: it literally makes us feel well. Architects, Ruggles said, as his talk ended, are the new leaders of the health and wellbeing movement.

This is a claim made by lots of people who are interested in traditional approaches to architecture and design, or at least in an architecture that operates at a more recognisably 'human' scale than the grand, ambitious visions of the twentieth century. To put it perhaps too simply, the argument goes that traditional and classical architectures are good because they are good for us; they align with human nature. Modern architecture is bad because it denies and excludes the forms we naturally yearn for and which we actually need to be surrounded by in order to stay well and happy. When, later on, I spoke to Nicholas Boys Smith, founder of the urban design social enterprise Create Streets,[14] who had also been at the event in Cambridge, he told me that his own ideas about the built environment were underpinned by a set of first principles and primary questions: 'Where are people happy? Where do people like to be? What do people want to be in? And what's good for people?' It seems hard to object to this. But words like 'happy' and 'good', for all their gentle appearance, can be quite forceful. On its website, Create Streets says that it's trying to support 'beautiful, sustainable places' that are 'correlated with good wellbeing and public health outcomes'.[15] It's not that people can't enjoy good wellbeing in tower blocks, Boys Smith said to me, just that it might take more work. 'The types of home that I think most of us tend to be most happy in', he went on, 'are ones in which it's quite quick and easy to retreat into the private realm, but also where one can quite rapidly advance through a portal into the public realm, where we can engage with everything else.' If you simply and undogmatically follow the evidence about which spaces are good for people, what they say they find beneficial, then you are likely to head down a particular aesthetic or structural path. 'The evidence', he said, 'supports a fairly traditional approach to urban morphology: block structure with clear private and public space; a clear framework of blocks and plots and streets, with greenery interwoven throughout; vertical infrastructure that encloses a square or a park or a street.'

This is all fair enough, I think. But even allowing that people *do* often say they favour more traditional or 'human-scale' developments, with natural materials, a gentler relationship to size, some loose feeling of 'heritage', 'belonging' and so on[16] – even if we accept all of this, we're still not obliged simply to take the public at their word. In fact, I think it's wholly possible that insofar as traditional buildings really do make people happy (or at least insofar as people *say* they make them happy, which is not the same thing), this is not because of any inbuilt biological predisposition. It's not some random preference, outside of culture and history, that we have to just accept at face value.* We could also argue – at least *I* would argue – that it's a product of the fact that we inhabit a stifling, backward-looking and rather stupid age, in which reactionary ideas about aesthetics and design dominate mainstream conversation, while the politically dodgy claims that 'old is good', 'heritage' is valuable, and so on, are simply out there, unquestioned, as if distributed through the water system as a collective moral nutrient. In this sense, 'traditional' style might make people happy because they have learned over time – they have been rigorously *taught* over time – to associate that style with what they are told elsewhere are good and positive attributes of society. Alternatively, it might not make people happy at all, but when asked in surveys about architectural preferences or invited to participate in experiments, they know the

---

* I put this argument to Boys Smith over email. He replied, pointing out that we don't have to take people's word for it – that we can also use pricing data as a guide to what economists call 'revealed preferences' (this is the idea that what people actually buy, and will pay more for, is a good guide to what they really value). I'm not convinced by this – the idea that behaviour is a reliable guide to desire is a typical economist's fallacy, in my view – but see his report 'Beyond Location', written with Alessandro Venerandi and Kieran Toms, in the April/May 2018 issue of *Land*, for more on this.

culturally appropriate response, and duly offer it. Either way, we can't simply conclude that people gravitate to traditional styles *naturally* or for no reason at all. To the extent that people do, indeed, often seem to favour traditional buildings, this is surely inseparable from the fact that they have been taught since early childhood to be repelled by anything new and modern; to internalise a dull, conservative horror at the more forward-looking, revolutionary, *social* forms of collective inhabitation that emerged, slowly, painfully and very partially, over the course of the twentieth century.

There is an intellectual heritage here. And a good deal of it passes through the conservative philosopher Roger Scruton, in particular his ideas about beauty. The thing about beauty, according to Scruton, is that it's not a subjective matter, where one opinion is as good as another; beauty, rather, is what Scruton calls an ultimate value, 'as important as truth and goodness'.[17] It is even, he says, 'a universal need of human beings'. Without it, we are in 'a spiritual desert'. His first book, *The Aesthetics of Architecture*, with which he began a career as one of the world's most influential proponents of traditional building, is very wrong, but also undeniably clever and original – as well as hugely influential.[18] In it, Scruton says that experiencing architecture is not a simple sensation, like being touched. Rather, it involves intellectual work: you have to think and reason when you experience a building. And like any piece of intellectual work, experiencing architecture can be done well or poorly; your experience can be right or wrong. This is different from the experience of looking at a tree, say, where a tree is a tree is a tree – an instance of what

Scruton calls 'literal' perception. When you are engaged in literal perception, you're taking in basic information. A tree. Fine. Nothing else to say. In an *imaginative* experience, by contrast, you have to *choose* an interpretation. In this sense, the experience of a building, Scruton says, 'admits of argument and proof, can be described as right, wrong, appropriate and misleading', and so on. He separates what he calls 'aesthetic' pleasures – which are basically intellectual – from more *sensual* ones, which are immediate and have no real relationship to thought. Getting into a nice hot bath, for Scruton, is a sensuous pleasure. You don't have to interpret your bath; it just feels nice on the bum. A truly *aesthetic* pleasure, on the other hand, the kind you take from a building, is an intellectual act. Architectural taste, in Scruton's view, is not a spontaneous thing like enjoying your bath; it is an act of *reasoning*.

Scruton sees taste in architecture as objective, but not in the sense that there is a 'truly' good architecture that you can simply recognise. He doesn't think that Roman columns are just objectively lovely. He means objective in the sense of morally correct architecture. A Georgian streetscape, in Scruton's terms, shouldn't be preferred by planners because it is somehow the nicest kind of street. It should be preferred because it is the most *good* kind of street. It's good in the same way that charity or love are good, i.e. eternally, universally, inarguably. This, for what it's worth, is Scruton's big departure from Immanuel Kant, who argued that aesthetics and morality were not the same thing at all. Aesthetic experience, says Scruton, is about the search for 'order and meaning'. A building either confirms our humanity or alienates us from it. A Georgian streetscape, for example, reflects 'the desire for a common public order'.

But compare that polite, well-ordered, mannerly Georgian frontage with, say, a public housing estate – 'the maddest of all Utopian schemes', says Scruton, 'where streets are replaced by empty spaces from which towers arise, towers bearing neither the mark of a communal order, nor any visible record of the individual house, and demonstrating in their every aspect the triumph of that collective individualism from which both community and individual are abolished'.

Scruton published *The Aesthetics of Architecture* in the same year that Margaret Thatcher became prime minister of the UK. His work caught a conservative zeitgeist that saw modern housing estates not simply as dysfunctional or ugly, but as morally wrong, even bad for people. British social historians remember the decade that followed as one in which the state started a process of almost total disinvestment in the provision of public housing, especially as it was manifested in modernist schemes, the dominant form of social housing since World War II. This all took place through a combination of privatisation and quasi-abandonment. Partly, this was simple Conservative Party ideology: public housing was a reminder that economic forces other than the market might produce attractive places to live, for lots of people, in surprisingly efficient ways. But it was also carried along by a series of specific arguments. In 1977, David Watkin, a historian, had suggested that architecture should have nothing to do with 'social policy' and that the mysterious individual genius of the architect was all that mattered.[19] In 1985, the geographer Alice Coleman published *Utopia on Trial*, which drew on the controversial concept of 'defensible space' to argue that the design of tower blocks made them susceptible to crime and social breakdown.[20] But the most important intellectual and political force undoubtedly came from people like Scruton, who argued that certain kinds of architecture produce certain kinds of people; that, to put it in plain terms, bad streets, and bad buildings, make for bad humans too.

As one contemporary observer astutely pointed out, there is a strange layering of often sophisticated moral philosophy and 'crude Thatcherism' in Scruton's writing.[21] The veneration of traditional architecture may well have been couched in a gentlemanly language of rights and expression and human nature, but the wrecking ball that came for the tower blocks of the 1950s and 1960s was moved as much by the desire for profit, and a general indifference to human misery, as it was by any high-flown ideas about man's timeless genius. In 2009, Scruton, whose ideas were by now mainstream among right-leaning politicians and intellectuals, made a documentary for the BBC, *Why Beauty Matters*. In the film, which is often unintentionally very funny, he goes on a walk around the centre of Reading. The town, he says, miserably, represents 'the greatest crime against beauty that the world has yet seen, and that is the crime of modern architecture'. The camera dwells on shots of admittedly not very lovely office buildings. 'Everywhere you turn', Scruton says, 'there is ugliness and mutilation . . . Everything has been vandalised.' Poor Reading! Traditional architecture, by contrast, with its ornament and detail 'satisfies our need for harmony'. It reminds us that we are not just animals with appetites, we have 'spiritual and moral needs too'. There is a close-up of a leaf and some dreamy choral music. Encounters with such beautiful things, intones Scruton, in full-on messianic mode, should be understood as 'calling us to the divine'.

You might laugh, but I want to take this school of thought seriously here, not least because of how influential it has been. After all, the idea that traditional building satisfies a very real inner desire, the idea that it organises our inbuilt, natural inclination towards harmony and order, that it resolves the dystopian nightmare of twentieth-century public housing in particular, has clear real-world effects. In 2022, the American Institute of Architects, the main professional body for architects in the US, threw its weight behind the bipartisan 'democracy in design' bill, legislation that tried to stop an incoming formal turn from modernism to classicism in the design code for US federal buildings.[22] In the UK in 2021, the then housing minister, Robert Jenrick, unveiled a national planning framework for new housing, asking councils to emphasise 'traditional stonework' in the south of England, while, in the north, new houses were to be designed in line with that region's 'redbrick heritage'.[23]

Roger Scruton died in 2020, leaving, whatever you may think of him, a remarkably influential legacy. But if you want to follow his influence today, if you're looking for people pursuing research programmes that trade in many of the same ideas, you need to set aside talk of the divine, or Kant, or what it might mean to encounter a nice leaf in Reading town centre on a Tuesday afternoon. You need to look instead for people who talk about architecture and the brain, and about landscape patterns, and the unconscious – and, in particular, about how a person's gaze can now be *minutely* tracked and measured as it moves across and through a visual scene.

'So this is Villa La Rotonda,' said Ann Sussman to me, down a Zoom connection from her home in Massachusetts. It was now some months since the Cambridge conference. 'It's a really famous building in Italy. George Washington hired an architect in 1800 and built a building like this. That's why we have the same elevation on every $20 bill.' We were looking at a shared screen, where I could see a front-on view of a beautiful white cubic structure, placed delicately on top of a grassy hill, as if part of a child's Lego set. The building was fronted by a classical portico, held up by six slender columns, and on top of the portico was the outline of a dome. This home had been designed in the late 1560s by Andrea Palladio, the most famous and successful architect of

Palladio's Villa La Rotonda, near Vicenza, Italy.

Renaissance Italy, in the countryside near the then Republic of Venice. On my screen, though, the image of the building was covered with yellow dots of varying sizes, which were connected by thin lines, like a network diagram. 'So this is really fascinating,' Ann went on. 'This technology is what Honda, BMW, GM, Procter & Gamble use.' She was showing me how she uses eye-tracking software – literally, software that tracks where you direct your gaze – to study how people are unconsciously attracted to particular design features. 'What the dots are doing', she explained, 'is tracking the fixations of how the research subject's brain, without her awareness, makes her look. You're really seeing your animal brain architecture at work here.' The idea, in other words, is that your brain knows what you're doing before you yourself do; that to know what really matters aesthetically, we don't need to ask you what you *think* you like, we just need to track where your brain tells you to look.

As Ann flicked through some more slides, we talked about the use of scientific tools in marketing and web design, and the effort that huge companies are putting into figuring out how long it takes you to pay attention to a particular on-screen button. Trying to understand how the subliminal brain works is a major growth area in business schools, with eye-tracking just the tip of the iceberg. The idea is that we don't necessarily know, consciously, what we like or what will capture our attention in a scene. In fact, when we take in a view, our gaze is not directed by what we think we want to look at; it's directed by an evolved capacity for identifying danger in the landscape. We're not aware of this. Instead, our evolved brain takes in the scene before we have any idea what's going on.

This evolutionary adaptation, it's claimed, is why we have a subliminal attraction to particular sorts of scenes, elevations and vistas – things like overlooks or open savannahs, from where danger is clearly visible. This is also why landscapes that don't look much like the places we were living in when our brain evolved this capacity – modern cities, for example – produce so much stress.

Now we were looking on our shared screen at an image of a flat and – I had to admit it – very uninviting modern building. 'Can you see', Ann said, very seriously now, 'how dangerous facades like this are for the nervous system? You're going to have more cortisol secretion.' She explained how companies like Apple can measure how much people smile when they see something. 'And what's amazing', she said, 'is you can really see the biological impact of your design intervention, because when you smile, that releases oxytocin. That's a hugging hormone.' In her book *Cognitive Architecture*, co-written with Justin B. Hollander, Ann argues that 'the repetitive parallel lines common to most modern built environments stress the brain'.[24] Parallel lines are unusual in nature; they don't feel natural to us. And so it requires work – demanding, stressful work – to take them in. Humans 'evolved to assess their environment', Sussman and Hollander write, 'the natural one, quickly and not the modern industrial or post-industrial one. Pointed shapes, such as barbs, thorns, quills, sharp teeth, were ever-present threats in our evolutionary past . . . We evolved for this past environment, and remain designed for it.'

This view has some pretty sharp consequences. In one reading, modernist building design – with its straight lines, its sometimes blank facades, its hidden doors and its lack of decorative features – seems so ill-suited to our evolved brain function that it might even be the outcome of some kind of neurological pathology. This is something Ann takes very seriously. 'Key fathers of modern architecture', she said to me, 'were German World War I vets.' And they all suffered from post-traumatic stress disorder. 'When you have PTSD,' she went on, 'your brain doesn't let you see reality normally or neurotypically.' I guess I looked sceptical at this point – and the truth is, I *was*. 'I was invited to present at a medical conference in 2019,' she said, 'and then I asked a psychologist who teaches at Harvard Medical School, and other leading trauma psychologists in New York, to look at my slideshow of modernist architecture. And this is what they said: "If you never told me who lived there, I could tell this person had been traumatised. Classic PTSD."' Architects such as Bauhaus founder Walter Gropius, she argues, who served for some years on the Western Front, designed buildings that resembled bunkers and trenches because of how the war had damaged their brains. 'Gropius', Ann said, definitively, 'was mentally ill. He'd wake up screaming in the middle of the night.' I guess I still looked sceptical. 'Look,' she said. 'Walt Disney decides in 1955 on an empty orange grove to make the most successful tourist destination in the world. He designs Disneyland Main Street, about a mile long, not a modern building on it. Why do you think he did that? Because he had an intuition that this is what people wanted. He sent his "Imagineers" all over Europe to look at where people were happiest, and then he replicated that to invent the happiest place on earth. When you go down a modern street, your brain, your body actually can't regulate your nervous system, because it doesn't have the fixations to make you feel safe, because of how we evolved for vigilance. What traditional architecture does is it gets us out of the vigilant state, because it gives us the subliminal fixations the brain desires. When you build modern architecture, by contrast, you're building stressful architecture.'

I took all this in, slowly.

'Traditional architecture', Ann said, with finality, 'externally expresses the hidden brain design that most naturally meshes with our nervous system.'

In the late 1960s and early 1970s, just as Roger Scruton, fresh from his PhD at Cambridge University, was introducing a course on aesthetics at Birkbeck College in London, a widespread panic emerged about the sustainability of human development on planet earth. If the post-war decades had established endless growth as the apparently normal state of economic affairs in Europe and North America, by the late 1960s, drawing on the more critical work of economists like J. K. Galbraith, as well as on Rachel Carson's surprise hit, *Silent Spring*, policy-makers and think tanks had begun to get skittish about how long all of this producing, consuming and growing could go on.[25] In 1972, the Club of Rome – a weird, self-appointed group of what today we would call 'thought leaders' – commissioned a report, *The Limits to Growth*, which used a computer model to predict a sharp decline in the earth's population as industrial and ecological capacity was reached.[26] When a series of rolling oil shocks emerged the following year, it seemed as if the capacity of the earth and its resources to endlessly sustain human activity, and human habitats, was suddenly, and quite radically, in question.

In 1969, the Glasgow-born landscape architect Ian McHarg published his landmark book, *Design with Nature*, a work that carried this widespread sense of ecological anxiety into the worlds of architecture and city planning.[27] Like many others, McHarg had come to see urbanisation and industrialisation as a kind of 'self-mutilation', a disaster for the natural world. He lamented the 'bondage' of industrial civilisation, and even described his home city, Glasgow, as a 'smear' on the surrounding countryside. *Design with Nature* was a kind of anti-urban polemic, a book about limiting the city and preserving 'the bounty of that great cornucopia [the countryside] which is our inheritance'. And it was a huge and instant success. Over the course of the 1970s, McHarg became an influential figure – 'one of the very few landscape architects since Frederick Law Olmsted Sr', says Anne Whiston Spirn, herself a very prominent US landscape architect, 'who have commanded widespread notice, respect and influence outside the design and planning fields'.[28]

McHarg was hardly the first planner or architect to foreground nature. But he was distinctive – and enormously successful – in how he wrapped an emergent sense of mid-century ecological crisis into these fields. He was not simply arguing, in that familiar hand-wringing sort of way, for a more 'sustainable' approach to planning. His was a sharper, perhaps nastier, interest in human civilisation as ecologically and biologically constrained. He was concerned with how the planet might yet remind us (or at least some of us) of that constraint, now that we seem to have forgotten it. Though this position is at least partly rooted in an understandable concern with preserving the natural environment, it also has that familiar chemical whiff of the jackboot about it. 'The real fundamental division in the world', McHarg wrote in a 1971 pamphlet, 'is between these people who are not planetary diseases and those who are necrotic patho-logical tissue walking around pretending to be men.'[29] This is, of course, a wholly fascist sentiment. As the historian Peder Anker makes clear, McHarg, who was much inspired by the South African racist and segregationist ecologist John Phillips, was working quite clearly in a British colonial tradition, contrasting the degenerate West with the 'harmo-nious naturalism of the Orient'.[30]

McHarg worked at famous universities; his books were reviewed in the mainstream papers; he had the ear of pol-iticians and policy-makers. If we wanted to, we could add his US-based interest in ecological design to a UK-based concern with aesthetic philosophy – equally mainstream and influential – and we could use these as the starting point for a genealogy of today's broadly conservative interest in traditional design and planning as a kind of biological necessity. But McHarg wasn't the only person with design training who was becoming anxious about the state of the planet in the 1960s and 1970s. On the opposite coast of the US, experiments in ecological design and living emerged not from the Ivy League, but from a more free-floating early internet culture, and what the writer Douglas Murphy calls the 'cybernetic ecology' of people like Buckminster Fuller and Stewart Brand.[31] By the 1980s, this mix of ideas and influences would lead to the bizarre 'Biosphere 2' experi-ment, in which a group of volunteers attempted to spend a year living sustainably in a sealed greenhouse, an event that was grounded in – this is Murphy again – 'an odd mix of space-age nostalgia, environmental utopianism and mass entertainment'.

This period also produced spaces like the New Alchemy Institute, a ranch and research centre concerned with the production of food, and how to build new communities around agricultural experiments. New Alchemy was founded, wrote the science writer Nicholas Wade in *Science*, after he visited in 1975, by 'a small group of people who consider that modern American agriculture is a mighty edifice built on sand'.[32] The institute – funded by, among others, the Rockefeller Brothers Fund – worked on organic farming methods, as well as on what its leaders called 'bioshelters', greenhouses that were designed to sustain an entire food ecosystem. It's true, wrote Wade, that like many of their contemporaries, the group did have an anti-technology, somewhat apocalyptic bent. But nonetheless, it was here that two of the founders of New Alchemy, John Todd and Nancy Jack-Todd, set out the first principles of what we today call 'biomimicry' or 'biomimetic design'.[33] And it was from here, finally, that a second, highly consequential tradition emerged for thinking about the nexus of ecology, design and human life.

Biomimetic design is design that mimics forms or processes from nature, whether this means mimicking the shape of a natural object, such as a leaf or peanut shell, or reproducing some process or principle, such as how a termite nest regulates heat. Crucially, biomimetic design does this (or is supposed to) not for aesthetic reasons, but out of a desire to reproduce some good or useful effect of the natural world. It may sound simple enough, but these principles have travelled a long way, from 1970s cyborg–hippie culture to the cutting-edge work of major international design firms today.

The materials scientist Julian Vincent gives the example of the 'Bundle Towers', a proposed replacement for the World Trade Center designed by Foreign Office Architects (FOA) in 2002.[34] Skyscrapers have developed over time to handle the challenge of height by using large structural beams at their edges. The higher a building goes, the more physical support you need at the edges, and so its interiors shrink, its occupants are further away from natural light, and so on. Taking a cue from how natural materials like bamboo solve the problem of growing upwards, FOA proposed a skyscraper composed of 'a bundle of interconnected structural tubes'; in other words, a series of thin, undulating rods that bumped into each other as they snaked upwards, thereby reducing the need for heavy structural materials at the perimeter. This is a classic biomimetic approach, looking at how a natural process has evolved to solve an environmental challenge – in this case, the need to remain stable while growing upwards – and modelling an architectural form to reproduce it.

Just as the roots of this approach are entangled in the early days of Silicon Valley, today much of the world of biomimetic architecture also leaks into a related set of 'computational' or 'generative' approaches to building design. This is partly because a lot of computational power is necessary to do the calculations that make biometric designs possible. But it's also because patterns generated in nature are, at least in principle, expressible in numbers: the patterns that appear on the wall of an expanding bubble, for example, as air pushes its wall outwards, can be set out mathematically and modelled with an equation.[35] This means you can take some material – a very thin film, for instance – and, using the parameters of your bubble-wall equation, realistically model what will happen to the film when it comes under the same constraint as the bubble (which is to say, how it would act if there was air expanding within it). Suddenly, a whole world opens up, in which architects are able to use the strict parameters provided by generative structures found in nature – a bubble expanding, a leaf growing, a river flowing towards the sea – to map out novel three-dimensional forms.

Take the Beijing National Aquatics Centre (also known as the Water Cube), built for the 2008 Olympic Games, with its famous soap-bubble exterior. This was designed using a proof from two physicists, who had established, for the first time, the science of how bubbles fill space as they expand.[36] As the engineering firm Arup put it: 'The building's form is inspired by the natural formation of soap bubbles. Arup's designers and structural engineers realized that a structure based on this unique geometry would be highly repetitive and buildable, while appearing organic and random.'[37]

Of course, the term 'inspired by' is doing a lot of work here. In the end, these designers were perhaps less interested in imitating nature than they were in making a cool, functional building for their client – which is fair enough. But in this sense, biomimetic architecture, for all its claims to being innovative and different, is generally still rooted in a very conventional notion of how architecture works. Ultimately, no matter how much your building looks like a peanut shell or an ant farm, somewhere a person in an expensive suit is maintaining a spreadsheet that ensures it's offering a reasonable return on investment. For other people in this emergent genre, though, such as the architect and theorist Achim Menges, what matters is following biological *principles* and letting the aesthetic and functional chips fall where they may. Consider a brick, he said to me in an interview. A brick at the top of a wall takes only a fraction of the load of one at the base; yet we build the two bricks exactly the same, using up the same resources, as if they all had to be so sturdy. An evolutionary system would probably not be so wasteful. *These* kinds of principles from nature are what matter, and are worth mimicking (I am paraphrasing Menges here), not a roof that looks like a forest canopy, for example.

Imagine if, rather than a blueprint for a building coming from the mind of a human designer, it just sort of *emerged* from a set of inputs, a bit like a flower emerges from the code of a germ cell. There are genetic rules governing what the flower will look like, obviously, but there is also some variety as the emerging bloom meets its local environmental conditions. In what Menges and his collaborators call 'morphogenetic computational design', architects use computers to mimic this kind of process in nature. If you think of a finished building as if it were a human, or a cat, or a nice oak tree, then think of the morphogenetic architect as someone trying *not* to create the organism, but rather to figure out the genetic code from which the organism sprang.[38] Of course, organisms don't simply emerge in their environment and then sit there unchanged; they respond to the environmental conditions they find themselves in. In the same way, the morpho-ecological approach works with materials that have an interactive, ongoing relationship to the environment – materials that will change and adapt over time.

This isn't new, exactly. The copper dome on a nice neo-classical building from the nineteenth century is green today because the oxidising metal, exposed to the elements, produces a patina to protect itself. The people who put that dome on there knew this was going to happen – they were planning on an environmental adaptation. But morpho-ecology goes a step further, even transforming architecture into something biological as such. Architects in this tradition aren't trying simply to figure out how human planning might be ecologically smarter, but to imagine how architects and designers could *make natural environments*. This means getting away from the constraints and rules of modernist design – this is where you work; this is where you sleep; this is the space for the factory; this is the space for the home – and producing heterogeneous spaces where things change over time, where the boundaries aren't clear, where buildings are 'constructed through social operations and the local experience of space–time'.[39] Instead of having a material that you can shape or form in particular ways, you let the material find its own form as it actually comes to exist in the world. Rather than being put into place by the master designer, the material, now, learns to organise itself.

This all gets super-technical, and super-philosophical, and super-weird, really quickly. We are talking about buildings growing, after all, and about using things like mushrooms and watery scum as building materials, but we're also talking about high-powered computing and extremely futuristic-looking design. In this world of generative architecture, the design historian Christina Cogdell points out, 'the lines between computation, architecture and biology begin to blur'.[40] One recent academic paper on artificial intelligence in architecture wondered, quite seriously, whether the capacity of neural networks to learn to generate images might mean that machines could even *hallucinate* buildings in the future.[41] This weird oscillation between machine and organism, between the dull mandates of geology and wild sci-fi phantasm, is absolutely characteristic, and has aesthetic consequences. As Cogdell puts it, generally 'the final products share a common aesthetic, one that entails an interconnected proliferation of component-based forms that morph through different curvatures, resulting in a stylized organic appearance'. In other words, what begins in a world of extremely dense philosophy and hugely sophisticated computing, in some of the world's finest architectural research institutions, often ends up as a fancy office building that's a bit curvy, or kind of looks like a shell.

As with all human endeavours, the gap between desire and reality is sometimes rather large here. But also, in a way, that doesn't really matter so much. What matters here is the *desire* that architecture should be something else: not an engineering practice involving materials, space, a certain amount of money, the needs of the clients, and so on, but a biological process in which an object produces and reproduces itself, in relationship to a natural environment, and according to a set of evolutionary processes which are themselves incrementally morphing over time, in a feedback loop with biological and environmental conditions. The usually stated aim, here, is that an architect should be less of a designer, less of an artist, and more of a scientific researcher. There's a certain abdication of agency here – even of humanity as such. I couldn't help but wonder, as I read these texts, if the desire to play with living systems, with life, doesn't betray a different kind of fantasy – whether the true desire here is not to be thought of as a biologist but, rather, as a minor god.

At the beginning of 2019, I saw an online advert for a conference on 'living architecture' in Seville. On a whim, I got on a plane and arrived – it was by now mid-March – in the middle of a religious festival, where groups of sinister-looking, besuited men paraded life-size effigies of Christ and the Virgin Mary through the steaming early-evening streets. The next morning, fuzzy with Catholicism and sherry, I took my seat among an audience of mostly local students in the university auditorium's gleaming white plastic chairs, to hear some of the leading proponents of a radical new approach to architecture and nature. The goal is not to create 'good architecture', the architect and designer Waltraut Hoheneder told the conference in a dazzling opening address. 'That was twenty years ago.' A plant, Hoheneder said, has basically the same problems as a house – how to manage water and solar energy, how to create shade. She talked about the structural use of hydrogels, mycelium, algae and 3D-printed calcium carbonate; she talked about no longer seeing growth as directional and economic but cyclical and biological; she talked about how water can transport nutrients and regulate temperature around a space; she talked about building in Antarctica and on the International Space Station; she talked about artificial life, and why we should think about buildings as partners, and also about fungal webs, and the moon. I scribbled frantically, half delirious with heat and manzanilla in the weirdly intense spring temperatures. 'What is the unit of design in nature?' asked the next speaker, the British experimental architect Rachel Armstrong. In Venice, she said, there are two architectures: on the surface, the Venetian Gothic that we all know; and then there is also the scum that reveals itself between high and low tide, forming a kind of 'second city'. In my notebook, I wrote WETNESS, VITALISM, GROWTH, and then, a bit overcome, left to walk under the orange trees, loosely in the direction of the Catedral de Santa María de la Sede, the world's largest Gothic cathedral, where I had planned to see (and vaguely curse) the tomb of Christopher Columbus.

On the way, though, I got lost, and more by accident than design I eventually found my way to Las Setas – the famous 'Mushrooms of Seville', an urban renewal project designed by the German architect Jürgen Mayer, which also claims to be the largest wooden structure in the world. Facing much technical complexity, it was finally completed in 2011, amid the familiar public controversies about cost overruns. It now claims to be more popular than the cathedral. There's apparently a market there, and a walkway along the top, but it was just so hot that day, and this ersatz wooden mushroom wasn't doing much to help me regulate my body temperature, so I left fairly quickly and sought out shelter instead in the dark little nineteenth- and twentieth-century bars, which were much cooler and full of sherry, cold meat and those weird little hard crackers that are so salty and moreish, and yet feel like they're going to break your teeth. As I lightly fractured some veneers, I was thinking hard about the politics of these experiments, and what it might actually mean to reimagine design as a process of nature, and where all of this might lead a person.

In 2008, the year of the Beijing Olympic Games, the architect and theorist Patrik Schumacher, then a partner in the firm of Zaha Hadid and now its leader following Hadid's death in 2016, proposed the term 'parametricism' or 'parametric architecture', which he then developed into a kind of oddball social theory. 'The key issues that avant-garde architecture and urbanism should be addressing', Schumacher wrote, 'can be summarized in the slogan: organizing and articulating the increased complexity of post-Fordist society. The task is to develop an architectural and urban repertoire that is geared up to create complex, polycentric urban and architectural fields which are densely layered and continuously differentiated.'[42] Society, in other words, is no longer neatly ordered along the industrial lines of the twentieth century; we no longer have the factory, and then the houses near the factory, and further on the town centre, where you spend your pay from the factory. What we have now is . . . well, something else. 'Interarticulate,' Schumacher commands his readers, 'hyberdize [sic], morph, deterritorialize, deform, iterate, use splines, nurbs, generative components, script rather than model.' This is all pretentious bollocks, obviously, but architectural theorists, for whatever reason, get the absolute horn for this kind of thing. Still, Schumacher has a strategic goal that is clear enough: he wants to remake the notion of style, away from being a set of aesthetic preferences or a question of fashion, and into something more like a programme of biological research.[43] Rather than having building design simply dissolve into a messy pluralism in the wake of modernism's failures – as critics like Charles Jencks argued in the 1990s – parametricism can be a hegemonic new style. What's driving Schumacher is an attempt to reconcile, on the one hand, a vision of society as something deeply complex and intertwined, where the different bits are not obviously separated from another, but nonetheless *some* kind of order is working itself out; and on the other, an architectural style that can meet this pattern through a form of 'organized (law-governed) complexity' that works like 'natural systems'. Society today, we might say, is more like a beehive than a factory, so why are we still designing factories rather than beehives? Or better still: why are we 'designing' at all, rather than taking the beehive as a model of how a complex natural system can *itself* generate the physical structure that houses it?

For a few years, parametricism was hot stuff at the self-consciously avant-garde architectural institutions. By 2016, though, Schumacher was desperately working to halt what he saw as its 'increasing marginalization' in the profession, which he blamed partly on the 2008 financial crash.[44] His response was 'Parametricism 2.0' – an attempt to move away from manifestos and engage in 'serious, relevant, high-performance work'. Moving from individual buildings to whole cities, he called for a 'parametric urbanism', in which unfettered free-market logic would resolve the complexities of urban planning. 'The market process', Schumacher wrote, 'is an evolutionary one'; like the unfolding of a genetic code, it involves mutation, selection, reproduction. Buildings or neighbourhoods are like new species settling into an ecological niche. Rethinking urban planning from such a perspective reduces disorienting visual chaos in cities, or what Schumacher calls 'garbage-spill urbanism'. The master architect is here in search of order, and he takes order to be natural. There are, needless to say, worrying antecedents to such views of the city. That same year, in a speech in Berlin of all places, Schumacher suggested privatising all urban space and eliminating social housing. Protests, predictably, ensued. 'I've been depicted as this kind of villain, as this fascist,' he complained to the *Guardian*.[45]

In the end, maybe precisely because he is so limited a thinker, Schumacher is a useful figure in terms of seeing how two apparently very different ways of thinking about the urban environment – one traditional and backward-looking; the other technology-driven and futuristic – are nonetheless united by a single political vision. In his writing, you get a clear distaste for the convivial mess of urban modernity, a pearl-clutching horror at the shonky utopianism that drove so much public design and planning in the middle decades of the twentieth century. This is precisely the same distaste and dislike, of course, that one gets from the clay-fingered scribblings of King Charles. Schumacher and the King are driven by a shared desire not only for hierarchy, rationality and order, but for the reproduction of these elements in the built environment, as they have been given to us in nature. Architecture reproduces the social order, and the social order is a product of nature. Nature – poor, benighted, built-over nature – is understood, by both, as a collection of technological instructions *and* a set of moral indictments. These are just two kinds of anti-urbanism, in other words, moved by the same central conceit: that the city is or should be a living thing; that tending it and cultivating it, as one might cultivate a vegetable plot or pasture, is the royal road to resolving the seemingly endless crises that puncture our increasingly fractious and anxious urban age.

In the end, it's not style that matters, for either traditionalism or parametricism; it's ideology. Patrik Schumacher's work – as far away from 'traditional' as it is possible to get – expresses the belief that we are biological creatures, living in ecological space; that our buildings should align with complex, natural, evolutionary processes because this is the form that our society is taking. Order, in this approach, is maintained not through a rigid, top-down hierarchical organisation, but through the gradual intertwining of bottom-up biological codes. For someone like Donald Ruggles, by contrast, traditional architecture expresses the fact that we have evolved to appreciate particular forms, and that if we don't continue to build those forms, which we call 'beautiful', then we are actively working against our nature, in a way that is likely to make us unwell.

For all that they may affect disdain for one another, what these positions share is an abhorrence of the twentieth century, as a period when architecture and biology became disastrously unhooked from one another. The parametric architect looks *forward*, into a radical future of daring and overbearing design; the urban traditionalist looks *back*, to what we used to know about columns, and facades, and cute little chimney-pots. But this is a trivial difference. What holds the two together – what, in the end, largely dominates architectural and urban thinking today – is a singular conviction that the central problem of architecture in the twentieth century is that it left nature too far behind.

Towards the end of writing this book, I went back to the Church of Christ the King in Turner's Cross for the first time in, I think, several decades. It was a miserable day in early January, the kind of bruisingly dark, wet morning that made me question my decision to leave my life in Bristol and return to live in Cork, the city where I had grown up. Finding myself unexpectedly at a loose end, with Christmas over and a new job yet to start, I decided to cycle to where I'd truly come from: the city's unglamorous southern suburbs and their rows of semi-detached and terraced post-war houses, but also to that strange grey ziggurat, looming over the slate roofs, which still seemed to be most plausibly explained as a kind of cosmic glitch, an error inserted from an entirely different timeline.

Inside, shaking off the rain, and not really sure why I'd come here, I realised that Christ the King – it was completely empty – is actually all triangles. They fold down, like inverted steps, from the ceiling to the aisles, only to then rise up again behind the altar in serrated concrete rows, forming a large tri-angular screen facing the nave, which is topped with a small, very plain golden cross. From this pinnacle, the congregation moves outwards, back towards the entrance, in neat, plain rows of wooden benches. Along the back wall, I found subtly decorative panels composed of three different cuts of stone: polished, whitewashed and rough. I noticed, too, for the first time, that the Stations of the Cross running up and down the sides of the church – that bane of childhood Good Friday services, as the priest moved with aching slowness between them – were carved directly into the stone and then painted over. On the noticeboard, a reliable lady advertised cleaning services; marriage counselling was offered to worried couples; there were several entreaties to the reader that they consider becoming a priest.

I sat down, heavily. It was hard to believe that when I was a child, this place had stood for everything that I fantasised (as adolescents always fantasise) I might one day get away from: provincial conservatism, inward-looking self-satisfaction, the dull reproduction of a reactionary moral system that even its own defenders didn't bother pretending to believe in. Obviously, I didn't get away (no one does), but now the church and its universe hit differently. The space was sadder and smaller than I remembered it, of course, as is always the case with one's childhood world – but somehow, too, as an enclosure the church seemed more morally and politically ambiguous, maybe even more hopeful, than I recalled. What world were they trying to bring into being, I wondered, the commissioners, designers, builders and worshippers at this giant, tomb-like monolith, in a then desperately poor country, only barely and partially independent, still bearing the scars of civil war? This was a world, certainly, no less than that materialised in the work of Antonio Gaudí, that was also wrestling with time – tied, in one sense, to the reproduction of a particular kind of clerical tradition, but also striving to represent the hopes and ambitions of a wider community that, suddenly, and perhaps unexpectedly, had become unmoored from its own fate.

Christ the King is an attempt to catechise a certain vision of modernity, industry, rationality – of new forms of collectivity, even new ways of being and living in space. The church's architect, Barry Byrne, says the historian Vincent L. Michael, embraced wholly the 'positivist discourse of twentieth-century modernism', for which 'societal ills became solvable design problems'.[46] His work in designing churches – Byrne was himself a progressive Catholic – was deeply congruent with the 'machine-age rationalism' of figures like Walter Gropius, Le Corbusier and Ludwig Mies van der Rohe, some of whom Byrne had met while on a European trip in 1924, which included a visit to the then-thriving Bauhaus. In Byrne's work, tradition or precedent, wrote Lewis Mumford, 'is in the nature of the Church's ceremonies and observances, rather than in the crystallization of these elements into some special architectural form in, say, the thirteenth century'.[47] For him, the church is not a set of spires and buttresses and gargoyles; it is simply 'a sanctuary surrounded by a congregation'. Here, for all the faults of the institution it sustains, is a provincial Irish Catholic church reaching out to European modernism, and to European urbanism between the wars. It's a building that, in the face of so many temptations otherwise, at least attempts something other than the simple reproduction of traditional form; that refuses the ineluctable working-through of fate, of history, of environmental conditions, of slowly developing human biology.

This message from 1931, the year of the church's construction, seems quite lost today amid a wider international debate about what form the city of the future should take, dominated by two different kinds of reactionary anti-urbanism: here, traditional and focused on human nature; there, future-oriented and concerned with ecological preservation. These are, ultimately, each in their own way, negative and fatalistic ideologies, one looking to the imagined certainties of the past, the other to a half-desired apocalypse in the coming decades. What each understands as nature or biology, whether it comes in the form of a Doric column or a soap bubble, is, in the end, little more than a miserable politics of inevitability, an attempt to quieten any loose talk of reason, modernity, collectivity, transcendence or change. And if we are not minded simply to defend words like 'reason' and 'progress' – which have themselves propelled a great deal of political violence – nonetheless, the Church of Christ the King, a piece of ecclesiastical architecture in provincial Ireland, offers an unexpected reminder that other futures are still imaginable, and that it might yet be possible to put a glitch in these deathly visions; that something unexpectedly grey and graceful, something clean and sharp and new, might yet cut through a landscape, and a timeline, that we have now been too long given to imagine as unchangeable, eternal, *natural.*

# Acknowledgements

I'm grateful, first, to everyone who took the time to talk to me during the research for this book, not all of whom made it to the page, but all of whom have nonetheless been critical in terms of helping me make better arguments. Even where there's been disagreement, I've tried to make sure people's voices and arguments are always represented seriously and with care. I hope this comes across!

Research for this book was funded through an award from the Leverhulme Trust, for which I am extremely grateful. I have written about William Lever's twentieth-century legacy a good deal in these pages. I am glad to see that the trust is currently foregrounding work on that legacy, and I look forward to seeing how this develops in the future.

Thanks to Chris Wellbelove, my agent, who was the first person to recognise there was actually a book here, and who then successfully nagged me into writing that book. I met Chris through a scheme run by the UK's Arts and Humanities Research Council and the BBC called 'New Generation Thinkers'. I'm extremely grateful to everyone involved in that scheme, working hard to keep it afloat amid difficult times for humanities research.

I'm grateful to everyone who has had an editorial hand in this book, especially, at Faber, Fred Baty and Alex Bowler, and at Basic, T. J. Kelleher and Lara Heimert. A great deal of what's on the page here is due to the careful ministrations of Fred and Lara in particular, though they bear no responsibility for the infelicities that remain. Copy editing by Connie Oehring and Ian Bahrami improved the text a good deal, and also saved me from a bunch of embarrassing errors (the embarrassing errors that remain are, obviously, my own fault).

I did the writing for this book in three exceptionally convivial and intellectually rich places: first, the School of Social Sciences at Cardiff University; second, at the Wellcome Centre for Cultures and Environments of Health at the University of Exeter; and now, having returned home, at the Radical Humanities Laboratory and the Department of Sociology and Criminology at University College Cork. There's no space to mention the many, many people at all three places who have helped me to think more sharply and carefully about the arguments I make here, but thank you to all!

Most of all, I am grateful to Neasa, Finbarr and Mary, with whom I lived in several different cities during the writing of this book. I do honestly sometimes wonder if the resolutely affirmative view of city life taken in this book comes in large part from having always shared urban space, first, with Neasa Terry, the best person I've ever met, and then sometime later with the other two as well, who also have their charms. But there's nothing much to be done about that now.

# Permissions

PHOTO CREDITS

p. 13: from Wikimedia user Golliday, shared under a CC BY-SA 3.0 licence. See: https://commons.wikimedia.org/wiki/File:Le_Corbusier_Haus,_Berlin.jpg.

p. 27: public domain image, via Google Art Project. See: https://commons.wikimedia.org/wiki/File:Albert_Bierstadt_-_Valley_of_the_Yosemite_-_Google_Art_Project.jpg.

p. 66: public domain image, first published by Swan Sonnenschein & Co., London, 1898. See: https://commons.wikimedia.org/wiki/File:Garden_Cities_of_Tomorrow,_No._2.jpg.

p. 70: public domain image, first published by the Association of All Classes of All Nations, London, 1838. See: https://commons.wikimedia.org/wiki/File:New_Harmony,_Indiana,_por_F._Bates.jpg.

p. 85: from 'Cognitive Maps in Rats and Men' by Edward C. Tolman; first published by the American Psychological Association in *Psychological Review*, 1948.

p. 88: from Wikimedia user Codera23, shared under a CC BY-SA 4.0 licence. See: https://commons.wikimedia.org/wiki/File:Salk_Institute_2.jpg.

p. 125: from Wikimedia user Garry Knight, shared under a

p. 131: public domain image, shared on Wikimedia by user
H005. See: https://commons.wikimedia.org/wiki/File:Torre_
Guinigi_from_Torre_Torre_dell%27Orologio.jpg.
p. 183: public domain image, first published by
Groombridge & Sons, London, 1855.
p. 221: from Wikimedia user Quinok, shared under a CC
BY-SA 4.0 licence. See: https://commons.wikimedia.org/
wiki/File:07-Villa-Rotonda-Palladio.jpg.

All other images courtesy of the author.

TEXT PERMISSIONS

Some sections in Chapter 1 appeared previously in 'A
Gigantic Vertical Zoo: Madness and the Green City', published in *Terrain: Anthropologie et Sciences Humaines*, Volume
76, in 2022. Small sections from Chapters 1, 2 and 3 have
appeared in 'A Forest, a Maze, a Garden, a City: Psychiatry's
Architectural Turn', in *Cultural Politics* (Duke University
Press), Volume 18, Issue 3, also in 2022. For another version
of the Jonas Salk story, see 'A City Is Not a Park', an episode
of *The Essay* for BBC Radio 3, also by Des Fitzgerald, first
broadcast in 2019.

# Notes

INTRODUCTION

1 For biographical detail here, I rely on Laura Wood Roper, *FLO: A Biography of Frederick Law Olmsted* (Johns Hopkins University Press, 1973).

2 Frederick Law Olmsted, 'Preliminary Report Upon the Proposed Suburban Village at Riverside, Near Chicago'. See *Olmsted: Writings on Landscape, Culture, and Society* (Library of America, 2015).

3 Frederick Law Olmsted, 'To Edward Everett Hale'. Ibid.

4 Dorceta E. Taylor, *The Rise of the American Conservation Movement: Power, Privilege and Environmental Protection* (Duke University Press, 2016).

5 Peter Hall, *Cities of Tomorrow: An Intellectual History of Urban Planning and Design in the Twentieth Century* (Blackwell, 1996).

6 Ebenezer Howard, *Garden Cities of To-Morrow* (MIT Press, 1965 (1898)).

7 Le Corbusier, *The City of Tomorrow and Its Planning* (The Architectural Press, 1979 (1929)).

8 Frank Lloyd Wright, *The Living City* (Horizon Press, 1958).

9 See https://twitter.com/BIG_Architects/status/1433023271352651779.

10 See https://cityoftelosa.com/#CityofTelosa.

11 Henry George, *The Writings of Henry George. Progress and Poverty: An Inquiry into the Cause of Industrial Depressions and of Increase of Want with Increase of Wealth: The Remedy* (Doubleday and McClure Company, 1898). See https://www.gutenberg.org/cache/epub/55308/pg55308-images.html.

12 Bjarke Ingels, *Yes Is More: An Archicomic on Architectural Evolution* (Taschen, 2009).

13 See http://cityoftelosa.com, accessed 19 April 2023.

14 See https://www.neom.com/en-us/regions/theline.

15 Tom Ravenscroft, 'Saudi Arabia Unveils Plans for Octagonal

# Notes

Floating Port City in Neom', *Dezeen*, 21 December 2022. https://www.dezeen.com/2022/12/21/oxagon-floating-port-city-neom-saudi-arabia/?li_source=base&li_medium=bottom_block_1.

16 Ruth Michaelson, '"It's Being Built on Our Blood": The True Cost of Saudi Arabia's $500bn Megacity', *Guardian*, 4 May 2020. https://www.theguardian.com/global-development/2020/may/04/its-being-built-on-our-blood-the-true-cost-of-saudi-arabia-5bn-mega-city-neom.

17 Mohammed Rasool, 'Saudi Arabia Sentences 3 Men to Death for Refusing to Vacate NEOM Development Site', *Vice*, 11 October 2022. https://www.vice.com/en/article/5d3kkd/neom-saudi-arabia-howeitat-tribe.

18 For an excellent sociological analysis of the possibilities and problems of green utopia, one that is perhaps more optimistic than the present text, see Lisa Garforth, *Green Utopias: Environmental Hope Before and After Nature* (Polity, 2018).

## I: LIVING IN THE CITY

1 On this voyage, see 'Bauhaus Aboard!' by 'GH', originally published as part of the 'Bauhaus 100' series on the Bauhaus Kooperation site: https://www.bauhauskooperation.com/kooperation/project-archive/magazine/discover-the-bauhaus/bauhaus-aboard/.

2 Eric Mumford, 'CIAM and the Communist Bloc, 1928–59', *Journal of Architecture*, 14: 237–54 (2009).

3 For biographical detail in this chapter, I draw especially on Nicholas Fox Weber, *Le Corbusier: A Life* (Knopf, 2008).

4 See Brian Ackley, 'Le Corbusier's Algerian Fantasy: Blocking the Casbah', *Bidoun* (Winter 2006). https://www.bidoun.org/articles/le-corbusier-s-algerian-fantasy.

5 See Simone Brott, 'The Le Corbusier Scandal, or, Was Le Corbusier a Fascist?', *Fascism*, 6(2): 196–227.

6 Le Corbusier, *The Athens Charter* (Grossman, 1973).

7 Peder Anker, *From Bauhaus to Ecohouse: A History of Ecological Design* (Louisiana State University Press, 2010).

8 Le Corbusier, *The City of Tomorrow*.

9 Ibid.

10 On Greek modernism, see Yorgos Simeoforidis and Yannis Aesopos, *Landscapes of Modernisation: Greek Architecture, 1960s and 1990s* (Metapolis Press, 1999).

11 On phytoncides, see Anna Lena Philips, 'A Walk in the Woods', *American Scientist*, 99(4), 301 (2011).

12 See Qing Li, *Into the Forest: How Trees Can Help You Find Health and Happiness* (Penguin, 2019).

13 Kristine Engemann et al., 'Residential Green Space in Childhood Is Associated with Lower Risk of Psychiatric Disorders from Adolescence into Adulthood', *PNAS*, 116 (11): 5, 188–93 (2019).

14 MaryCarol R. Hunter, Brenda W. Gillespie and Sophie Yu-Pu Chen, 'Urban Nature Experiences Reduce Stress in the Context of Daily Life Based on Salivary Biomarkers', Frontiers in Psychology, 10 (2019). https://www.frontiersin.org/articles/10.3389/fpsyg.2019.00722.

15 I'm referring here to work by Roger Ulrich in the first instance and Edward O. Wilson – both of whom I consider in a bit more detail in Chapter 3.

16 See Nadia Khomami, 'London Garden Bridge Project Collapses in Acrimony After £37m Spent', *Guardian*, 14 August 2017.

17 United Nations Human Settlements Programme, *World Cities Report 2022* (United Nations, 2022).

18 See Mark Spence, 'Dispossesing the Wilderness: Yosemite Indians and the National Park Ideal, 1864–1930', *Pacific Historical Review*, 65(1): 27–59 (1996).

19 Dorceta Taylor, *The Rise of the American Conservation Movement* (Duke, 2016).

20 See Thomas Fisher, 'Frederick Law Olmsted and the Campaign for Public Health', *Places Journal*, November 2010.

21 See 'The Greatest Glory of Nature', in Charles Beveridge (ed.), *Olmsted: Writings on Landscape, Culture, and Society* (Library of America, 2015).

22 See Richard Grusin, 'Reproducing Yosemite: Olmsted, Environmentalism, and the Nature of Aesthetic Agency', *Cultural Studies*, 12(3): 332–59 (1998).

23 See Theodore S. Eisenman, 'Frederick Law Olmsted, Green Infrastructure, and the Evolving City', *Journal of Planning History*, 12(4): 287–311 (2013).

24 Donna Haraway, 'Teddy Bear Patriarchy: Taxidermy in the Garden of Eden, New York City, 1908–1936', *Social Text*, 11: 20–64 (1985). See also Anna Bramwell, *Ecology in the Twentieth Century: A History* (Yale, 1989).

25 On the history of health professionals and urban green space in the

Notes

UK, see Clare Hickman, '"To Brighten the Aspect of Our Streets and Increase the Health and Enjoyment of Our City": The National Health Society and Urban Green Space in Late-Nineteenth Century London', *Landscape and Urban Planning*, 118: 112–19 (2013).

26 Select Committee, *Report from the Select Committee on Public Walks*, 1833.

27 See 'The People's Park at Birkenhead, Near Liverpool', in Beveridge (ed.), *Olmsted*.

28 Hickman, '"To Brighten the Aspect of Our Streets"'.

29 On this history, see Hazel Conway, *People's Parks: The Design and Development of Victorian Parks in Britain* (Cambridge University Press, 1991).

30 Haraway, 'Teddy Bear Patriarchy'. See also Bramwell, *Ecology in the Twentieth Century*.

31 Hickman, '"To Brighten the Aspect of Our Streets"'.

32 See again the work of Clare Hickman, *Therapeutic Landscapes* (Manchester University Press, 2014).

33 See Charles E. Beveridge and Paul Rocheleau, *Frederick Law Olmsted: Designing the American Landscape* (Rizzoli, 1995).

34 Feargus O'Sullivan, 'Paris Wants to Grow "Urban Forests" at Famous Landmarks', *City Lab*, 19 June 2019. https://www.citylab.com/environment/2019/06/paris-trees-famous-landmarks-garden-park-urban-forest-design/591835/.

35 Lewis Mumford, *The Culture of Cities* (Harvest/HBJ, 1970).

36 Steven Vogel, *Thinking Like a Mall* (MIT, 2016).

37 See the *Times* Editorial Board, 'Editorial: If We Want Wildlife to Thrive in L.A., We Have to Share Our Neighborhoods with Them', *Los Angeles Times*, 7 November 2022.

38 Christine Dell'Amore, 'Wild Animals Are Adapting to City Life in Surprisingly Savvy Ways', *National Geographic Magazine*, 7 June 2022.

39 William Cronon, *Uncommon Ground: Rethinking the Human Place in Nature* (Norton, 1995).

40 Tom Ravenscroft, 'Vincent Callebaut Proposes a Roof That Generates Energy and Food for Notre-Dame Cathedral', *Dezeen*, 9 May 2019.

## 2: THE GARDEN BATHED IN SUNLIGHT

1 Rohan Varma, 'Architecture as an Agent of Change: Remembering Charles Correa, "India's Greatest Architect"',

*ArchDaily*, 16 June 2016. https://www.archdaily.com/789384/
architecture-as-agent-of-change-remembering-charles-correa-india.

2 Joseph Rykwert, 'Charles Correa Obituary', *Guardian*, 19 June
2015. https://www.theguardian.com/artanddesign/2015/jun/19/
charles-correa.

3 'Royal Gold Medal', https://www.architecture.com/awards-and-
competitions-landing-page/awards/royal-gold-medal, accessed 19
April 2023.

4 HRH the Prince of Wales, 'A Speech by HRH the Prince of Wales
at the 150th Anniversary of the Royal Institute of British Architects
(RIBA), Royal Gala Evening at Hampton Court Palace' (1984).

5 Hugh Pearman, 'Prince Rains on 150th Parade', *RIBAJ*, 13 August
2018. https://www.ribaj.com/culture/ribaj-125-archive-september-
2018-prince-charles-hampton-court-speech.

6 Pearman, 'Prince Rains on 150th Parade'.

7 HRH The Prince of Wales, *A Vision of Britain: A Personal View of
Architecture* (Doubleday, 1989).

8 'History: The Masterplan', https://poundbury.co.uk/about/history/.

9 Léon Krier, *Albert Speer: Architecture 1932–1942* (Monacelli, 2016).

10 Owen Hatherley, 'King Charles Has Some Very Strange Ideas
About How Cities Should Look', *Jacobin*, September 2022. https://
jacobin.com/2022/09/king-charles-architecture-cities-poundbury-
krier-conservative.

11 Léon Krier, 'TRADITION – MODERNITY – MODERNISM:
Some Necessary Explanations. Statement Prepared for the Skidmore,
Owings & Merrill Architectural Institute'. *Architectural Design*, 57
(1987): 38–43.

12 Hatherley, 'King Charles Has Some Very Strange Ideas'.

13 Here I am drawing on Lawrence Goldman, 'The Social Science
Association, 1857–1886: A Context for Mid-Victorian Liberalism',
*The English Historical Review*, 101(398): 95–134 (1986).

14 On urban mortality in the period, see Simon Szreter, 'Mortality
and Public Health, 1815–1914', in A. Digby, C. Feinstein and
D. Jenkins (eds), *New Directions in Economic and Social History*
(Palgrave, 1992).

15 Benjamin Ward Richardson, *Hygeia, A City of Health* (1876). See
https://www.gutenberg.org/cache/epub/12036/pg12036-images.html.

16 James H. Cassedy, 'Hygeia: A Mid-Victorian Dream of a City of
Health', *Journal of the History of Medicine and Allied Sciences*, 17(2):
217–28 (1962).

# Notes

17  On Howard's biography, see Robert Beevers, *The Garden City Utopia* (Palgrave, 1988). See also sections on Howard in Hall, *Cities of Tomorrow*.

18  Howard, *Garden Cities of To-Morrow*.

19  In this section I am drawing on a brilliant PhD dissertation: see Jeremy David Rowan, 'Imagining Corporate Culture: The Industrial Paternalism of William Hesketh Lever at Port Sunlight, 1888–1925' (LSU Doctoral Dissertations, 2003).

20  Here and elsewhere I draw on David J. Jeremy, 'The Enlightened Paternalist in Action: William Hesketh Lever at Port Sunlight Before 1914', *Business History*, 33(1): 58–81 (1991).

21  'History of the Trust', https://www.leverhulme.ac.uk/history-trust, accessed 19 April 2023.

22  See https://www.leverhulme.ac.uk/history-trust#:~:text=The%20 Leverhulme%20Trust%20was%20established,Margarine%20 Unie%20to%20form%20Unilever. See also Josephine Tierney, 'Report of Scoping Survey of the Lever Brothers' Plantations in the Solomon Islands and the Congo, 1900–1930', available at https://royalafricansociety.org/wp-content/uploads/2022/05/ University-of-Liverpool-Scoping-Report-Lever-Bros-Plantations-in- the-Congo-and-Solomon-Islands-1900-to-1930.pdf (2021).

23  Amy Sergeant, 'Lever, Lifebuoy and Ivory', *Early Popular Visual Culture*, 9(1): 37–55 (2011).

24  See Elizabeth Outka, *Consuming Traditions: Modernity, Modernism and the Commodified Authentic* (Oxford University Press, 2008).

25  Amanda Rees, 'Nineteenth-Century Planned Industrial Communities and the Role of Aesthetics in Spatial Practices: The Visual Ideologies of Pullman and Port Sunlight', *Journal of Cultural Geography*, 29(2): 185–214 (2012).

26  William Lever, 'Mr. Lever's Address on Visit of International Housing Conference to Port Sunlight, 9 August 1907' (1907). Available at Warwick Digital Collections: https://wdc.contentdm. oclc.org/digital/collection/health/id/68/.

27  Ibid.

28  Jeremy, 'The Enlightened Paternalist in Action'.

29  See Reuben Loffman and Benoît Henriet. '"We Are Left with Barely Anything": Colonial Rule, Dependency, and the Lever Brothers in the Belgian Congo, 1911–1960', *Journal of Imperial and Commonwealth History*, 48(1): 71–100 (2020).

30  See Jules Marchal, *Lord Leverhulme's Ghosts: Colonial Exploitation in the Congo* (Verso, 2017).

3: LIKE A RAT IN A MAZE

1  Dora Vargha, 'Between East and West: Polio Vaccination Across the Iron Curtain in Cold War Hungary', *Bulletin of the History of Medicine*, 88(2): 319–43 (2014). Here I also draw on Barry Trevelyan, Matthew Smallman-Raynor and Andrew D. Cliff, 'The Spatial Dynamics of Poliomyelitis in the United States: From Epidemic Emergence to Vaccine-Induced Retreat, 1910–1971', *Annals of the Association of American Geographers*, 95(2): 269–93 (2005).

2  See Christos Lynteris, *Visual Plague: The Emergence of Epidemic Photography* (MIT Press, 2022).

3  For versions of the Salk story, see John Paul Eberhard, 'Architecture and Neuroscience: A Double Helix' in Sarah Robinson and Juhani Pallasmaa (eds), *Mind in Architecture: Neuroscience, Embodiment, and the Future of Design* (MIT Press, 2015); or Emily Badger, 'Corridors of the Mind: Could Neuroscientists Be the Next Great Architects?', *Pacific Standard* (2017), https://psmag.com/social-justice/corridors-of-the-mind-49051. Notably, the story appears fleetingly in an exhaustive biography by Charlotte DeCroes Jacobs (*Jonas Salk: A Life*, Oxford University Press, 2015), and then only as something mentioned by Salk some years later.

4  On this history, see Dora Vargha, *Polio Across the Iron Curtain: Hungary's Cold War with an Epidemic* (Cambridge University Press, 2018).

5  Carolina A. Miranda, 'Louis Kahn's Salk Institute, the Building That Guesses Tomorrow, Is Aging – Very, Very Gracefully', *Los Angeles Times*, 22 November 2016. https://www.latimes.com/entertainment/arts/miranda/la-et-cam-salk-institute-louis-kahn-20161107-html-story.html.

6  Luke Fiederer, 'AD Classics: Salk Institute/Louis Kahn', *ArchDaily*, 27 August 2017. https://www.archdaily.com/61288/ad-classics-salk-institute-louis-kahn.

7  See 'Remarks by Jonas Salk, On the Occasion of the Presentation of the 25th Year Award for the Design of the Salk Institute by Louis I. Kahn at the American Institute of Architects Awards Ceremony. AIA Convention in Boston, Massachusetts. June 19, 1992', part of the Salk Papers, held in Special Collections and Archives at the library of UC San Diego.

# Notes

8   See 'Remarks by Jonas Salk, In Response to the Salk Institute's
    Receiving the American Institute of Architects' 25-Year Award
    at the Accent on Architecture Gala Celebration for Excellence in
    Architecture, Kennedy Center, Washington, D.C., January 22,
    1992', ibid.

9   See the 'Mission' section of their website: https://www.anfarch.org/
    mission.

10  See Alison Whitelaw, 'Introducing ANFA, the Academy of
    Neuroscience for Architecture', *Intelligent Buildings International*, 5
    (suppl. 1): 1–3 (2013).

11  Florian Lederbogen and colleagues, 'City Living and Urban
    Upbringing Affect Neural Social Stress Processing in Humans',
    *Nature*, 474: 498–501 (2011).

12  Kristine Engemann and colleagues, 'Residential Green Space in
    Childhood Is Associated with Lower Risk of Psychiatric Disorders
    from Adolescence into Adulthood', *PNAS*, 116 (11): 5, 188–93
    (2019).

13  Gregory N. Bratman and colleagues, 'Nature Experience Reduces
    Rumination and Subgenual Prefrontal Cortex Activation', *PNAS*,
    112 (28): 8,567–72 (2015).

14  See Felicity Callard and Daniel Margulies, 'The Subject at Rest: Novel
    Conceptualizations of Self and Brain from Cognitive Neuroscience's
    Study of the "Resting State"', *Subjectivity*, 4: 227–57 (2011).

15  Paul Dudchenko, *Why People Get Lost: The Psychology and
    Neuroscience of Spatial Cognition* (Oxford University Press, 2010).

16  Willard S. Small, 'An Experimental Study of the Mental Processes of
    the Rat', *American Journal of Psychology*, 11(2): 133–65 (1900); and
    Willard S. Small, 'An Experimental Study of the Mental Processes of
    the Rat II', *American Journal of Psychology*, 12(2): 206–39 (1901).

17  Edward C. Tolman, 'Cognitive Maps in Rats and Men', *Psychological
    Review*, 55(4): 189–208 (1948).

18  John O'Keefe and Jonathan Dostrovsky, 'The Hippocampus as a
    Spatial Map. Preliminary Evidence from Unit Activity in the Freely-
    Moving Rat', *Brain Research*, 34(1): 171–5 (1971).

19  John O'Keefe and Lynn Nadel, *The Hippocampus as a Cognitive Map*
    (Oxford University Press, 1978).

20  For a good guide to some of this history, see Rodrigo Mara's PhD
    thesis: 'The Cognitive Roots of Space Syntax' (University College
    London, 2009). https://core.ac.uk/download/pdf/1687777.pdf.

21  Eleanor A. Maguire and colleagues, 'Navigation-Related Structural

Change in the Hippocampi of Taxi Drivers', *PNAS*, 97(8): 4,398–403 (2000).

22  Rowan Moore, 'The Royal College of Physicians – Just What the Doctors Ordered', *Observer*, 7 September 2014.

23  In these sections, I draw on my notes of the talks, which capture the content of what was being said but not exact quotes.

24  Robert E. L. Faris and H. Warren Dunham, *Mental Disorders in Urban Areas: An Ecological Study of Schizophrenia and Other Psychoses* (University of Chicago Press, 1939).

25  For more on this, and especially for an elaboration of the historical background, see a book I wrote with Nikolas Rose, *The Urban Brain* (Princeton University Press, 2022).

26  Charles Montgomery, *Happy City: Transforming Our Lives Through Urban Design* (Penguin, 2013).

27  Roger S. Ulrich, 'Visual Landscapes and Psychological Well-Being', *Landscape Research*, 4(1): 17–23 (1979).

28  To cite just one example, Byoung-Suk Kweon, Roger S. Ulrich, Verrick D. Walker and Louis G. Tassinary, 'Anger and Stress: The Role of Landscape Posters in an Office Setting', *Environment and Behavior*, 40(3): 355–81 (2008).

29  Kevin Baker, '"Welcome to Fear City" – The Inside Story of New York's Civil War, 40 Years On', *Guardian*, 18 May 2015.

30  Otto Saumarez Smith, 'The Inner City Crisis and the End of Urban Modernism in 1970s Britain', *Twentieth Century British History*, 27(4): 578–98 (2016). He is, in fact, a member of the same distinguished extended family as the architect George Saumarez Smith, whom we met in the previous chapter.

31  Jane Jacobs, *The Death and Life of Great American Cities* (Random House, 1961).

32  Robert Caro, *The Power Broker: Robert Moses and the Fall of New York* (Knopf, 1974).

33  Roger S. Ulrich, 'Biophilia, Biophobia and Natural Landscapes', in Edward O. Wilson and Stephen R. Kellert (eds), *The Biophilia Hypothesis* (Island Press, 1995).

34  Edward O. Wilson, *Biophilia: The Human Bond with Other Species* (Harvard University Press, 1984).

35  Lauren Greyson, *Vital Reenchantments: Biophilia, Gaia, Cosmos and the Affectively Ecological* (Punctum Press, 2019).

36  Rachel Kaplan and Stephen Kaplan, *The Experience of Nature: A Psychological Perspective* (Cambridge University Press, 1989).

37  Heather Ohly et al., 'Attention Restoration Theory: A Systematic
    Review of the Attention Restoration Potential of Exposure to
    Natural Environments', *Journal of Toxicology and Environmental
    Health*, Part B, 19: 7, 305–43 (2016).

38  Bill McKibben, *The End of Nature* (Random House, 1989).

39  For a full account of this perspective (what sociologists sometimes call
    the 'postnaturalist' view), see Garforth, *Green Utopias*, Chapter 6.

40  William Cronon, *Nature's Metropolis: Chicago and the Great West*
    (W. W. Norton, 1992).

## 4: THE CONQUERED CITY

1  See https://www.mvrdv.nl/projects/456/marble-arch-hill.

2  Ibid.

3  Jonathan Prynn, 'Marble Arch "Mound" Plan to Lure Visitors
   Back to West End with 25m-High Hill Set to Provide Sweeping
   Views', *Evening Standard*, 16 February 2021. https://www.
   standard.co.uk/news/london/marble-arch-mound-oxford-street-
   westminster-b919890.html.

4  See https://twitter.com/danbarker/status/1419787260107558918.

5  See https://www.westminster.gov.uk/news/update-marble-arch-
   mound-monday-26-july.

6  Mark Brown, 'Marble Arch Mound: Deputy Council Leader Resigns
   Over £6m Cost', *Guardian*, 13 August 2021. https://www.
   theguardian.com/uk-news/2021/aug/13/marble-arch-mound-
   deputy-council-leader-resigns-over-cost.

7  Patrick Butler and Mark Brown, 'Marble Arch Mound Draws
   Crowds Keen to See How Bad It Is', *Guardian*, 23 August 2021.
   https://www.theguardian.com/uk-news/2021/aug/23/not-pretty-
   marble-arch-mound-draws-crowds-keen-to-see-how-bad-it-is.

8  Jill Starley-Grainger, 'A Review of London's Worst-Ever Tourist
   Attraction and Where to Go Instead', *EuroNews*, 27 August 2021.
   https://www.euronews.com/travel/2021/09/25/the-mound-is-
   london-s-worst-ever-tourist-attraction-here-are-the-best-alternatives.

9  See https://westminster.moderngov.co.uk/documents/s44227/
   Westminster%20City%20Council%20Internal%20Review%20
   Report%20Part%201.pdf.

10 Huw Lemmey, 'An Exclusive Interview with the Marble Arch
   Mound', *Frieze*, 12 January 2022. https://www.frieze.com/article/
   exclusive-interview-marble-arch-mound.

11  Sumana Roy, *How I Became a Tree* (Yale University Press, 2021).

12  See https://www.gov.uk/government/news/millions-of-funding-for-projects-in-england-to-plant-hundreds-of-thousands-of-trees.

13  Alexandra Kelley, 'Is Trump Really Planting a Billion Trees?', *The Hill*, 30 September 2020. https://thehill.com/changing-america/sustainability/environment/518994-is-trump-really-planting-a-billion-trees.

14  Will Feuer, 'Salesforce CEO Marc Benioff Says Over 300 Companies Have Agreed to Help Plant One Trillion Trees', CNBC, 23 January 2020. https://www.cnbc.com/2020/01/23/salesforce-ceo-marc-benioff-300-companies-to-help-plant-1-trillion-trees.html.

15  Jean-François Bastin et al., 'The Global Tree Restoration Potential', *Science*, 365 (6448): 76–9 (2019).

16  Steffan Messenger, 'Climate Change: Corporate Mass Tree Planting "Damaging" Nature', BBC, 10 November 2021. https://www.bbc.co.uk/news/uk-wales-59220669.

17  Rowan Moore, 'Why the Marble Arch Mound Is a Slippery Slope to Nowhere', *Observer*, 24 July 2021. https://www.theguardian.com/artanddesign/2021/jul/24/why-the-marble-arch-mound-is-a-slippery-slope-to-nowhere.

18  Ali Karimi, 'Cultivating the Arts: The Tree Out of Context', *Architectural Review* 12 October 2021. https://www.architectural-review.com/essays/ecology/cultivating-the-arts-the-tree-out-of-context.

19  Jonathan Bate, 'Review: *The Overstory* by Richard Powers – *Moby-Dick*, with Tree-Huggers', *The Times*, 24 March 2018

20  Katya Kupelian and Abby Narishkin, 'Look Inside the New $1.3 Billion Complex at Singapore's Changi Airport, with a 130-Foot Indoor Waterfall', *Business Insider*, 17 April 2019.

21  I am relying here on Google Translate: see https://www.stefanoboeriarchitetti.net/project/san-siro-uno-stadio-bosco-per-milano/. This proposal was not successful, but discussion on it was reignited in 2022, as the winning proposal continued to run into difficulties: https://www.thestadiumbusiness.com/2022/11/04/forest-stadium-vision-set-to-be-presented-for-stadio-giuseppe-meazza/.

22  See https://twitter.com/JustinTrudeau/status/1177613585381543936.

23  Toby Berrett, 'Meet "Sussex on Ecosia", the Sussex Students Saving the World with a Search Engine', *The Tab*, 2018.

24  See https://tred.earth/tred-card/.

25  Marine Le Pen, leader of the party once known as the Front

National, and which now openly calls itself an environmental party, describes Europe as 'the world's leading ecological civilisation'. See https://www.nytimes.com/2019/10/17/world/europe/france-far-right-environment.html.

26 Paris Marx, 'Jeff Bezos' "O'Neill Colony" Dreams Ignore the Plight of Millions Living on Earth Now', *NBC News*, 15 May 2019. https://www.nbcnews.com/think/opinion/jeff-bezos-blue-origin-space-colony-dreams-ignore-plight-millions-ncna1006026.

27 David Harvey, *The Urban Experience* (Johns Hopkins University Press, 1989).

28 Luke Turner, *Out of the Woods* (Weidenfeld & Nicolson, 2019).

29 I am drawing here on the work of the historian Steve Hindle. See 'Imagining Insurrection in Seventeenth-Century England: Representations of the Midland Rising of 1607', *History Workshop Journal*, 66(1): 21–61 (2008).

30 See Joan Thirsk, 'Arthur Standish', *Oxford Dictionary of National Biography*.

31 Quoted in Thirsk, ibid.

32 Arthur Standish, 'New Directions of Experience . . .' (1613) (Ann Arbor, Text Creation Partnership). Available at: https://quod.lib.umich.edu/e/eebo2/B08132.0001.001?view=toc.

33 Sir Anthony Fitzherbert, *The Boke of Husbandry* (1531). https://quod.lib.umich.edu/e/eebo/A00884.0001.001/1:4.86?rgn=div2;view=fulltext.

34 Peter Warde, 'Fear of Wood Shortage and the Reality of the Woodland in Europe, *c.*1450–1850', *History Workshop Journal*, 62(1): 28–57 (2006).

35 Karl Marx, *Capital, Volume 1* (1867). See https://www.marxists.org/archive/marx/works/1867-c1/ch01.htm#S1.

36 John Evelyn, *Sylva, Or a Discourse of Forest Trees and the Propagation of Timber* (1662). https://www.gutenberg.org/files/20778/20778-h/20778-h.htm.

37 See James C. McKusick, 'John Evelyn: The Forestry of Imagination', *English Faculty Publications*, 17 (2013). https://scholarworks.umt.edu/eng_pubs/17.

38 See 'Kilcash', in Eiléan Ní Chuilleanáin, *The Girl Who Married the Reindeer* (Galley Press, 2001). See also Matthew Rowney, 'Broken Arbour: "The Ruined Cottage" and Deforestation', *European Romantic Review*, 26(6): 719–41 (2015). I'm grateful to Ger Mullaly for pointing this connection out to me.

39  Oliver Rackham, *Trees and Woodland in the British Landscape* (Weidenfeld & Nicolson, 2001 (1975)).

40  George Perkins Marsh, *Man and Nature or, Physical Geography as Modified by Human Action* (1864). https://www.gutenberg.org/files/37957/37957-h/37957-h.htm.

41  See Andrea Wulf, *The Invention of Nature* (Vintage, 2016).

42  See Leo Marx, *The Machine in the Garden: Technology and the Pastoral Ideal in America* (Oxford University Press, 1964).

43  Harriet Ritvo, *The Dawn of Green: Manchester, Thirlmere and Modern Environmentalism* (University of Chicago Press, 2009).

44  Not only did Haeckel popularise in Germany a variety of social Darwinism that ascribed different value to different 'races', he was also enthusiastic about killing sickly infants and was a founder of the aggressively imperialist and racist Pan-German League. His popular book *The Riddle of the Universe*, meanwhile, which had sold half a million copies by the time Hitler came to power, was received by an enthusiastic German public as 'a scientific religion which established the truth of German romantic nationalism, Aryan superiority, and the true value of the folk' (quoted from George J. Stein, 'Biological Science and the Roots of Nazism', *American Scientist*, 76(1): 50–8 (1988)).

45  See Paul Warde, Libby Robin and Sverker Sörlin, *The Environment: A History of the Idea* (Johns Hopkins University Press, 2018).

46  See Hickman, *Therapeutic Landscapes*.

47  See Kirsten McEwan et al., 'A Pragmatic Controlled Trial of Forest Bathing Compared with Compassionate Mind Training in the UK: Impacts on Self-Reported Wellbeing and Heart Rate Variability', *Sustainability*, 13(3): 1,380 (2021).

48  Glen Moore and Cassandra Atherton, 'Eternal Forests: The Veneration of Old Trees in Japan', *Arnoldia*, 77(4): 24–31 (2020).

49  See Robert H. Sharf, 'Is Mindfulness Buddhist? (And Why It Matters)', *Transcultural Psychiatry*, 52(4): 470–84 (2015).

50  See http://forest-medicine.com/epage01.html.

51  Samantha Walton, *Everybody Needs Beauty: In Search of the Nature Cure* (Bloomsbury, 2021).

52  Mark Jackson, *The Age of Stress: Science and the Search for Stability* (Oxford University Press, 2013).

53  See Vadim Saraev et al., 'Valuing the Mental Health Benefits of Woodlands', Research Report, Forest Research, Edinburgh (2021).

54  Walton, *Everybody Needs Beauty*.

# Notes

55  Richard Mabey, *Nature Cure* (Vintage, 2008).

56  Sigmund Freud, *Civilization and Its Discontents* (Penguin Freud Library, Vol. 12, 1991).

57  Matt Ffytche, *Critical Lives: Sigmund Freud* (Reaktion Books, 2022).

58  Sara Maitland, *Gossip from the Forest: The Tangled Roots of Our Forests and Fairytales* (Granta, 2006).

5: SAVE ME

1  I'm grateful to Yvonne Lynch for additional help with this background. Any outstanding inaccuracies, as well as the wider interpretation, are wholly my own.

2  I am taking these extracts from Adrienne LaFrance, 'When You Give a Tree an Email Address', *The Atlantic*, 10 July 2015.

3  For a really good academic analysis of these emails and their relationship to urban conviviality, see Elizabeth Straughan, Catherine Phillips and Jennifer Atchison, 'Finding Comfort and Conviviality with Urban Trees', *Cultural Geographies* (2022). https://doi.org/10.1177/14744740221136284.

4  Per Bolund and Sven Hunhammar, 'Ecosystem Services in Urban Areas', *Ecological Economics*, 29(2): 293–301 (1999).

5  Catherine Phillips and Jennifer Atchison, 'Seeing the Trees for the (Urban) Forest: More-Than-Human Geographies and Urban Greening', *Australian Geographer*, 51: 155–68 (2020).

6  See again Vadim Saraev et al., cited in the previous chapter. For a useful summary from a public health perspective, see Danielle Shanahan et al., 'Toward Improved Public Health Outcomes from Urban Nature', *American Journal of Public Health*, 105: 470–7 (2015).

7  See https://www.gov.uk/government/publications/enabling-a-natural-capital-approach-enca-guidance/enabling-a-natural-capital-approach-guidance#introduction-to-natural-capital.

8  Hillary Angelo, *How Green Became Good: Urbanized Nature and the Making of Cities and Citizens* (University of Chicago Press, 2021).

9  Sonja Dümpelmann, *Seeing Trees: A History of Street Trees in New York City and Berlin* (Yale University Press, 2019).

10  India Block, 'Paris Plans to Go Green by Planting "Urban Forest" Around Architectural Landmarks', *Dezeen*, 26 June 2019.

11  Adam Nossiter, 'The Greening of Paris Makes Its Mayor More Than a Few Enemies', *New York Times*, 5 October 2019.

12  Jaime Velázquez, 'Madrid Building a Huge Urban Forest in a Bid to Combat Climate Change', *Euronews*, 19 July 2021.

13  Michael L. Treglia et al., *The State of the Urban Forest in New York City* (The Nature Conservancy, 2021). See also this discussion on the website of The Nature Conservancy: https://www.nature.org/en-us/about-us/where-we-work/united-states/new-york/stories-in-new-york/future-forest-nyc/.

14  Hall, *Cities of Tomorrow*.

15  Nikolas C. Heynen, 'The Scalar Production of Injustice Within the Urban Forest', *Antipode* 35(5): 980–98 (2003).

16  See Matthew Gandy, *Concrete and Clay: Reworking Nature in New York City* (MIT Press, 2003).

17  See Joanna Dean, 'Seeing Trees, Thinking Forests: Urban Forestry at the University of Toronto in the 1960s', in Alan MacEachern and William J. Turkel (eds), *Method and Meaning in Canadian Environmental History* (Nelson, 2009). Dean includes the enticing detail that Jorgensen was an associate of the University of Toronto's then star professor, gnomic media theorist Marshall McLuhan, having been tasked with advising on tree management around the celebrity academic's home. 'Urban Forest', Dean points out, a conjunction of apparent opposites, seems very close to some of McLuhan's own coinages, such as 'Global Village'. In this sense, you might even say that the concept of the urban forest, in spite of its earthy connotations, is actually little more than a side-product of Cold War media theory.

18  See Paul E. Waggoner and J. D. Ovington, *Proceedings of the Lockwood Conference on the Suburban Forest and Ecology* (The Connecticut Agricultural Experiment Station, Bulletin 652 (1962)).

19  Matthew Gandy, *Natura Urbana: Ecological Constellations in Urban Space* (MIT Press, 2022).

20  See Rowan A. Rowntree, 'Urban Forest Ecology: Conceptual Points of Departure', *Arboriculture & Urban Forestry*, 24(2): 62–71 (1998).

21  See Michael Williams, 'Sauer and Man's Role in Changing the Face of the Earth', *Geographical Review*, 77(2): 218–31 (1987).

22  Preston E. James, 'Man's Role in Changing the Face of the Earth: A Review', *Economic Geography*, 33(3): 267–74 (1957).

23  Ibid.

24  H. C. Darby, 'The Clearing of the Woodland in Europe', in W. L. Thomas (ed.), *Man's Role in Changing the Face of the Earth* (University of Chicago Press, 1956).

25 Lewis Mumford, 'The Natural History of Urbanization', ibid.

26 For an introduction to this perspective, see Nik Heynen, Maria Kaika and Erik Swyngedouw, *In the Nature of Cities* (Routledge, 2006).

27 Matthew Gandy and Sandra Jasper, *The Botanical City* (Jovis Verlag, 2020).

28 Richard Deakin, *Flora of the Colosseum of Rome* (Groombridge, 1855).

29 See https://savesheffieldtrees.org.uk/history/.

30 Ellie Violet Bramley, 'For the Chop: The Battle to Save Sheffield's Trees', *Guardian*, 25 February 2018. https://www.theguardian.com/uk-news/2018/feb/25/for-the-chop-the-battle-to-save-sheffields-trees.

31 Sir Mark Lowcock, KCB (Independent Chair), *Sheffield Street Trees Inquiry* (2023). See https://www.sheffield.gov.uk/sites/default/files/2023-03/sheffield_street_trees_inquiry_report.pdf.

32 See https://www.sheffield.gov.uk/content/dam/sheffield/docs/libraries-and-archives/archives-and-local-studies/research/Park_Hill_and_Hyde_Park_Study_Guide_v_1-12.pdf.

33 Bart Bryant-Mole, 'AD Classics: Park Hill Estate / Jack Lynn and Ivor Smith, *ArchDaily*: https://www.archdaily.com/791939/ad-classics-park-hill-estate-sheffield-jack-lynn-ivor-smith.

34 BBC, 'Park Hill'. https://www.bbc.co.uk/southyorkshire/content/articles/2007/03/07/park_hill_feature.shtml.

35 See https://www.sheffield.gov.uk/content/dam/sheffield/docs/libraries-and-archives/archives-and-local-studies/research/Park_Hill_and_Hyde_Park_Study_Guide_v_1-12.pdf.

36 See John Boughton, *Municipal Dreams: The Rise and Fall of Council Housing* (Verso, 2018).

37 Owen Hatherley, 'Regeneration? What's Happening in Sheffield's Park Hill Is Class Cleansing', *Guardian*, 28 September 2011. https://www.theguardian.com/commentisfree/2011/sep/28/sheffield-park-hill-class-cleansing.

38 Paul Dobraszczyk, 'Sheffield's Park Hill: The Tangled Reality of an Extraordinary Brutalist Dream', *Guardian*, 14 August 2015. https://www.theguardian.com/cities/2015/aug/14/park-hill-brutalist-sheffield-estate-controversial-renovation.

39 Stefi Orazi, *Modernist Estates: The Buildings and the People Who Live in Them* (Frances Lincoln, 2015).

6: THE TWENTIETH CENTURY DID NOT TAKE PLACE

1 Lisa Abend, 'Inside Barcelona's Unfinished Masterpiece', *Time*, 8 July 2019. https://time.com/sagrada-familia-barcelona/.

2 Stephen Burgen, 'Huge Star Atop Sagrada Família Rekindles Residents' Complaints', *Guardian*, 29 November 2021. https://www.theguardian.com/world/2021/nov/29/ huge-star-atop-sagrada-familia-rekindles-residents-complaints.

3 Lewis Mumford, 'A Modern Catholic Architect', *Commonweal*, 2 March 1927.

4 See https://turnerscross.com/architecture/barry-byrne/.

5 Mark Burry, 'Antoni Gaudí and Frei Otto: Essential Precursors to the Parametricism Manifesto', *Architectural Design*, 86(2): 30–5 (2016).

6 See also Christina Cogdell, *Toward a Living Architecture? Complexism and Biology in Generative Design* (University of Minnesota Press, 2018).

7 See https://sagradafamilia.barcelona-tickets.com/sagrada-familia-tower-interiors/.

8 Javier Senosiain, *Bio-Architecture* (Routledge, 2003).

9 See, for example, the website of the Traditional Architecture Group, which is a society linked to the Royal Institute of British Architects (the main professional body for UK architects). http:// traditionalarchitecturegroup.org/about.

10 India Block, 'Trump Orders New Government Buildings Must Be "Beautiful"', *Dezeen*, 21 December 2020.

11 See https://www.johnsimpsonarchitects.com/news-defence-national-rehabilitation-centre-jsa.html.

12 https://www.thednrc.org.uk/facts-figures/press-releases/22/ Handover-of-the-gift-of-the-Defence-and-National-Rehabilitation-Centre-by-the-Duke-of-Westminster.

13 Donald H. Ruggles, *Beauty, Neuroscience & Architecture: Timeless Patterns and Their Impact on Our Well-Being* (University of Oklahoma Press, 2018).

14 Create Streets is an organisation that both advocates for an approach to urban design that it calls 'gentle density' and provides services to clients broadly based on this approach. Its website says that it exists 'to help solve the housing crisis and to help neighbourhood [*sic*], communities, landowners, councils and developers create and manage beautiful, sustainable places of gentle density that will be

popular, are likely to be correlated with good wellbeing and public health outcomes and which are likely to prove good long term investments based on the historical data of value appreciation and maintenance costs'. Create Streets is by no means a simplistic or dogmatic 'traditionalist' organisation, and I think it would understand itself as being led by evidence for what people want in planning and design. But I don't think it does great violence to say that it is a rather conservative (small 'c') organisation. In 2021, indeed, the Conservative government appointed its founder, Nicholas Boys Smith, as chair of the new Office for Place, a public body intended, according to the then housing minister Robert Jenrick, to correct 'post-war mistakes' and 'put beauty back at the heart of how we build'.

15 See 'Our Story': https://www.createstreets.com/front-page-2/about-us/our-story/.

16 These themes have been at the centre of a range of public and government reports in the UK in recent years, as the housing market has failed badly to keep up with demand and a sense of anxiety has set in with regard to the quality and range of new-build communities. See, for example, the Royal Institute of British Architects' report 'The Ten Primary Characteristics of Places People Want to Live', published in response to a government report on making Britain's new housing development less grimly homogenous: https://www.architecture.com/knowledge-and-resources/resources-landing-page/ten-characteristics-of-places-where-people-want-to-live. See also 'Living with Beauty', the final report from the government's 'Building Better, Building Beautiful' commission – co-chaired by Nicholas Boys Smith – on improving the design of new homes and neighbourhoods: https://www.gov.uk/government/groups/building-better-building-beautiful-commission.

17 Roger Scruton, *Beauty: A Very Short Introduction* (Oxford University Press, 2009).

18 Roger Scruton, *The Aesthetics of Architecture* (Princeton University Press, 2013 (1979)).

19 David Watkin, *Morality and Architecture* (University of Chicago Press, 1984).

20 Alice Coleman, *Utopia on Trial: Vision and Reality in Planned Housing* (Hilary Shipman, 1985).

21 Alex Potts, 'The New Right and Architectural Aesthetics', *History Workshop*, 12: 159–62 (1981).

22  National Civic Art Society, 'Americans' Preferred Architecture for Federal Buildings', October 2020.

23  Martyn Brown, 'New Homes Need to Be Built in Keeping with Traditional Architectural Styles', *Express*, 21 July 2021.

24  Ann Sussman and Justin B. Hollander, *Cognitive Architecture: Designing for How We Respond to the Built Environment* (Routledge, 2014).

25  Matthias Schmelzer, '"Born in the Corridors of the OECD": The Forgotten Origins of the Club of Rome, Transnational Networks, and the 1970s in Global History', *Journal of Global History*, 12(1): 26–48 (2017).

26  On this history, see also Garforth, *Green Utopias*, pp. 31–46

27  Ian McHarg, *Design with Nature* (Wiley, 1995 (1969)).

28  Anne Whiston Spirn, 'Ian McHarg, Landscape Architecture and Environmentalism: Ideas and Methods in Context', in Michael Conan (ed.), *Environmentalism in Landscape Architecture* (Dumbarton Oaks, 2001).

29  Ian McHarg, *Man: Planetary Disease* (US Agricultural Service, 1971).

30  Peder Anker, *From Bauhaus to Ecohouse: A History of Ecological Design* (Louisiana State University Press, 2010).

31  Douglas Murphy, *Last Futures: Nature, Technology and the End of Architecture* (Verso, 2016).

32  Nicholas Wade, 'New Alchemy Institute: Search for an Alternative Agriculture', *Science*, 187 (4,178): 727–9 (1975).

33  D. C. Wahl, 'Bionics vs. Biomimicry: From Control of Nature to Sustainable Participation in Nature', in C. A. Brebbia (ed.), *Design and Nature III: Comparing Design in Nature with Science and Engineering* (WIT Press, 2006).

34  Julian Vincent, 'Biomimetic Patterns in Architectural Design', *Architectural Design*, 79 (6): 74–81 (2009).

35  A. O. Maksimov and T. G. Leighton, 'Pattern Formation on the Surface of a Bubble Driven by an Acoustic Field', *Proceedings of the Royal Society A*, 468: 57–75 (2012).

36  Philip Ball, 'Beijing Bubbles', *Nature*, 448: 256 (2007).

37  See https://www.arup.com/projects/chinese-national-aquatics-center.

38  Achim Menges, 'Biomimetic Design Processes in Architecture: Morphogenetic and Evolutionary Computational Design', *Bioinspiration & Biomimetics*, 7(1) (2012).

39  Michael Hensel and Achim Menges, *Morpho-Ecologies: Towards a Discourse of Heterogeneous Space in Architecture* (AA Publications, 2006).

40  Cogdell, *Toward a Living Architecture?*

41  Matias del Campo and Neil Leach, 'Can Machines Hallucinate Architecture? AI as Design Method', in M. del Campo and N. Leach (eds), *Machine Hallucinations: Architecture and Artificial Intelligence* (Wiley, 2022).

42  Patrik Schumacher, *Parametricism as Style – Parametricist Manifesto* (2008): http://www.patrikschumacher.com/Texts/Parametricism%20 as%20Style.htm.

43  Patrik Schumacher, 'Patrik Schumacher on Parametricism – "Let the Style Wars Begin"', *Architects Journal*, 6 May 2010.

44  Patrik Schumacher, 'Introduction: Parametricism 2.0 – Gearing Up to Impact the Global Built Environment' (2016): https:// www.patrikschumacher.com/Texts/Parametricism%202_0_ Gearing%20up%20to%20Impact%20the%20Global%20Built%20 Environment.html.

45  Aaron M. Renn, 'Interview: Architect Patrik Schumacher: "I've Been Depicted as a Fascist"', *Guardian*, 17 January 2018.

46  Vincent L. Michael, 'Expressing the Modern: Barry Byrne in 1920s Europe', *Journal of the Society of Architectural Historians*, 69 (4): 534–55 (2010).

47  Mumford, 'A Modern Catholic Architect'.

# Index

# Index

# Index

# Index

# Index